Thomas Z

major contentions

Thomas Szasz

primary values and major contentions

edited by Richard E. Vatz and Lee S. Weinberg

 Prometheus Books

700 East Amherst St. Buffalo, New York 14215

Published 1983 by Prometheus Books

Library of Congress Catalog Card Number: 82-62083

ISBN 0-87975-187-8 (Cloth)
ISBN 0-87975-188-6 (Paper)

Printed in the United States of America on acid-free paper.

CONTENTS

FOREWORD

I have devoted much of my professional life to an effort to clarify what is conventionally considered to be the riddle of mental illness. Perhaps because I was strongly influenced by an empiricist-rationalist education, and perhaps because I was endowed with a stubborn sense of independence, it seemed to me obvious, even before I reached my teens, that what people call mental illness is not like ordinary illness: typically, neither the so-called patients nor their would-be healers behave like ordinary patients and doctors.

That much has been obvious to many other people as well, of course. The vexing problems that insight creates have, however, been evaded by some such reasoning as this: "Mental patients behave the way they do because they have a mental illness. The illness is due to, or is a manifestation of, a brain disease. They must be treated for that disease to help them recover from it. It is the task of psychiatric science to discover the causes of mental illness, and of psychiatric practice to provide scientifically rational care for mental patients."

This reasoning sounds very persuasive. If it didn't, it would not have persuaded generations of psychiatrists to follow the path it laid out for them, nor would it have persuaded generations of lay persons to accept the coercive social practices based on it. However, this reasoning is persuasive not because it is sound but because it is rhetorically powerful.

It is possible, indeed it is likely, that there are brain diseases as yet undiscovered by medical science. But that fact has no bearing on what is conventionally considered to be the problem of mental illness.

What, then, is the so-called problem of mental illness really about? It is

9

about two disconcerting facts. The first fact is that there is no mental illness: The term is simply a socially validated verbal construct. The second one is that psychiatric inquiry and practice are not empirical, rational, or scientific: Indeed, how could they be if their aim is to empirically investigate and treat an alleged disease, mental illness, that cannot be empirically identified? Such reflections have led me to look for the answer to the riddle of mental illness in scrutinizing not the *condition* of mental illness, which has proved so elusive and refractory a quarry to scientific investigation, but the observable facts or practices associated with this *idea*. By observable facts I refer to two simple sets of objectively verifiable phenomena: What so-called mentally ill persons (especially *qua* mental patients) do, and what other persons (especially, but not solely, psychiatrists) do when they call individuals mentally ill and treat them as mental patients. Because of the sorts of things these protagonists in the drama of psychiatry actually do, matters psychiatric have always been deeply involved with legal, moral, and political considerations and hence, inevitably, with profoundly important and yet often elusive linguistic considerations as well.

What, then, do mental patients and psychiatrists do? Many so-called mental patients engage in disturbing or illegal behavior: they starve themselves, attack members of their families, commit arson or theft, kill prominent persons. The psychiatrists reciprocate with two characteristic acts: they inculpate and imprison the innocent, calling it civil commitment and psychiatric treatment; and they exculpate and imprison the guilty, calling it the insanity defense and criminal commitment. Although psychiatrists perform many other acts as well, these two sets of psychiatric performances stand as important reminders of what I regard as the central moral-philosophical act of psychiatry: transforming individuals from responsible moral agents into non-responsible, insane patients. To be sure, psychiatrists claim that it is not they but the dreaded illness they call "psychosis" that transforms men and women from moral agents into organisms that deserve neither blame nor praise but only pity and therapy. This controversy will not, of course, be further pursued here, especially since the reader will find it amply illuminated in the materials assembled in this volume.

I should like to close with expressing my appreciation and thanks to my good friends Richard Vatz and Lee Weinberg for this synoptic presentation of my views. It is particularly gratifying to me that this exposition and interpretation of my writings should have been undertaken by a professor of rhetoric and a professor of legal studies. Their professional identities symbolize and forewarn of the cognitive quantum jump that is expected of the reader interested in transcending the perspectives of conventional psychiatry.

Thomas S. Szasz, M.D.
Upstate Medical Center
State University of New York

PREFACE

Having taught thousands of students to grapple with the ideas of Thomas Szasz, we have repeatedly encountered three problems with the available published materials: first, Szasz's own writings are voluminous and cannot practically be read in a single term; second, students who have grasped some of Szasz's ideas begin to demand answers to a variety of questions concerning "what Szasz would think about" certain specific issues; and third, both friendly and hostile student readers frequently want to know the nature of the major criticisms levelled at Szasz by other professionals and how such criticisms might be answered.

These difficulties are not dissimilar to the problems encountered in endless debates, discussions, and arguments on Szasz that we have had with scores of colleagues. In fact, with colleagues and other professionals there has been the additional obstacle that, as Charles Krauthammer wrote in *The New Republic,* "Szasz is the kind of author no one reads, but everyone knows about. . . ." Students and professionals alike are in need of an introduction to the writings of Szasz illustrating his value system, the central tenets of his view of human behavior, and the nature of the debate over these views. This has been our goal in preparing the present volume. There is no single volume that comprehensively presents Szasz's basic premises and arguments by carefully selecting samples of his own writings as well as those of his critics and defenders. The need for such a volume is evident in view of the fact that Szasz's work is studied, taught, and criticized in a wide range of disciplines including: psychiatry, sociology, rhetoric, law, criminal justice, political science, health science, psychology, philosophy, and others. His ideas cut across academic disciplines; his writings are assigned to

11

college classes in a variety of subject areas; and his work has achieved a readership in an equally broad array of professions both in the United States and abroad. (Much of Szasz's work has been translated and made available to readers in Asia and Europe).

To accomplish the above stated goals for students, professionals, and other interested readers we have undertaken a complete examination of virtually all of Szasz's writings in order to identify his primary values (Part One), his central contentions (Part Two), some of the major criticisms levelled against him on these two fronts, and responses to these criticisms (Part Three). To distill the ideas of Thomas Szasz into one compact volume required careful selection and editing to assure that no central components were omitted, inadequately explained, or unnecessarily repeated. We have organized this material into categories that we believe most clearly reflect the major values and contentions contained in Szasz's prolific writings. In addition, the reader has been provided with sub-headings or brief summary statements which will further explicate crucial elements of Szasz's thought. It should be noted that the excerpts from Szasz's work contained herein have been edited only to delete footnotes and to provide continuity within the organization of the present volume.

We come from the disciplines of rhetoric, politics, and law, which, along with the mental health fields, are perhaps the areas most conspicuously enriched by the work of Thomas Szasz. To us the personal and professional benefits of his work have been, and continue to be, profound. While neither we nor the readers of this book should unquestioningly accept all of his arguments (Szasz discourages such sycophancy), we hope that this volume captures the essence and richness of Thomas Szasz so that others may enjoy the same stimulation and insight that his works have afforded us over the years.

Richard E. Vatz, Ph.D.
Towson State University

Lee S. Weinberg, J.D., Ph.D.
University of Pittsburgh

INTRODUCTION

Since the publication in 1961 of *The Myth of Mental Illness,* which served originally to thrust him into the center of the debate over the nature of "mental illness" and the proper role of psychiatry, the ideas of Dr. Thomas Szasz have enlightened, provoked, inspired, challenged, and angered millions of readers, not only those within psychiatry but also many outside its confines. Through nearly a score of books and over four hundred articles and reviews, Szasz has sought to demystify and demythologize the "science" of psychiatry by revealing it as an essentially political and moral enterprise operating under the mask of medicine. The primary approach taken by Szasz in his voluminous writing might best be characterized as rhetorical in that he analyzes the ways in which language and symbols have been used by psychiatry to influence the allocation of power; to control the lives, percep-tions, and self-perceptions of millions of people; and to interact with the legal system in the assignment of responsibility for human actions. While rhetorical analysis constitutes the common methodological thread running through all of Szasz's work, strict libertarianism constitutes the political thread, and individual responsibility the moral thread. Recognition of this linkage of rhetoric, politics, and ethics provides the starting point for an understanding of Szasz's thought.

For Szasz, the central struggle faced by each human being is to defend against those who would impose upon him their own definitions of who he is and what constitutes his best interests. The battlefield upon which this struggle for definition is fought is largely linguistic and the ultimate meaning of behavior and events is established by the victors in the battle of words. Reality, from the rhetorical perspective of Szasz, is imbedded in the language used to describe it, and one cannot escape from this reality unless one controls the language itself (Szasz: "the struggle for definition is veritably the struggle for life itself. . . . In ordinary life, the struggle is not for guns but for words: whoever first defines the situation is the victor; his adversary, the victim. . . . In short, he who first seizes the word imposes reality on the other; he who defines thus dominates and lives; and he who is defined is subjugated and may be killed" [*Second Sin*]).

Thus, in his best known work, *The Myth of Mental Illness*, Szasz argues that "mental illness" is a myth; that is, the behaviors that "mental health" professionals and others define as "mental illness" are simply misunderstood and/or disapproved language and action. This defining, Szasz believes, is strategic rhetoric that serves the purposes of the definers and those who benefit from the definitions, often at the expense (economic, political, moral, or otherwise) of the defined. Moreover, he maintains, the labelling of people as "sick" or "disturbed" is successfully accomplished largely because psychiatry has managed to clothe itself in "the logic, imagery, and the rhetoric of science, and especially medicine" (*Ideology and Insanity*). Yet, Szasz points out, the connection between psychiatry, science, and medicine is at best tenuous: "Not only is there not a shred of evidence to support this [connection], but, on the contrary, all the evidence is the other way, and supports the view that what people now call mental illnesses are, for the most part, *communications* expressing unacceptable ideas, often framed in an unusual idiom" (*Ideology and Insanity*). However invalid or misleading, the rhetoric of mental illness is persuasive to many, primarily due to its "scientific" status.

Central to the rhetorical method of Szasz is the concept of metaphor, which he employs in most of his analyses. In stating that "mental illness" is a myth, therefore, Szasz is not arguing that the behavior labelled "mental illness" does not occur, but rather that "mental illness" and related categories are purely metaphoric explanations, not medical ones. As Szasz states (and states often), we have incorrectly, either innocently or not so innocently, taken this metaphoric "illness" to be literal illness. The seemingly endless array of categories and sub-categories of mental "illnesses" and "disorders," which psychiatrists continue to "discover" and revise, are in fact nothing more than descriptions of the unlimited variety of human behaviors, especially those violating social or psychiatric norms. This misleading literalization of metaphor furthers the interests of psychiarists and society, if not the interests of the "mentally ill." To Szasz, the use of strategic metaphors—especially the camouflaged use of such metaphors—deprives humankind of its greatest freedom: autonomy. Unlike religious and democratic political persuaders who claim no false identity and implicitly recognize man's autonomy, psychiatrists present themselves as scientists and explicitly deny the right of autonomy to those whom they choose to define and control.

Having devoted much attention to the argument that everything considered bad is not "sickness," Szasz more recently has argued in *The Myth of Psychotherapy* that everything considered good is not "therapy." Thus, only through rhetoric and mystification does the conversation of a troubled person with a listener become "therapy" within which "symptoms" are "diagnosed" by physicans. In short, Szasz's penetrating rhetorical analysis demonstrates how ". . . coercion and conversation become analogized to medical treatment," with the result being that anything at all can become a form of "therapy" if carried out under the watchful eye of an appropriately credentialed physician, psychiatrist, or, in fact, any other "therapist." Thus, reading can become "bibliotherapy," volleyball can become "recreational therapy," and solicitation of a variety of sex partners can become "sex therapy." No one is suggesting that these activities cannot make a person happier or at least feel better; they unquestionably may have this effect. The point is that these activities are in no way medical, because, in order to be medical, they must be applied to an illness, and since the "patients" being "treated" with these "therapies" have only metaphoric "illnesses," these activities, at best, can only be metaphoric "therapies." In a sense, the concept of "sex therapy" represents to Szasz the ultimate extent to which the "mental illness" ideologues have run amuck: the medicalization of sexual knowledge and behavior. Szasz attacks the pseudo-medical pretentions of sexologists in general, and Masters and Johnson in particular. Of the latter, Szasz writes, "They are the foremost base rhetoricians of modern sexology . . . [who] are skillful in concealing and communicating their sexual ethic and sexual prescriptions as if they were the results of their 'scientific research' and the products of their 'professional' expertise" (*Sex by Prescription*).

Szasz's comprehensive rhetorical insights and unmaskings regarding behavioral medicine are perhaps even more apparent in his analysis of sexology than of "mental illness," though the logic and conclusions are virtually the same. For if the medical metaphor is employed for understanding sex, then any deviation from the norm may be looked upon as an "illness," with the sufferer becoming a "patient." He or she would then seek "doctors" who specialize in sexual "dysfunctions" (a category comprised of virtually inexhaustible maladies). If, on the other hand, a metaphor of interpersonal relations is used, individual differences will no longer be considered diseases, but may be understood as disagreements of preference or freedom of choice. A humorous but instructive illustration of these competing perspectives took place when Dr. Szasz appeared on a television talk show in Baltimore. A female caller asked his advice on what she believed to be a medical problem in her marriage: her husband insisted that she watch him masturbate. Dr. Szasz asked her "Do you want to watch him?" When she replied "No," his "medical" advice was "Then don't!" Beyond this initial humorous response, Dr. Szasz explained that the caller needed to discuss *this* marital disagreement with her husband, as she would *any* marital disagreement.

A doctor is no more required when reaching agreement on sexual issues than would be the case if a couple sought to reach agreement on budgetary matters or any other marital issue. Just as the medical metaphor for sex results in the transformation of prostitutes into "sexual surrogates" and pornography into "sexual therapy," the caller's disagreement with her husband regarding his sexual conduct was transformed in her mind into a disease requiring medical advice and, perhaps, care.

While many of the works of Thomas Szasz should be characterized primarily as theoretical rather than activist in nature, Szasz does not shrink from making specific recommendations to policy makers — especially when individual liberties are threatened by a legal system that typically accepts the medicalization of deviant behavior. Szasz has argued against involuntary treatment or hospitalization, which he claims violate even the traditional *medical* norms supporting patient autonomy. Thus, while rejecting the medical model for behavior, Szasz insists on a medical model for consent, which, he maintains, should be adopted even by those who accept the former if they are to be consistent. Whereas psychiatrists often claim that, unlike other patients, "mental patients" lack the rationality to judge what is in their best interests, Szasz claims that psychiatrists have no special insight into rationality or what constitutes the patient's best interests. Moreover, he claims that we must presume a patient's automony and rationality to the point that whatever choices they make will, *ipso facto,* be assumed to be in their best interests. Therefore, the ethical issue of who has the right to determine a person's best interest has been resolved by Szasz in favor of the individual. This argument, in effect, eliminates any subsequent debate as to whether in a particular instance a person (who has the "right" to decide what is in his best interest) has chosen "correctly."

Thus far we have seen individual freedom afforded protection through Szasz's notion of autonomy; but, to Szasz, autonomy is a double-edged sword protecting freedom on the one hand, while requiring responsibility on the other. On the issue of criminal responsibility in particular, Szasz has sought, in *Law, Liberty, and Psychiatry* and elsewhere, explicitly to oppose the availability of the insanity defense by arguing that one always has the choice of committing or not committing a criminal act. An individual's health, "mental" or otherwise, should not serve to excuse him.

Much like the general controversy surrounding mental illness, the issue of legal sanity rests upon an attempt to reconcile two incompatible and competing assumptions: 1) that criminal behavior is a result of free choices made by autonomous human beings, and 2) that there is "mental disease" that strikes some people, making them criminal offenders, and therefore mitigates their criminal responsibility. Further, this second assumption implies that however vague or broad the range of diseases may be, there are medical experts who can diagnose not only their existence, but whether they have destroyed a lawbreaker's autonomy.

Szasz argues that the choice of assumptions regarding individual autonomy has critical implications for the legal system. In fact, he emphasizes the decisive importance of autonomy assumptions for questions of legal sanity, just as he does for questions of the rights of the "mentally ill" in general. Like infancy and involuntary intoxication, the plea of insanity is an assertion that the accused lacked autonomy, i.e., the mental ability to choose or formulate a criminal intent. Unlike infancy, however, where one need only prove the fact of infancy and not that the defendant's thoughts were "infant thoughts," in insanity the existence of "insane thoughts" constitutes proof that insanity is present! Any one of these three types of incapacity would function as a complete defense to a criminal charge, provided that the existence of the incapacity could be successfully argued. Writers as far back as Aristotle argued that blameworthiness was a condition antecedent to the attachment of criminal responsibility, and, in turn, is conditioned upon the existence of free choice. Thus, in a sense, autonomy was and is the *sine qua non* of criminal law. Without the assumption that people possess free choice, Szasz implies, the whole of criminal law is vitiated.

The views of Thomas Szasz, which have been compiled in this volume, are well within the mainstream of traditional American beliefs and values regarding individual freedom. That this is not recognized may be due in part to the fact that, as earlier noted, Szasz has been subjected to more criticism than thoughtful study. Ironically, this has led his critics to call him a "radical psychiatrist." In fact, nothing could be further from the truth, for a basic conservatism is central to Szasz's work. All of his writing reflects one major rhetorical-philosophical argument: human freedom is based upon the right to define oneself and one's own best interests without the interference of others, and the obligation to take responsibility for the choices one has made without psychiatric or other forms of exculpation.

PART ONE
PRIMARY VALUES

Introduction

In Part One the reader is introduced to Thomas Szasz's central values, which serve as the foundation for his major contentions and policy recommendations regarding the proper role of law, medicine, and the state *vis-à-vis* human behavior. Chapter 1 presents Szasz's advocacy of his most cherished value: autonomy.

The significance to Szasz of the idea of autonomy can hardly be overstated. In his writings one finds repeated references to the crucial nature of this value; numerous policies are supported and justified in its name. Szasz defines autonomy as ". . . freedom to develop one's self—to increase one's knowledge, improve one's skills, and achieve responsibility for one's conduct. And it is freedom to lead one's own life, to choose among alternative courses of action so long as no injury to others results" (*The Ethics of Psychoanalysis*).

In two senses Szasz's writings clearly show his commitment to the principle of autonomy. In the *normative* sense of autonomy, Szasz believes that people ought to be free to make choices about their lives. In the *descriptive* sense of the term, he believes that when people act without physical coercion, such actions should be interpreted as representing freely chosen behavior.

For Szasz, the idea of (descriptive) autonomy comes close to defining the essential nature of human behavior; it is a paramount concept in all of his writings and it is the cornerstone principle of all of his arguments. Both non-criminal behavior and criminal behavior represent choices for which individuals bear total responsibility unless coerced, not unless "irrational" or "ill" or both. Behavior that is offensive, befuddling, or otherwise upsetting, but not illegal, should not be interfered with (e.g. by involuntary hospitalization or other incarceration), thus ensuring the (normative) autonomy of humanity.

In this chapter we present Szasz's discussion of what he regards as the most conspicuous violation of both types of autonomy: societal and psychiatric interference with and/or persecution of those who wish to commit suicide. Last, we set forth Szasz's argument that psychiatry need not violate the principle of autonomy. Here he specifically explains how psychiatry may indeed *promote* autonomy.

In Chapter 2 passages have been included illustrating Szasz's strong adherence to authenticity and humanism. Like Erving Goffman, Szasz writes that one must not misrepresent oneself to others. Szasz maintains that physicians are inauthentic in a variety of ways, ranging from the more obvious act of cloaking nonmedical endeavors in medical or scientific garb to the less obvious attempt to camouflage specific interests (e.g., the court-appointed psychiatrist who hides his allegiance to the court from the accused), and subtle misrepresentations of the nature of their quasi-medical work (e.g., the representation of an abortion as a *medical* as opposed to a *surgical* procedure). These deceptions, writes Szasz, promote the subjugation of freedom and constitutional rights. Furthermore, the crucial aid of seductive rhetoric serves to minimize criticism. When forcible drugging is called "drug therapy" and forced interrogations are called "psychiatric examinations," the traditional muckrakers seem paralyzed. As Szasz indicates in these excerpts, the medical-scientific imprimatur is for many so mystifying that there is a general suspension of the critical faculties necessary to unmask patently nonmedical, heinous practices.

Finally, in this chapter we offer Szasz's views on humanism, an often abused concept. It is here that Szasz most eloquently expresses his belief that humanism represents a sincere, non-ritualistic celebration of freedom, a freedom inextricably linked to honest uses of language and rhetoric.

1

Autonomy

When the psychiatrist approves of a person's actions, he judges that person to have acted with "free choice"; when he disapproves, he judges him to have acted without "free choice." It is small wonder that people find "free choice" a confusing idea: It looks as if "free choice" is something that qualifies what a person being judged (often called the "patient") *does* — when it is actually what a person making the judgment (often a psychiatrist or other mental health specialist) *thinks.*[1]

One person's liberty may be enhanced at the expense of another's, as, for example, the master's is at the expense of the slave's. Thus liberty may be in conflict with liberty. Is is not so with dignity. One person's dignity is never enhanced by another's indignity. Hence, in ordering our values, perhaps we should place dignity even above liberty.[2]

Autonomy is a double-edged sword of freedom and responsibility.

Descriptive Autonomy: Man's actions represent free choices for which he is responsible, but for which he may rhetorically seek to avoid responsibility, most prominently through attributing behavior to literal and/or figurative gods. The traditional Judeo-Christian monotheistic god would be an example of the former, while physicians might be classified as the latter.

23

The crucial moral characteristic of the human condition is the dual experience of freedom of the will and personal responsibility. Since freedom and responsibility are two aspects of the same phenomenon, they invite comparison with the proverbial knife that cuts both ways. One of its edges implies options: we call it freedom. The other implies obligations: we call it responsibility. People like freedom because it gives them mastery over things and people. They dislike responsibility because it constrains them from satisfying their wants. That is why one of the things that characterizes history is the unceasing human effort to maximize freedom and minimize responsibility. But to no avail, for each real increase in human freedom—whether in the Garden of Eden or in the Nevada desert, in the chemical laboratory or in the medical laboratory—brings with it a proportionate increase in responsibility. Each exhilaration with the power to do good is soon eclipsed by the guilt for having used it to do evil.

Confronted with this inexorable fact of life, human beings have sought to bend it to their own advantage, or at least to what they thought was their advantage. In the main, people have done so by ascribing their freedom, and hence also their responsibility, to some agency outside themselves. They have thus projected their own moral qualities onto others—moralizing them and demoralizing themselves. In the process, they have made others into puppeteers and themselves into puppets.

Evidently, the oldest scheme for constructing such an arrangement is religion: only deities have free will and responsibility; people are mere puppets. Although most religions temper this imagery by attributing some measure of self-action to the puppets, the importance of the underlying world view can hardly be exaggerated. Indeed, people still often try to explain the behavior of certain self-sacrificing persons by saying that they are carrying out God's will; and, perhaps more important still, people often claim to be carrying out God's will when they sacrifice others, whether in a religious crusade or in a so-called psychotic episode. The important thing about this imagery is that it makes us witness to, and even participants in, a human drama in which the actors are seen as robots, their movements being directed by unseen, and indeed invisible, higher powers.

If stated so simply and starkly, many people nowadays might be inclined to dismiss this imagery as something only a religious fanatic would entertain. That would be a grave mistake, as it would blind us to the fact that it is precisely this imagery that animates much contemporary religious, political, medical, psychiatric, and scientific thought. How else are we to account for the systematic invocation of divinities by national leaders? Or the use of the Bible, the Talmud, the Koran, or other holy books as guides to the proper channeling of one's freedom to act in the world? One of the universal solvents for guilt, engendered by the undesirable consequences of one's actions, is God. That is why religion used to be, and still is, an important social institution.

But the belief in deities as puppeteers and in people as puppets has diminished during the past few centuries. There has, however, been no corresponding increase in the human acceptance of, and tolerance for, personal responsibility and individual guilt. People still try to convince themselves that they are not responsible, or are responsible only to a very limited extent, for the undesirable consequences of their behavior. How else are we to account for the systematic invocation of Marx and Mao by national leaders? Or the use of the writings of Freud, Spock and other ostensibly scientific works as guides to the proper channeling of one's freedom to act in the world? Today, the universal solvent for guilt is science. That is why medicine is such an important social institution.

For millennia, men and women escaped from responsibility by theologizing morals. Now they escape from it by medicalizing morals. Then, if God approved a particular conduct, it was good; and if He disapproved it, it was bad. How did people know what God approved and disapproved? The Bible—that is to say, the biblical experts, called priests— told them so. Today, if Medicine approves a particular conduct, it is good; and if it disapproves it, it is bad. And how do people know what Medicine approves or disapproves? Medicine—that is to say, the medical experts, called physicians—tells them so.

The extermination of heretics in Christian pyres was a theological matter. The extermination of Jews in Nazi gas chambers was a medical matter. The inquisitorial destruction of the traditional legal procedures of Continental courts was a theological matter. The psychiatric destruction of the rule of law in American courts is a medical matter. And so it goes.[3]

Normative autonomy: Human actions should be interfered with or constrained *only* when those actions violate the freedom of others, or when interference is requested. Simply because an attempt is made to justify the interference by referring to it as "medical" makes it no more acceptable philosophically.

How medicine, the art of healing, has changed from man's ally into his adversary, and how it has done so during the very decades when its powers to heal have advanced the most momentously during its whole history—that is a story whose telling must await another occasion, perhaps even another narrator. It must suffice here to note that there is nothing new about the fact that in human affairs the power to do good is usually commensurate with, if not exceeded by, the power to do evil; that human ingenuity has created, especially in the institutions of Anglo-American law and politics, arrangements that have proved useful in dividing the power to do good into its two basic components— namely, *good* and *power*; and that these institutional arrangements, and the moral principles they embody, have sought to promote the good by depriving its producers and purveyors of power over those desiring to receive or reject their services. The most outstanding monument to that effort on the part of rulers to protect their subjects from those who would do them good, even if it meant doing them in, is the First Amendment clause guaranteeing that "Congress shall make no law respecting an establishment of religion, or prohibiting the free exercise thereof." Let me indicate briefly how I think that guaranty, and the moral and political principles it embodies, applies to our contemporary conditions.

Everyone now recognizes the reality of spiritual suffering—that is, of the fact that men, women, and children may be, and often are, distressed because they can neither find nor give meaning to their lives, or because they can neither accept nor create satisfactory standards for regulating their personal conduct. Although these circumstances result in untold suffering, no one in the United States—certainly, no judical or legal authorities—would contend that such unhappiness justifies the forcible imposition of certain religious beliefs and practices on the sufferers. Such an intervention, even if it proved "helpful" in relieving the suffering, would violate the First Amendment guaranty against the "establishment of religion."

This principle applies, and ought to be applied, to medical or so-called therapeutic interventions as well. I maintain, in other words, that suffering caused by illness—regardless of whether it is actual bodily illness or alleged mental illness—cannot be the ground, in American law, for depriving a person of liberty, even if the incarceration is called *hospitalization,* and even if the intervention is called *treatment.* I contend that such use of state power—whether rationalized as the necessary deployment of the police power or as the therapeutic application of the principle of *parens patriae*—is contrary to the ideas and ideals enshrined in the First Amendment to the Constitution.

To join this argument, we need not consider what the state might do, or ought to do, *to citizens* who are *not* suffering in order to do something *for* those who *are.* The recipients of social security or welfare payments are not subjected to the police power of the state: they are not incarcerated and are not compelled to submit to medical treatments. However, we must consider what is being done in the United States—and, of course, elsewhere too—to people who are suffering, or who are alleged to be suffering, ostensibly to help them. It is precisely at this point that the theology of medicine—and especially the theology of psychiatry and of therapy—is writ clear and large.

For example, on February 6, 1976, *Psychiatric News,* the official newspaper of the American Psychiatric Association, published a front-page interview conducted by Robert Pear of the *Washington Star* with Dr. Judd Marmor, the president of the American Psychiatric Association. After alluding to my objections to involuntary psychiatric interventions, Pear asks Marmor, "But if a person who is supposedly ill doesn't recognize his illness and doesn't request treatment—should society intervene?" To which Marmor replies, "Yes, because these individuals are suffering and it's in the nature of their suffering very often that they are in no position to evaluate the fact that they are mentally ill."

This modern therapeutic view seems to me identical to the traditional theological view acccording to which some persons are suffering and it's in the nature of their suffering very often that they are in no position to evaluate the fact that they have strayed from the true faith.

The framers of the Constitution opposed such sophistry and such policy. They reasoned—I think rightly—that even if the case were exactly as Marmor, for example, presents it, it should be enough for those solicitous for the welfare of such "sufferers" to offer them their "help." That would remove the sufferers' supposed ignorance about their own suffering and about the help available for its relief. Neither the existence of such suffering, real or alleged, nor the existence of help for it, real or alleged, could justify, in this view, an alliance between church and state and the use of the state's power to impose clerical help on unwilling clients. Just so, I insist, it cannot justify imposing clinical help on them.

How, then, has it come about that medicine has succeeded where religion has failed? How has therapy been able to breach the wall separating church and state where theology has been unable to do so? Briefly put, medicine has been able to achieve what religion has not, primarily by a radical violation of our vocabulary, of our conceptual categories; and secondarily, through the subversion of our ideals and institutions devoted to protecting us from reposing power in those who would help us whether we like it or not. We have done it before to the blacks. Now we are doing it to each other, regardless of creed, color, or race.

How was slavery justified and made possible? By calling blacks *chattel* rather than *persons.* If blacks had been recognized as persons, there could have been no selling and buying of slaves, no fugitive slave laws—in short, there could have been no American slavery. And if plantations could be called *farms,* and forcing blacks to work on them could be called guaranteeing them their *right to work,* then slavery might still be regarded as compatible with the Constitution. As it is, no term can now conceal that slavery is involuntary servitude. Nothing can. Whereas anything can now conceal the fact that institutional psychiatry is involuntary servitude.[4]

Violations of descriptive and normative autonomy are made possible by rhetorical deceptions and mystifications.

How are involuntary psychiatric interventions—and the many other medical violations of individual freedom—justified and made possible? By calling people *patients,* imprisonment *hospitalization,* and torture *therapy*; and by calling uncomplaining individuals *sufferers,* medical and mental-health personnel who infringe on their liberty and dignity *therapists,* and the things the latter do to the former *treatments.* This is why such terms as *mental health* and the *right to treatment* now so effectively conceal that psychiatry is involuntary servitude.

It is at our own peril that we forget that language is our most important possession or tool; and that whereas in the language of science we explain events, in the language of morals we justify actions. We may thus explain abortion as a certain type of medical procedure but must justify permitting or prohibiting it by calling it *treatment* or the *murder of the unborn child.*

In everday life, the distinction between explanation and justification is often blurred, and for a good reason. It is often difficult to know what one should do, what is a valid justification for engaging in a particular action. One of the best ways of resolving such uncertainty is to justify a particular course of action by claiming to explain it. We then say we have had no choice but to obey the Truth—as revealed by God or Science.

Another reason for concealing justifications as explanations is that, rhetorically, a justification offered as such is often weak, whereas a justification put forth as an explanation is often very powerful. For example, formerly, if a man had justified his not eating by saying that he wanted to starve himself to death, he would have been considered mad; but if he had explained it by saying that he was doing so the better to serve God, he would have been regarded as devoutly religious. Similarly, today, if a slender woman justifies her not eating by saying she wants to lose weight, she is considered to be a madwoman suffering from anorexia nervosa; but if she explains it by saying that she is doing so to combat some political wrongdoing in the world, she is regarded as a noble protester against injustice.

To be sure, people do suffer. And that fact—according to doctors and patients, lawyers and laymen—is now enough to justify calling and considering them patients. As in an earlier age through the universality of sin, so now through the universality of suffering, men, women, and children become—whether they like it or not, whether they want to or not—the patient-penitents of their physician-priests. And over both patient and doctor now stands the Church of Medicine, its theology defining their roles and the rules of the games they must play, and its canon laws, now called *public health* and *mental health* laws, enforcing conformity to the dominant medical ethic.

My views on medical ethics depend heavily on the analogy between religion and medicine—between our freedom, or the lack of it, to accept or reject theological and therapeutic intervention. It seems obvious that in proportion as people value religion more highly than liberty, they will seek to ally religion with the state and support state-coerced theological practices; similarly, in proportion as they value medicine more highly than liberty, they will seek to ally medicine with the state and support state-coerced therapeutic practices. The point, simple but inexorable, is that when religion and liberty conflict, people must choose between theology and freedom; and that when medicine and liberty conflict, they must choose between therapy and freedom.

If Americans were confronted with this choice today, and if they regarded religion as highly as they regard medicine, they would no doubt try to reconcile what are irreconcilable—by calling incarceration in ecclesiastical institutions *the right to attend church* and torture on the rack *the right to practice the rituals of one's faith.* If the latter terms were accepted as the proper names of the former practices, coerced religious observance and religious persecution could be held to be constitutional. Those subjected to such practices could then be categorized as persons *guaranteed their right to religion,* and those who object to such violations of human rights could be dismissed as the subverters of a free society's commitment to the practice of *freedom of religion.* Americans could then look forward breathlessly to the next issues of *Time* and *Newsweek* celebrating the latest breakthrough in *religious research.*

And yet, perhaps it is still not too late to recall that it was respect for the cure of souls, embraced and practiced freely or not at all, that inspired the framers of the Constitution to deprive clerics of secular power. It was enough, I assume they reasoned, that theologians had spiritual power; they needed no other for the discharge of their duties. Similarly, it is respect for the cure of bodies (and "minds"), embraced and practiced freely or not at all, that inspires me to urge that we deprive clinicians of secular power. It is enough, I believe, that physicians have the power inherent in their scientific knowledge and technical skills; they need no other for the discharge of their duties.

Let me hasten to say that I am not denying the scientific or technical aspects of medicine. On the contrary, I believe—and it is rather obvious—that the genuine diagnostic and therapeutic powers of medicine are much greater today than they have ever been in the history of mankind. That, precisely, is why its religious or magical powers are also much greater. Anyone who interprets my efforts to explain, and sometimes to reduce, the magical, religious, and political dimensions of medicine as an effort to cast aspersions on, or to belittle, its scientific and technical dimension does so at his own peril. [These views are] addressed to those persons who understand the difference between why a priest wears a cassock and a surgeon a sterile gown, between why an orthopedic surgeon uses a cast and a psychoanalyst a couch. Unfortunately, many people don't.

Why don't they? Why indeed should they? Why should anyone want to distinguish between technical and ceremonial acts, roles, and words? There is probably only one reason—namely, the desire to be free and responsible. If a person longs to submit to authority, he will find it useful to bestow ceremonial powers on those who wield technical skills, and vice versa; it will make the authorities seem all the more useful as priests and physicians.

People who possess certain intellectual knowledge or technical skills are obviously superior, at least in those respects, to people who do not. Thus, unless people long for a dictatorship of technicians—say, of physicians—they ought to make sure that the expert's favorable social position due to his having special skills is not further enhanced by attributing ceremonial powers to him as well. Conversely, unless they long to be fooled by fakers—say, by psychiatrists—they ought to make sure that the expert's favorable social position due to his having special ceremonial skills, or to such skills being attributed to him by others, is not further enhanced by crediting him with technical powers he does not possess.

Formerly, people victimized themselves by attributing medical powers to their priests; now, they victimize themselves by attributing magical powers to their physicians. Faced with persons endowed with such superhuman powers—and, of course, benevolence—ordinary men and women are inclined to submit to them with that blind trust whose inexorable consequence is that they make slaves of themselves and tyrants of their "protectors." That is why the framers of the Constitution urged their fellow Americans to respect priests for their faith but to distrust them for their power. To enable them to do so, they erected a wall separating church and state.

I hold, similarly, that people should respect physicians for their skill but should distrust them for their power. But unless the people erect a wall separating medicine and the state, they will be unable to do so and will succumb precisely to that danger from which the First Amendment was supposed to protect them.[5]

The most conspicuous violation of both senses of autonomy is manifested in the societal and psychiatric perspectives and practices regarding suicides. This violation requires for its successful perpetration profound rhetorical deception.

In 1967, an editorial in the *Journal of the American Medical Association* declared that "the contemporary physician sees suicide as a manifestation of emotional illness. Rarely does he view it in a context other than that of psychiatry." It was implied, the emphasis being the stronger for not being articulated, that to view suicide in this way is at once scientifically accurate and morally uplifting. I shall try to show that it is neither and that, instead, this perspective on suicide is both erroneous and evil—erroneous because it treats an act as if it were a happening and evil because it serves to legitimize psychiatric force and fraud by justifying it as medical care and treatment.

It is difficult to find a "responsible" medical or psychiatric authority today that does not regard suicide as a medical, and specifically as a mental health, problem.

For example, Ilza Veith, the noted medical historian, declares that "the act [of suicide] clearly represents an illness and is, in fact, the least curable of all diseases." Of course, it was not always thus. Veith herself remarks that "it was only in the nineteenth century that suicide came to be considered a psychiatric illness."

If so, we might ask, What was discovered in the nineteenth century that required removing suicide from the category of sin or crime and putting it into that of illness? The answer is, nothing. Suicide was not *discovered* to be a disease; it was *declared* to be one. The renaming and reclassifying as sick of a whole host of behaviors formerly considered sinful or criminal is the very foundation upon which modern psychiatry rests. The process of reclassification affects our views on suicide. I shall [show this] by citing some illustrative opinions.

Bernard R. Shochet, a psychiatrist at the University of Maryland, asserts that "depression is a serious systemic disease, with both physiological and psychological concomitants, and suicide is a part of this syndrome." This claim, as we shall see again and again, serves mainly to justify subjecting the so-called patient to involuntary psychiatric interventions, especially involuntary mental hospitalization: "If the patient's safety is in doubt, psychiatric hospitalization should be insisted on."

Harvey M. Schein and Alan A. Stone, psychiatrists at Harvard University, express the same views. "Once the patient's suicidal thoughts are shared," they write, "the therapist must take pains to make clear to the patient that he, the therapist, considers suicide to be a maladaptive action, irreversibly counter to the patient's sane interests and goals;

that he, the therapist, will do everything he can to prevent it; and that the potential for such an action arises from the patient's illness. It is equally essential that the therapist believe in the professional stance; if he does not, he should not be treating the patient within the delicate human framework of psychotherapy."

It seems to me that if a psychiatrist considers suicide a "maladaptive action," he himself should refrain from engaging in such action. It is not clear why the patient's placing confidence in his therapist to the extent of confiding his suicidal thoughts to him should *ipso facto* deprive the patient from being the arbiter of his own best interests. Yet this is exactly what Schein and Stone insist on. And again the thrust of the argument is to legitimize depriving the patient of a basic human freedom—the freedom to change therapists when patient and doctor disagree on therapy: "The therapists must insist that patient and physician— *together*—communicate the suicidal potential to important figures in the environment, both professional and family. . . . Suicidal intent must not be part of therapeutic confidentiality." And later, they add: "Obviously this kind of patient must be hospitalized. . . . The therapist must be prepared to step in with hospitalization, with security measures, and with medication. . . ." Many other psychiatric authorities could be cited to illustrate the current unanimity on this view of suicide.

Lawyers and jurists have eagerly accepted the psychiatric perspective on suicide, as they have on nearly everything else. An article in the *American Bar Association Journal* by R. E. Schulman, who is both a lawyer and a psychologist, is illustrative. Schulman begins with the premise that no one could claim that suicide is a human right: "No one in contemporary Western society," he writes, "would suggest that people be allowed to commit suicide as they please without some attempt to intervene or prevent such suicides. Even if a person does not value his own life, Western society does value everyone's life."

I should like to suggest, as others have suggested before me, precisely what Schulman claims no one would suggest. Furthermore, if Schulman chooses to believe that Western society—which includes the United States with its history of slavery, Germany with its history of National Socialism, and Russia with its history of Communism—really "does value everyone's life," so be it. But to accept that assertion as true is to fly in the face of the most obvious and brutal facts of history.

Moreover, it is mischievous to put the matter as Schulman phrases it. For it is not necessarily that the would-be suicide "does not value his own life" but rather that he may no longer want to live it as he must and may value ending it more highly than continuing it.

Schulman, however, has abandoned English for newspeak. That is illustrated by his concluding recommendation regarding treatment.

"For those," he writes, "who complete the suicide, that should be the *finis* as the person clearly intended. For those unsuccessful suicides, the law should uniformly ensure that these people be brought to the attention of the appropriate helping agency. This is not to say that help should be forced upon these people but only that it should be made available. . . ." It is sobering to see such writing in the pages of the *American Bar Association Journal;* it calls to mind what has been dubbed the Eleventh Commandment—"Don't get caught!"

The amazing success of the psychiatric ideology in converting acts into happenings, moral decisions into medical diseases, is thus illustrated by the virtually unanimous acceptance in both medical and legal circles of suicide as an "illness" for which the "patient" is not responsible. If, then, the patient is not responsible for it, someone or something else must be. Psychiatrists and mental hospitals are thus often sued for negligence when a depressed patient commits suicide, and they are often held liable.

How deeply the psychiatric perspective on suicide has penetrated into our culture is shown by the following two cases: in the first, a woman attributed her own suicide attempt to her physician; in the second, a woman attributed her husband's suicide to his employer.

A waitress was given diet pills by a physician to help her lose weight. She then attempted suicide, failed, and sued the physician for giving her a drug that "caused" her to be emotionally upset and attempt suicide. The court held for the physician. But the fact remains that both parties, and the court as well, accepted the underlying thesis— which is what I reject—that attempted suicide is *caused* rather than *willed.* The physician was held not liable, not because the court believed that suicide was a voluntary act, but because the plaintiff failed to show that the defendant was negligent in the "treatment" he prescribed.

In a similar case, the widow of a ship captain sued the shipping line for the suicide of her husband. She claimed that the captain leaped into the sea because "he was in the grip of an uncontrollable impulse at the time" and that the employer was responsible for that "impulse." Before the case could come to trial, the ship's doctor tried to assert the physician-patient privilege and declined to testify. The court ruled that in a case of this type there was no such privilege under admiralty law. I don't know whether or not the plaintiff has ultimately succeeded in her suit. But again, whatever the outcome, the proposition that suicide is an event brought about by certain antecedent *causes* rather than that it is an act motivated by certain *desires* (in this case, perhaps the ship captain's wish not to be reunited with his wife) is here enshrined in the economics, law and semantics of a civil suit for damages.

When a person decides to take his life and when a physician decides to frustrate him in this action, the question arises, Why should the physician do so?

Conventional psychiatric wisdom answers, Because the suicidal person suffers from a mental illness whose symptom is his desire to kill himself; it is the physician's duty to diagnose and treat illness; *ergo,* he must prevent the patient from killing himself and at the same time must treat the underlying disease that causes the patient to wish to do away with himself. That looks like an ordinary medical diagnosis and intervention. But it is not. What is missing? Everything. The hypothetical suicidal patient is not ill: he has no demonstrable bodily disorder (or if he does, it does not cause his suicide); he does not assume the sick role—he does not seek medical help. In short, the physician uses the rhetoric of illness and treatment to justify his forcible intervention in the life of a fellow human being—often in the face of explicit opposition from his so-called patient.

I object to that as I do to all involuntary psychiatric interventions, and especially involuntary mental hospitalization. I have detailed my reasons why elsewhere and need not repeat them here. For the sake of emphasis, however, let me state that I consider counseling, persuasion, psychotherapy, or any other voluntary measure, especially for persons troubled by their own suicidal inclinations and seeking such help, unobjectionable, and indeed generally desirable. However, physicians and psychiatrists are usually not satisfied with limiting their help to such measures—and with good reason: from such assistance the individual may gain not only the desire to live, but also the strength to die.

However, we still have not answered the question posed above, Why should a physician frustrate an individual from killing himself? Some might answer, Because the physician values the patient's life, at least when the patient is suicidal, more highly than does the patient himself. Let us examine that claim. Why should the physician, often a complete stranger to the suicidal patient, value the patient's life more highly than does the patient himself? He does not do so in medical practice. Why then should he do so in psychiatric practice, which he himself insists is a form of medical practice? Let us assume that a physician is confronted with an individual suffering from diabetes or heart failure who fails to take the drugs prescribed for his illness. We know that that can happen, and we know what happens in such cases—the patient does not do as well as he might, and he may die prematurely. Yet it would be absurd for a physician to consider, much less to attempt, taking over the conduct of such a patient's life, confining him in a hospital against his will in order to treat his disease. Indeed, an attempt to do so would bring the physician into conflict with both the civil and the criminal law. For, significantly, the law recognizes the medical patient's autonomy despite the fact that, unlike the suicidal individual, he suffers from a real disease and despite the fact that, unlike the nonexistent disease of the suicidal individual, his illness is often easily controlled by simple and safe therapeutic procedures.

Nevertheless, the threat of alleged or real suicide, or so-called dangerousness to oneself, is everywhere considered a proper ground and justification for involuntary mental hospitalization and treatment. Why should that be so?

Surely, the answer cannot be that the physician values the suicidal individual's life more highly than does that individual himself. If he really did, he could prove it—and indeed would have to prove it—by the means we usually employ to judge such matters. Here are some examples.

Because of famine, a family is starving: the parents go without food and may perish so that their children might survive. A boat is shipwrecked and is sinking: the captain goes down with the ship so that his passengers might survive.

Were the physician sincere in his claim that he values the would-be suicide's life so highly, should we not expect him to prove it by some similar act of self-sacrifice? A person may be suicidal because he has lost his money. Does the psychiatrist give him his money? Certainly not. Another may be suicidal because he is alone in the world. Does the psychiatrist give him his friendship? Certainly not.

Actually, the suicide-preventing psychiatrist does not give anything of his own to his patient. Instead, he uses the claim that he values the suicidal individual's life more highly than that individual does himself to justify his self-serving strategies; the psychiatrist aggrandizes himself as a *suicidologist*—as if new words were enough to create new wisdoms—and he enlists the economic and police powers of the state on his own behalf, using tax monies to line his own pockets and to hire underlings to take care of his patient, and psychiatric violence to guarantee himself a patient upon whom to work his medical miracles.

Let me suggest what I believe is likely to be the most important reason for the profound anti-suicidal bias of the medical profession. Physicians are committed to saving lives. How then should they react to people who are committed to throwing away their lives? It is natural for people to dislike, indeed to hate, those who challenge their basic values. The physician thus reacts, perhaps "unconsciously" (in the sense that he does not articulate the problem in these terms) to the suicidal patient as if the patient had affronted, insulted, or attacked him. The physician strives valiantly, often at the cost of his own well-being, to save lives; and here comes a person who not only does not let the physician save him but, *horribile dictu,* makes the physician an unwilling witness to that person's deliberate self-destruction. That is more than most physicians can take. Feeling assaulted in the very center of their spiritual identity, some take to flight, while others counterattack.

Some physicians will thus avoid dealing with suicidal patients. That explains why many people who end up killing themselves have a record of having consulted a physician, often on the very day of their suicide. I surmise that those people go in search of help only to discover that the physician wants nothing to do with them. And in a sense it is right that it should be so. I do not blame the doctors. Nor do I advocate teaching them suicide prevention—whatever that might be. I contend that because physicians have a relatively blind faith in their lifesaving ideology—which, moreover, they often need to carry them through their daily work—they are the wrong people for listening and talking to individuals intelligently and calmly about suicide. So much for those physicians who, in the face of the existential attack that they feel the suicidal patient launches on them, run for their lives. Let us now look at those who stand and fight back.

Some physicians (and other mental health professionals) declare themselves ready and willing to help not only suicidal patients who seek assistance, but all persons who are, or are alleged to be, suicidal. Since they too seem to perceive suicide as a threat, not just to the suicidal person's physical survival but to their own value system, they strike back and strike back hard. That explains why psychiatrists and suicidologists resort, apparently with a perfectly clear conscience, to the vilest means: they must believe that their lofty ends justify the basest means. Hence, we have the prevalent use of force and fraud in suicide prevention. The upshot of that kind of interaction between physician and patient is a struggle for power. The patient is at least honest about what he wants: to gain control over his life and death—by being the agent of his own demise. But the psychiatrist is completely dishonest about what he wants: he claims that he only wants to help his patient, but actually he wants to gain control over the patient's life in order to save himself from having to confront his doubts about the value of his own life. Suicide is medical heresy.[6]

●   ●   ●

The absurdity of the medical-psychiatric positon on suicide . . . ends in extolling mental health and physical survival over every other value, particularly individual liberty. In regarding the desire to live, but not the desire to die, as a legitimate human aspiration, the suicidologist stands Patrick Henry's famous exclamation, "Give me liberty, or give me death!" on its head. In effect, he says, *"Give him commitment, give him electroshock, give him lobotomy, give him lifelong slavery, but do not let him choose death!"* By so radically illegitimizing another person's (but not his own) wish to die, the suicide-preventer redefines the aspiration of the Other as not an aspiration at all: the wish to die becomes something an irrational, mentally diseased being *displays* or something that *happens* to a lower form of life. The result is a far-reaching infantilization and dehumanization of the suicidal person.

For example, Phillip Solomon writes that physicians "must protect the patient from his own [suicidal] wishes"; while to Edwin Schneidman, "suicide prevention is like fire prevention." Solomon thus reduces the would-be suicide to the level of an unruly child, while Schneidman reduces him to the level of a tree! In short, the suicidologist uses his professional stance to illegitimize and punish the wish to die.

There is of course nothing new about any of this. Do-gooders have always opposed personal autonomy or self-determination. In "Amok," written in 1931, Stefan Zweig puts these words into the mouth of his protagonist:

> Ah, yes, "It's one's duty to help." That's your favorite maxim, isn't it? . . . Thank you for your good intentions, but I'd rather be left to myself. . . . So I won't trouble you to call, if you don't mind. Among the "rights of man" there is a right which no one can take away, the right to croak when and where and how one pleases, without a "helping hand."

But that is not the way the scientific psychiatrist or suicidologist sees the problem. He might agree (I suppose) that in the abstract man has the right Zweig claimed for him. But in practice suicide (so he says) is the result of insanity, madness, mental illness. Furthermore, it makes no sense to say that one has a right to be mentally ill, especially if the illness is one that, like typhoid fever, threatens the health of other people as well. In short, the suicidologist's job is to try to convince people that wanting to die is a disease.

•   •   •

I submit that preventing people from killing themselves is like preventing people from leaving their homeland. Whether those who so curtail other people's liberties act with complete sincerity or with utter cynicism hardly matters. What matters is what happens—the abridgement of individual liberty, justified, in the case of suicide prevention, by psychiatric rhetoric; and, in the case of emigration prevention, by political rhetoric.

In language and logic, we are the prisoners of our premises, just as in politics and law we are the prisoners of our rulers. Hence, we had better pick them well. For if suicide is an illness because it terminates in death, and if the prevention of death by any means necessary is the physician's therapeutic mandate, then the proper remedy for suicide is indeed liberticide.[7]

Psychiatry *could* (but does not) honorably serve the ends of descriptive and normative autonomy.

In psychiatry the burning question is: Which methods are justified, and which are not, for promoting and enforcing so-called mental health? I am opposed to coercive methods in the mental health field. I also believe it is important for lawyers, psychiatrists, and the public to think about this problem and to reach conclusions of their own.

The redefinition of moral values as health values will now appear in a new light. If people believe that health values justify coercion, but that moral and political values do not, those who wish to coerce others will tend to enlarge the category of health values at the expense of the category of moral values. We are already far along this road.[8]

•   •   •

Why do I place so much emphasis on autonomy? What is the special merit of this moral concept? Let us define what we mean by autonomy, and its value will then become evident. Autonomy is a positive concept. It is freedom to develop one's self—to increase one's knowledge, improve one's skills, and achieve responsibility for one's conduct. And it is freedom to lead one's own life, to choose among alternative courses of action so long as no injury to others results.

In a modern society, based more on contract than on status, the autonomous personality will be socially more competent and useful than its heteronomous counterpart. Moreover, and very significantly, autonomy is the only positive freedom whose realization does not injure others. Other freedoms—for example, to struggle for nationalistic or religious goals—are likely to injure others; indeed, many such goals cannot be pursued meaningfully unless there is opposition to them. To be sure, self-development may also "injure" others; the better bricklayer might displace the one who is less proficient.

But there is a radical difference between the injury inflicted on others by an individual who has superior skill and by one who coerces them or harms them bodily. Indeed, to argue that, because of his excellence, the more proficient person harms his less skillful fellows is like accepting the proposition that a sadist is one who refuses to hurt a masochist. Of course it is true that a less proficient person may indeed suffer in a freely competitive society that makes no provisions for the dignified survival of those who, for any number of reasons, fare badly in competition. This is, however, better corrected by rewarding poor players for playing better than by penalizing good players for playing well.

Because of the intimate, personal relationship between psychotherapist and patient, the concept of freedom is not an abstract, academic issue in analysis. Though at first the analyst occupies a role somewhat external to the analysand's struggles for freedom—from his inhibitions, symptoms, or "internal object"—the situation soon changes. In the first place, the patient has real, extra-analytic relationships—with his mother, father, brother, employer, wife, son, and so forth; second, he has a real relationship with the analyst. In various ways, the analysand is likely to feel constrained and imprisoned, not so much by his "inner personality structure" as by actual persons. The question is: What will be the analyst's attitude toward the people in the patient's life? And, as analyst, what will be his attitude toward the patient? In both ways, the analyst is bound to influence the patient in his search for or avoidance of personal freedom.

If he practices autonomous psychotherapy, the analyst must support the patient's aspirations toward freedom from coercive objects. This does not mean that he must encourage the patient to behave in any particular way—for example, to rebel against a domineering parent, spouse, or employer. But it does mean that the analyst must candidly acknowledge and interpret the nature of the patient's significant relationships, leaving him absolute freedom to endure, modify, or sever any given relationship.

The same problem is likely to arise in the analytic situation itself. If the patient feels habitually constrained in his human relationships, he will almost surely also feel constrained by the analyst. This will be an integral part of the analysand's transference neurosis. The reason for it is that we all tend to play the games we are used to playing. Thus, the patient will come to feel that the analyst is constraining him. Herein lies the most critical reason for avoiding all coercion in analysis. Indeed, this is why I insist that analysis cannot be *anything but* autonomous psychotherapy.

If the analyst lays down restrictive rules, as Freud advocated, he cannot show the patient the difference between transference and reality; how can he, when in fact there is no difference? Conversely, if the analytic situation is contractual and free of coercion, the patient will realize it. The analytic relationship will thus not only provide the conditions necessary for a certain kind of learning experiences, but will also furnish a model of the autonomous, noncoercive relationship.

The ethic of the analytic relationship is communicated by what actually occurs between analyst and analysand. What distinguishes this enterprise from others is that, although the analyst tries to help his client, he does not "take care of him." The patient takes care of himself. Furthermore, the analysand realizes that he is "expected to recover," not in any medical or psychopathological sense, but in a purely moral sense, by learning more about himself and by assuming greater responsibility for his conduct. He learns that only self-knowledge and responsible commitment and action can set him free. In sum, autonomous psychotherapy is an actual small-scale demonstration of the nature and feasibility of the ethic of autonomy in human relationships.

The analyst conducts himself autonomously and responsibly, subordinates himself to the terms of a contract regardless of the patient's subsequent conduct, and avoids coercing the patient in any way. Given these conditions, the patient will have an opportunity to free himself of those constraints that prevent him from becoming the autonomous, authentic person he wishes to be.[9]

2

Authenticity and Humanism

Much of what now passes as mental illness is actually force and fraud — the so-called patient trying to coerce others by pretending to be sick. Similarly, much of what now passes as psychiatry is also force and fraud — the so-called psychiatric physician trying to coerce others by pretending to be a healer combating a pestilential epidemic.

Some would cite the nastiness of the madman to justify the behavior of the psychiatrist. Others would cite the nastiness of the psychiatrist to justify the behavior of the madman. The upshot is that either madness or mad-doctoring is glamorized and romanticized, when, in fact, both are too often displays of deplorable behavior.[1]

Mental illness is coercion concealed as loss of self-control; institutional psychiatry is countercoercion concealed as therapy.

Mental illness is self-enhancing deception, self-promotive strategy.[2]

Not only is the metaphor of health misused in psychiatry, but so too is the metaphor of growth. Psychiatrists, and so-called mental health professionals generally, are fond of speaking of the "growth, development, and maturity of the personality." However, the whole point of being a person is being able and free to

41

make choices and to be responsible for their consequences. An acorn does not choose to become an oak tree; but a young person does choose to become a doctor or a dentist, a priest or a politician— a tolerant or tyrannical adult.[3]

AUTHENTICITY

Legal and ethical issues should be addressed as such. Moral issues are fabricated as medical issues by deceptive physicians who disguise their moral judgments and solutions as medical diagnoses and treatments.

Like politicians, psychiatrists must often choose between being popular and being honest; though they may strive valiantly to be both, they are not likely to succeed. There are good reasons why that should be so. Men need rules to live by. They need authority they can respect and that is capable of compelling conformity to rules. Hence, institutions, even institutions ostensibly devoted to the study of human affairs, are much better at articulating rules than at analyzing them. [Let us look at some of the] history of our attitudes toward contraception and abortion.

Although it was widely practiced, birth control was regarded as vaguely reprehensible until well past the Second World War. Only in 1965 did the Supreme Court strike down as unconstitutional a Connecticut statute against the dissemination of birth-control information and devices.

In 1959, I polled the opinion of members of the American Psychoanalytic Association on several topics, some pertaining to the moral aspects of psychoanalytic practices. Among the questions I asked was, "Do you believe that birth-control information should be unrestrictedly available to all persons eighteen years of age and over?" The questionnaire, which was to be returned unsigned, was sent to 752 psychoanalysts; 430, or 56 percent, replied. Thirty-four analysts, or 9 percent of those responding, asserted that they did *not* believe that adult Americans should have free access to birth-control information.

In this connection, it is significant that only in 1964 did the House of Delegates of the American Medical Association approve a resolution endorsing the general availability of contraceptive information and measures. Until that time, the American Medical Association *opposed* free access by American adults to birth control information!

The story about abortion is similar. In my poll, I also asked, "Do you regard the legally restricted availability of abortion as socially desirable?" Two hundred and two, or nearly 50 percent of the analysts who responded, opposed the repeal of legal restrictions on abortion. (Only seven analysts identified themselves as Roman Catholics.)

In 1965, the year after the Committee on Human Reproduction of the American Medical Association recommended the resolution on contraception just mentioned, it introduced a proposal for more "liberal" abortion laws—that is, for laws expanding the medical and psychiatric grounds for therapeutic abortions. The House of Delegates refused to approve that recommendation. Without discussion or dissent, the delegates agreed that "it is not appropriate at this time for the American Medical Association to recommend the enactment of legislation in this matter."

In 1970, after New York State removed abortion from the purview of the criminal law, the American Psychoanalytic Association issued its "Position Statement on Abortion" affirming that "We view a therapeutic abortion as a medical procedure to be agreed upon between a patient and her physician; and one which should be removed entirely from the domain of the criminal law."

The point I am making here, and have been making for some time, is simply that contraception and abortion, and suicide too, are not medical but moral problems. To be sure, the procedure of aborting a pregnancy is surgical; but that makes abortion no more a medical problem than the use of the electric chair makes capital punishment a problem of electrical engineering. The question is, What is abortion—the killing of a fetus or the removal of a piece of tissue from a woman's body?

Likewise, it is undeniable that suicide, if successful, results in death. But if the suicidal act is regarded as a disease because it is the proximate cause of death, then all other acts or events—from highway traffic to avalanches, from poverty to war—that may also be the proximate causes of death would also have to be regarded as diseases. Just so, say the modern manufacturers of madness, the community psychiatrists and the epidemiologists of mental illness, who push tirelessly for a 100 percent incidence of mental illness. I say all that is malicious nonsense.[4]

The ethical psychiatrist will not misrepresent ethical and legal judgments as medical, nor misrepresent whose agent he is.

The concept of illness, whether bodily or mental, implies deviation from a clearly defined norm. In the case of physical illness, the norm is the structural and functional integrity of the human body. Although the desirability of physical health, as such, is an ethical value, what health is can be stated in anatomical and physiological terms. What is the norm deviation from which is regarded as mental illness? This question cannot be easily answered. But whatever this norm may be, we can be certain of only one thing: namely, that it must be stated in terms of psychosocial, ethical, and legal concepts. For example, notions such as "excessive repression" or "acting out an unconscious impulse" illustrate the use of psychological concepts for judging so-called mental health and illness. The idea that chronic hostility, vengefulness, or divorce are indicative of mental illness is an illustration of the use of ethical norms (that is, the desirability of love, kindness, and a stable marriage relationship). Finally, the widespread psychiatric opinion that only a mentally ill person would commit homicide illustrates the use of a legal concept as a norm of mental health. The norm from which deviation is measured, when one speaks of a mental illness, is a *psychosocial and ethical* one. Yet, the remedy is sought in terms of *medical* measures which—it is hoped and assumed—are free from wide differences of ethical value. The definition of the disorder and the terms in which its remedy is sought are therefore at odds with one another. The practical significance of this covert conflict between the alleged nature of the defect and the remedy can hardly be exaggerated.

Having identified the norms used for measuring deviations in cases of mental illness, we shall now turn to the question; Who defines the norms and hence the deviation? Two basic answers may be offered. First, it may be the person himself—that is, the patient—who decides that he deviated from a norm. For example, an artist may believe that he suffers from a work inhibition. He may implement this conclusion by seeking help *for* himself from a psychotherapist. Second, it may be someone other than the patient who decides that the latter is deviant— for example, relatives, physicians, legal authorities, society generally. A psychiatrist may then be hired by persons other than the patient to do something *to* the patient in order to correct the deviation.

These considerations underscore the importance of asking the question, "Whose agent is the psychiatrist?" and of giving a candid answer to it. The psychiatrist (or nonmedical psychotherapist) may be the agent of the patient, the relatives, the school, the military services, a business organization, a court of law, and so forth. In speaking of the psychiatrist as the agent of these persons or organizations, it is not implied that his values concerning norms, or his ideas and aims concerning the proper nature of remedial action, must coincide with those of his employer. For example, a patient in individual psychotherapy may believe that his salvation lies in a new marriage; his psychotherapist need not share this hypothesis. As the patient's agent, however, he must not resort to social or legal force to prevent the patient from putting his beliefs into action. If his *contract* is with the patient, the psychiatrist (psychotherapist) may disagree with him or stop his treatment, but he cannot engage others to obstruct the patient's aspirations. Similarly, if a psychiatrist is retained by a court to determine the sanity of an offender, he need not fully share the legal authorities' values and intentions in regard to the criminal, nor the means deemed appropriate for dealing with him. The psychiatrist cannot testify, however, that the accused is not insane, but that the legislators are—for passing the law which decrees the offender's actions illegal. Such an opinion could be voiced, of course, but not in a courtroom, and not by a psychiatrist who is there to assist the court in performing its daily work.[5]

Just as a disagreement should not masquerade as a medical judgement, punishment for deviance should not masquerade as therapy or treatment, which are deceptions designed to create quiesence in patients and others.

Total institutions, though similar to one another in the scope and degree of control which staff exercises over inmates, can be divided into two groups. In one group the inmate is expected to live up to and incorporate into himself a staff-sponsored ideal of himself and of his correct behavior. Mental hospitals and "brainwashing camps" illustrate this type of institution. In the other type—a prison, for example—this is not expected of the inmate.

This significant distinction between two types of total institutions may also be formulated in terms of honesty and deceit. It seems to me that prisons—evil as they may be—must be credited with addressing their inmates honestly. The nature of the imprisonment is clearly defined. It is as if society were to say to the inmate: "You are confined here for such-and-such reasons. As long as you are incarcerated, you must behave thus. After you have spent a certain number of months or years here, you will be set free again."

In contrast, the relationship between the mental hospital and its inmates is suffused with dishonesty and deceit. Usually, the patient is not told the true reason for his detainment. Nor is he given explicit directions about the way he must behave. Finally, his discharge is not predicated upon objective criteria, such as confinement for a given period of time. It depends instead upon the judgment by the staff of a transformation of his personality.

Much of the renaming that has characterized the history of modern psychiatry—like calling insane asylums hospitals—has served to disguise the actual functions of the institution behind a facade of benevolence toward the patients. Attention was thus diverted from the conflicts of interest between staff and inmates. Over one hundred years ago, in Mrs. Packard's famous fight against her false commitment, we find this issue displayed quite nakedly.

Mrs. Packard quotes Dr. McFarland, the superintendent of the Jacksonville (Illinois) Insane Asylum where she was confined, as having commented on her manuscript as follows:

> I should like to remark here, that I don't like your calling this place a *prison*, so much; for it isn't so. And as I'm to superintend these manuscripts for the press, I'm not willing you should call it a prison. You may call it a place of confinement, if you choose, but not a prison [italics in the original].

This problem has hardly changed since then. Psychiatrists still resort to the tactic of mislabeling in order to mislead both patients and public. Only the rationalizations, the grounds given for the mislabeling, have changed somewhat. A century ago it was justified by humanitarian motives; today by modern *medical* knowledge.

The committed mental patient is disenfranchised and subjected to coercive "treatments." His relationship to his superiors invites comparisons with other types of oppressor-oppressed relationships. The master-slave pattern is one of the most extreme forms of this type of relationship and, perhaps for that reason, one of the most illuminating.

Let us consider the traditional attitudes of psychiatrists and lay persons toward the insane in this light. Even today, many people regard hospitalized mental patients as Plato regarded slaves. They are treated as if they did not know how to be anything but patients, and as if the psychiatrist-patient arrangement served their needs. Occasionally, there is protest. The misery of the patients is exposed. But the basic pattern of oppression continues. Like slavery, commitment is justified by appeal to the public interest. Mental patients annoy "normal" people. They are often said to be "dangerous." Hence, their confinement is required for the public good.

What is the evidence for this? First, there are the constant semantic efforts to embellish psychiatric oppression as benevolence. Words like "patient," hospital," and "treatment" instead of "inmate," "prison," "asylum," and "punishment" are examples. Second, there is the violence—indeed the brutality—and also the completely unproved efficacy, of such "treatments" as lobotomy, convulsions induced by insulin, metrazol, and electricity, and most recently, the chemical straitjackets. Do the patients so treated feel that they have been helped? Rarely. Could it be that this was never the intention? Or if it was, help meant teaching them to accept their oppressed, submissive status uncomplainingly.[6]

HUMANISM

Humanism is a discriminating value used as a label indiscriminately.

Humanism is a celebration of freedom and its hallmark is an abiding concern for clear and honest *uses* of language (not reason).

I must confess that I am not sure any more what the term *humanism* means. I know, of course, that all of us here are humanists and that it is good to be a humanist. But frankly I am troubled by that sort of use of the term *humanism*—that is, by the fact that humanism implies an idea or ideal that no one—in his right mind, if I may put it that way—can be against. I think we should try to transcend humanism as a mere rhetoric of self-approbation and give it a stricter meaning.

Although you may accept the necessity of this task without further discussion, let me cite in support of my foregoing assertion the principal definitions of humanism offered by *Webster's Third New International Dictionary*: ". . . (2) devotion to human welfare: interest in or concern for man (3) a doctrine, set of attitudes, or way of life centered upon human interests and values: as (*a*) a philosophy that rejects supernaturalism, regards man as a natural object, and asserts the essential dignity and worth of man and his capacity to achieve self-realization through the use of reason and scientific method—called also *naturalistic humanism, scientific humanism* . . . (*c*) a philosophy advocating the self-fulfillment of man within the framework of Christian principles—called also *Christian humanism.* . . ."

The first three characterizations of humanism are so framed as to command nearly universal assent; why should anyone be opposed to a "concern for man"? The fourth definition narrows the field to those who reject fundamentalistic religions; and the fifth, to those who embrace Christianity. None of them are of much help. Moreover, there are those who speak of *socialist humanism, existentialist humanism,* and so forth—each of those terms referring to views of the world, and of man in it, from the particular normative perspective of the speaker and his ethical system. The term *humanism* in most of those contexts and phrases is simply a tautology. That contention is supported by the fact that no one, to my knowledge, has ever advocated an ethic of inhumanism or has ever called himself an *inhumanist.*

All this points to the importance of language in coming to grips with what is humanism, or at least with what we want to say about it in such a way as to render both assent to it and dissent from it intelligible and, at least in principle, respectable.

Although the contemporary concept of humanism is shrouded in considerable confusion and controversy, the humanists of the past—particularly those of Athens and Rome, and of the Renaissance and the Enlightenment—are like stars in the firmament with whose aid we can steer our course through the troubled seas of modern ideologies.

Moreover, although books—and, indeed, whole lives—have been devoted to the exploration and exposition of those by-gone humanisms and humanists, it is fair to say that those great epochs and their representative thinkers shared one characteristic—namely, an abiding concern for language and, more specifically, a concern for individual freedom as expressed by clear and forthright speech and for self-restraint as expressed by the disciplined and aesthetic use of language. A few illustrations, to convey the spirit rather than the substance of this outlook on life, will have to suffice here.

"A slave," said Euripides, "is he who cannot speak his thought." The right of a citizen to say what he pleased was fundamental in Athens. The Greeks, Edith Hamilton tells us, "had no authoritative Sacred Book, no creed, no ten commandments, no dogmas. The very idea of orthodoxy was unknown to them." This pervasive sense of spiritual freedom and responsibility enabled the Greeks to see the world clearly: hence their unsurpassed power as artists, whether in fashioning stones or words. In Rome, Cicero, Seneca, and Plutarch continued the Greek tradition of humanism, laying the foundations for the ground on which, fifteen centuries later, the Enlightenment humanists made their stand and from which they drew their initial sustenance. *"Homo res sacra homini"* ("Man is sacred thing to man"), said Seneca, who, in his own life, labored to oppose the fraudulent rhetoric of demagogy with clear and simple speech.

The modern age and, with it, modern humanism were ushered in with the rediscovery of the ancient classics, with the struggles that accompanied the translations of the Bible into the "vulgar" European tongues, and with the reemphasis by the *philosophes* of the intimate connection between clear thought and clear speech.

Both classical and Renaissance humanists thus displayed deep concern not only for human freedom and dignity but also for the disciplined and honest use of language. The essential, perhaps even organic, unity between man and his language has been severed in the modern age, with many contemporary humanists displaying unconcern for language and many contemporary students of language displaying unconcern for humanism.

In proportion, then, as a person uses language poorly or well, he thinks poorly or well; and, accordingly, we tend to attribute a diminished or enhanced human stature to him. Children, uneducated people, foreigners, and madmen thus tend to be seen as possessing a diminished human stature; whereas novelists, playwrights, composers, philosophers, and scientists tend to be seen as possessing an enhanced human stature. I am not asserting that the proper or accomplished use of language is sufficient for qualifying a person as a humanist, but I am suggesting that it may be necessary for it.

In short, I believe there is a pressing need among contemporary humanists for a fresh emphasis on language; for although rationality, reasoning, and thinking occupy important positions in the modern humanist credo, language, writing, and speaking are conspicuous by their absence from it. But it is idle, or worse, to persist in characterizing people according to how they reason when all that we can observe is how they use language.[7]

The essential humanist will fight for the freedom from invidious labelling, rather than fighting paternalistically for the freedom from *unhappiness* of those so labelled.

The struggle for human liberty and dignity is now being waged on many fronts and in many different ways. As humanists — as linguistic humanists, if I may suggest a tentative self-description some of us might find fitting — we could, and should, be in the vanguard of those whose weapons are pens, not swords; typewriters and books, not demonstrations and bombs. That means that we must defend human rights because the victims are human beings. If you find that assertion contrived or opaque, may I remind you that it is currently popular for humanists and civil libertarians to champion the "rights of the mentally ill" and the rights of other victimized groups such as homosexuals, drug addicts, blacks, women, and so forth. From the point of view I am trying to articulate, all that is a grave mistake. We should reject slogans such as "protecting the rights of the mentally ill" (and of other victimized groups); instead, we should protect the rights of people to reject being called or categorized as mentally ill (or anything else) against their will (except as part of the process of the administration of the criminal law). In other words, we should stand steadfast for the right of men and women to reject those involuntary identifications or diagnoses that have traditionally justified and made possible, and often continue to justify and make possible, their inferior or subhuman treatment at the hands of those who ostensibly care for them but who actually scapegoat them.

Specifically, we should insist that the members of certain victimized groups have no right to treatment, to abortion or day-care centers, to methadone, or to any other service or special consideration; what they do have a right to, however, is to be considered and called persons or human beings. Moreover, as there are no rights without corresponding duties, this position — in contrast to the currently popular paternalistic-therapeutic position toward the insane, the poor, women, and so forth — implies, first, that, however different certain members of these groups might be from us, we should refuse to regard them as *a priori* better or worse, more or less deserving, than anyone else in society; and, second, that these victims should accept the same obligation of regarding themselves as neither inherently better than or superior to, nor worse than or inferior to, others. We cannot have our cake and eat it too; we cannot preach humanism and practice male or female chauvinism, paternalism, or therapeutism.[9]

Inauthenticity, is the great corruptor of language and, hence, the greatest corruptor of humanism.

I should like to return to my proposition that high among the humanist's concerns should be language and, in particular, his own disciplined use of it. That this is not a novel idea I not only acknowledge but emphasize. I respect intellectual tradition too highly to believe that a humanist should even aspire to novelty. I believe that, instead, he should try to reaffirm and rearticulate the wisdom of the humanists who have gone before him and should build on the solid, albeit familiar, foundation that they have laid down for us.

Accordingly, I should like to cite some observations on language that best express those timeless principles and practices to which, as humanists, we must perpetually recommit ourselves.

"A Chinese sage of the distant past," as Erich Heller tells it,

> was once asked by his disciples what he would do first if he were given power to set right the affairs of the country. He answered: "I should certainly see to it that language is used correctly." The disciples looked perplexed. "Surely," they said, "this is a trivial matter. Why should you deem it so important?" And the Master replied: "If language is not used correctly, then what is said is not what is meant, then what ought to be done remains undone; if this remains undone, morals and art will be corrupted; if morals and art are corrupted, justice will go astray; if justice goes astray, the people will stand about in helpless confusion."

In our own day, George Orwell was obsessed — in the loftiest sense of this word — by the idea that language was the very soul of man. "Newspeak" is not a warning about an imaginary, future threat to human dignity; it is the imaginative rendering of an ancient, perhaps perennial, human proclivity to corrupt and control man by corrupting and controlling his language. Orwell's short essay "Politics and the English Language" may well serve as a manifesto for linguistic humanists. In it, he writes:

> The inflated style is itself a kind of euphemism. A mass of Latin words falls upon facts like soft snow, blurring the outlines and covering up all the details. The great enemy of clear language is insincerity. When there is a gap between one's real and one's declared aims, one turns as it were instinctively to long words and exhausted idioms, like a cuttlefish squirting out ink. In our age there is no such thing as "keeping out of politics." All issues are political issues, and politics itself is a mass of lies, evasions, folly, hatred, and schizophrenia. When the general atmosphere is bad, language must

suffer. I should expect to find — this is a guess which I have not sufficient knowledge to verify — that the German, Russian, Italian languages have all deteriorated in the last ten or fifteen years. as a result of dictatorship.

Orwell concludes with a recommendation we might well adopt as our credo:

> . . . one ought to recognize that the present political chaos is connected with the decay of language, and that one can probably bring about some improvement by starting at the verbal end. If you simplify your English, you are freed from the worst follies of orthodoxy. You cannot speak any of the necessary dialects, and when you make a stupid remark its stupidity will be obvious, even to yourself. Political language . . . is designed to make lies sound truthful and murder respectable, and to give an appearance of solidity to pure wind. One cannot change this all in a moment, but one can at least change one's own habits.

Everything Orwell says here about political language applies also, perhaps with even greater force, to the languages of the so-called behavioral sciences and, among them, especially to that of psychiatry. Yet it is to behavioral scientists, and especially to psychiatrists — who call and consider themselves humanists and are generally so considered by others — that the modern humanist movement has often looked for inspiration and guidance. That is a grievous error: among the enemies of humanism, psychiatry — that is to say, the ideology of mental health and mental illness and the psychiatric deceptions and coercions justified in its name — is one of the most dangerous and most powerful. Terence, we might here recall, said, "I am a man, nothing human is alien to me." The psychiatrist has inverted that. He declares, "I am a psychiatrist, nothing alien is human to me," thus reasserting the old, barbaric view of the human.

Recognizing an adversary concealed as a ally, unmasking a foe masquerading as a friend, is, however, half the battle. As for the rest of it — the battle against one of the most vicious contemporary sociopolitical creeds that wages war against human freedom and dignity by corrupting language — everything, or very nearly everything, remains to be done. I am confident, however, that if we succeed in this struggle — or, better, in proportion as we succeed in it — it will be not because we are reasonable or well-meaning, rational or liberal, religious or secular, but rather because we protect and perfect our souls by protecting and perfecting our language.[10]

Psychiatry should and could serve the values of authenticity and freedom.

Although the concept of "psychiatric symptom" is generally well enough understood, it is necessary to say a few words about what I shall mean and not mean when I use the expression. In conformity with common usage, I shall speak of "symptoms" to denote ideas, feelings, inclinations, and actions that are considered undesirable, involuntary, or alien. But in whose judgment?

The judgment that conduct is inappropriate and hence a "symptom" may be made by a number of persons: the client himself; his relatives; an expert sympathetic with his desires; an expert openly or covertly antagonistic to him; or, finally, by society in general, through its duly appointed agents (for example, a court psychiatrist). Unfortunately, people tend to use the concept of psychiatric symptom (or diagnosis) without paying much attention to the problem of who judges whom. It is not surprising, then, that an individual frequently considers his own conduct appropriate and "normal" while others consider it inappropriate and a symptom of "mental disease."

In the following discussion, I shall confine myself to those instances in which the client regards some aspect of his own conduct as a psychiatric symptom or at least concurs in such a judgment made by others. In other words, I shall not consider those cases in which some aspect of a person's conduct is labeled a "symptom" by an observer, but is considered satisfactory by the subject.

Keeping in mind, then, that we shall speak of "psychiatric symptoms" only when such categorization of behavior agrees with the subject's own judgment of his conduct, let us ask this question: What distinguishes the varied phenomena that may be classed as psychiatric symptoms? All entail an essential restriction of the patient's freedom to engage in conduct available to others similarly situated in his society.

Phenomenologically, psychiatric symptoms are endlessly diverse. The hysteric is paralyzed; he cannot speak, walk, or write. The phobic cannot engage in certain acts; he must avoid touching various objects, going into the street, or being alone. The obsessive-compulsive is compelled to attend to trivia; he must check and recheck his acts, must think particular thoughts, or perform ritual acts. The hypochondriac must attend to his health; the paranoid, to his persecutory objects; the schizophrenic, to his waking dreams.

The common element in these and other so-called psychiatric symptoms is the expression of loss of control or freedom. Each symptom is experienced or defined by the patient as something he cannot help doing or feeling or as something he must do. The alcoholic, for example, asserts that he cannot stop drinking; the habitually tardy person, that he cannot help being late; the volatile person, that he cannot control his temper; the hallucinating person, that he cannot shut out "voices" and "visions"; the depressed person, that he cannot experience pleasure or self-esteem; and so forth.

What matters to us about psychiatric symptoms, then, is that the patient experiences them or defines them as (more or less) involuntary occurrences; furthermore, since he is not free to engage in or refrain from the particular act or experience, he usually claims that he ought not be responsible for it and its consequences.

To illuminate the significance of loss of freedom in the psychiatric symptom, let us compare symptoms with habits and work. We shall consider three concrete examples: hypochondriasis, habitual ill temper, and overcommitment to work (for example, by a physician). The hypochondriac makes a career of being sick, the ill-tempered person of being nasty, and the doctor, of being helpful; they resemble one another in their overcommitment to a particular role. However, these three types of persons may differ in the degree of commitment to their role, that is, in the degree of their freedom to engage in other activities. For example, the hypochondriac is regarded as hypochondriacal to the extent that he feels compelled to ruminate on his ailments or discomforts. In other words, to the extent that he is a "prisoner" of his "symptoms," we judge such a person hypochondriacal or not.

The difference between symptom and habit is largely a matter of convention and judgment: those used to an authoritarian type of family may accept an ill-tempered father as one with a bad habit; those unaccustomed to such a family may see him as a person with a mental sickness. The ill-tempered person himself is likely to consider his behavior beyond his control and hence similar to a symptom.

Finally, we usually regard commitment to work as something freely chosen and voluntary; however, work, too, may be qualified as behavior over which one has no control. Interestingly, overcommitment to work may be either extolled or criticized; for Albert Schweitzer, it is a response to a "calling," but for the ordinary businessman or physician who overworks, it is "enslavement" to his job.

We must keep in mind that personal conduct is also a form of communication and, as communication, is always qualified as free and voluntary or unfree and involuntary. The possession or lack of freedom of one person has a crucial effect on the degree of liberty of those people with whom he associates. Hence, the concept of liberty is bound to play a significant role in psychiatry and psychotherapy.

Indeed, perhaps the best way to classify psychotherapies is from the point of view of freedom. We may thus distinguish between two groups—one aimed at increasing the patient's personal freedom, the other aimed at diminishing it. Pre-Freudian psychotherapies were characteristically repressive; they tended to abridge the patient's freedom of feeling, thought, and action. Freud's great contribution lies in having laid the foundations for a therapy that seeks to enlarge the patient's choices and hence his freedom and responsibility.

Although never clearly articulated, the aim of psychoanalytic treatment was, from the start, to "liberate" the patient. At first, Freud wanted to free the patient from the pathogenic influence of traumatic memories. Of course, this was only freedom from symptoms, in the traditional medical sense. But let us not scoff at it. Even then Freud was trying to free the patient from burdens of bad memories, which is, after all, a sort of *moral* burden. Nor is this idea outdated. Some contemporary workers hold that the pychotherapist ought to do just the opposite. The "bad" memories prove that the patient is "sinful"; hence, he should not be freed from them, but be held more responsible for them than he has been willing to be. Still, the aim as well as the result would be greater moral freedom for him.

Not long after the traumatic-memory phase of psychoanalysis, Freud developed the view that neurosis is largely a matter of inhibition; the neurotic patient is sick because he is oversocialized. The aim of therapy should be to release some of the inhibitions so that the patient may become more spontaneous and creative—in a word, freer. This idea was prevalent in analytic circles in the 1920s and 1930s. Wilhelm Reich was its main advocate. Although he failed to temper freedom with responsiblity, his work, and especially his book *Listen, Little Man!* is more important in the history of psychoanalysis than many a psychoanalytic classic. Indeed, when ego-analysis was a new discovery, most analysts believed that the aim of analysis was the destruction of the patient's (archaic) superego. Nor was this idea entirely bad. Again, my point is that the analysts were then still engaged in playing the freedom game. They wanted to liberate the patient with the automatic, unconscious influences exerted on him by his infantile introjects or, in plain English, from the ideas that had been drilled into him as a child.

Since Freud's death, the aim of analysis has been to free the patient from the constricting effects of his neurosis (the term "neurosis" meaning unconsciously determined, stereotyped behavior, in contrast to "normal," freely chosen, consciously determined conduct). Again we have the notion of freedom. Actually, the modern psychoanalytic idea of normality is somehow the same as freedom— not, of course, economic or political freedom, but personal freedom. According to this view, neurotic conduct is automatic or habitual, whereas non-neurotic or normal conduct is discriminating and selective.

Although central to the theory of psychoanalytic treatment, the precise meaning or nature of freedom in this context was not made explicit, nor was it articulated into a coherent ethical system. Yet I contend that, as psychotherapy, psychoanalysis is meaningless without an articulated ethic. Herein lies the moral and political and, at the same time, the scientific signficance of the psychoanalytic situation; it is a model of the human encounter regulated by the ethics of individualism and personal autonomy. The aim of psychoanalytic treatment is thus comparable to the aim of liberal political reform. The purpose of a democratic constitution is to give a people constrained by an oppressive government greater freedom in their economic, political, and religious conduct. The purpose of psychoanalysis is to give patients constrained by their habitual patterns of action greater freedom in their personal conduct.[11]

PART TWO

MAJOR CONTENTIONS

Introduction

Throughout his writings, Thomas Szasz argues for policies and practices that reflect his deep commitment to autonomy, authenticity, and humanism. Chapters 3 through 6 present the specific positions that form the core of Szasz's general arguments against the medicalization and the control of deviant behavior and the growing power of the "therapeutic state."

Szasz's claim (first articulated over twenty-five years ago), that mental illness is a myth, has been met with substantial hostility among his psychiatric peers and other mental health professionals. While his colleagues now consider many of his ideas less heretical, a large majority still reject even his basic contentions, at least publicly, and an overwhelming majority reject political, legal, and medical implications of these views.

In Part Two we present those of Szasz's writings which focus upon his seminal contention that mental illness is a myth; his other major contentions are featured as well. Chapter 3, by design the lengthiest chapter, specifically presents a clear articulation by Szasz of his major theme that behaviors resulting in people being called "mentally ill" are not *medically* caused and, therefore, cannot be *medically* treated. We then present selections in Chapter 3 in which he accounts for such behavior through exclusively nonmedical explanations: games, lies, and communication. The section on mental illness as communication is unusually complex and sophisticated but necessary if one is to understand Szasz's perspective, through which unusual, bizarre, or idiosyncratic behaviors are viewed as strategic communication rather than illness. Finally, since schizophrenia has emerged as the cornerstone and central paradigm of the traditional and conventional view of mental illness, the remaining portion of Chapter 3 is devoted to a presentation of

Szasz's specific attack on this "sacred symbol of psychiatry." The special emphasis given to schizophrenia does not suggest that it is different from other mythological "mental illnesses"; rather it is given because psychiatrists have presented schizophrenia as the most common, serious, and indisputably medical mental illness.

Chapter 4 demonstrates that Szasz extrapolates the above analysis when arguing for his position that if mental illness is a myth, then mental therapy must also be a myth. In the selections presented here, Szasz explains that it is not logically possible to provide "therapy" for something that is not an "illness." In subsequent selections he elaborates on the persuasive functions of "psychotherapies," ranging from self-serving purposes of the therapist to simply giving advice to people with problems. Psychotherapy, thus, becomes another type of game, and the administration of drugs becomes the justification for the medical profession's domination of those people who are viewed as mentally ill, but who in fact are simply experiencing "problems in living." As Szasz has long argued (illustrations can be found in this chapter's concluding passages), that such persuasion is viewed as medicine is attributable to the often overlooked power of rhetoric and mystification.

Chapter 5 answers the question, What is deviant behavior if it is not "illness"? Szasz contends in these representative excerpts that deviant behavior is freedom of choice; therefore, whether the behavior consists of ingesting large quantities of drugs (including alcohol), performing too many or too few or unacceptable sex acts, committing suicide, or breaking the law, it is still behavior that the individual chooses to engage in and could choose to refrain from if he so desired. It is at this point that we present Szasz's critical notion of autonomy as a two-edged sword when applied to deviant behavior, wherein freedom is protected but responsibility is required. Thus, the ingestion of drugs and alcohol by adults, as well as other deviant behavior that is purely self-regarding, should be considered legal and not subject to interference; but if criminal acts are committed under the influence of drugs, this fact should not serve to mitigate responsibility for such acts.

The legal implications of the above contentions are examined in Chapter 6, in which Szasz asserts that forensic psychiatry is fraudulent and should be eliminated. If mental illness and therapy are myths and deviant behavior is freedom of choice, then the law should not recognize claims of insanity as defenses to crime, nor should courts inquire of psychiatrists as to the mental states of defendants in assessing their competency to stand trial. Moreover, since psychiatrists do not have a base of scientific or medical knowledge from which to identify the purely intrapersonal thought processes of persons accused of crime, they should never be permitted to testify as experts in these areas.

Szasz charges that forensic psychiatry provides a pseudo-scientific, justificatory basis for depriving citizens of their constitutional rights and freedoms through involuntary civil commitment—the most pernicious outrage of institutional psychiatry, and one supported by the therapeutic state.

Finally, in Chapter 7, we pose three questions most commonly asked of us by students and colleagues who are interested in criticisms of psychiatry in general and the practical and political significance of "mental health treatment." The answers are provided in selections from Szasz wherein these issues are addressed.

3

Mental Illness Is a Myth

Bodily illness is something the patient *has,* whereas mental illness is really something he *is* or *does.* If neurosis and psychosis were diseases, like pneumonia and cancer, it should be possible for a person to have *both* a neurosis and a psychosis. But the rules of psychiatric syntax make it absurd to assert such a diagnostic combination. Actually, we use the words "neurotic" and "psychotic" (and other psychiatric diagnostic terms) to characterize persons, not to name diseases.[1]

Mental illness is a false definition of a problem about one's self and others. We don't say: "I live badly. I am immoral"; instead we say: "I am confused. My mind doesn't work properly. I am sick." And we don't say: "You live badly. You are immoral"; instead we say: "You are confused. Your mind doesn't work properly. You are sick."[2]

MENTAL ILLNESS AS DISEASE

By historical and traditional criteria, "mental illness" is not illness but a bogus invention that allows behavior, any behavior, to be categorized as "disease."

Psychiatry is conventionally defined as a medical specialty concerned with the diagnosis and treatment of mental diseases. I submit that this definition, which is widely accepted, places psychiatry in the company of alchemy and astrology and commits it to the category of pseudoscience. The reason for this is that there is no such thing as "mental illness." Psychiatrists must now choose between continuing to define their discipline in terms of nonexistent entities or substantives, or,redefining it in terms of the actual interventions or processes in which they engage.

In the history of science, thinking in terms of entities has always tended to precede thinking in terms of processes. Alchemists and astrologers thus spoke of mysterious substances and concealed their methods from public scrutiny. Psychiatrists have similarly persisted in speaking of mysterious mental maladies and have continued to refrain from disclosing fully and frankly what they do. Indeed, whether as theorists or therapists, they may do virtually anything and still claim to be, and be accepted as, psychiatrists. The actual behavior of a particular psychiatrist may thus be that of a physician, psychologist, psychoanalyst, policeman, clergyman, historian, literary critic, friend, counselor, or teacher — or sundry combinations of these roles. A physician is usually accepted as a psychiatrist so long as he insists that what concerns him is the problem of mental health and mental illness.[3]

• • •

Until the middle of the nineteenth century, and beyond, illness meant a bodily disorder whose typical manifestation was an alteration of bodily structure: that is, a visible deformity, disease, or lesion, such as a misshapen extremity, ulcerated skin, or a fracture or wound. Since in this original meaning of it, illness was identified by altered bodily structure, physicians distinguished diseases from nondiseases according to whether or not they could detect an abnormal change in the structure of a person's body. This is why, after dissection of the body was permitted, anatomy became the basis of medical science: by this means, physicians were able to identify numerous alterations in the structure of the body which were not otherwise apparent. As more specialized methods of examining bodily tissues and fluids developed, the pathologist's skills in detecting hitherto unknown bodily diseases grew explosively. Anatomical and pathological methods and criteria continue to play a constantly increasing role in enabling physicians to identify alterations in the physiochemical integrity of the body and to distinguish between persons who display such identifiable signs of illness and those who do not.

It is important to understand clearly that modern psychiatry — and the identification of new psychiatric diseases — began not by identifying such diseases by means of the established methods of pathology, but by creating a new criterion of what constitutes disease: to the established criterion of detectable alteration of *bodily structure* was now added the fresh criterion of alteration of *bodily function;* and, as the former was detected by observing the patient's body, so the latter was detected by observing his behavior. This is how and why conversion hysteria became the prototype of this new class of diseases— appropriately named "mental" to distinguish them from those that are "organic," and appropriately called also "functional" in contrast to those that are "structural." Thus, whereas in modern medicine new diseases were *discovered*, in modern psychiatry they were *invented*. Paresis was *proved* to be a disease; hysteria was *declared* to be one.

It would be difficult to overemphasize the importance of this shift in the criteria of what constitutes illness. Under its impact, persons who complained of pains and paralyses but were apparently physically intact in their bodies—that is, were healthy, by the old standards— were now declared to be suffering from a "functional illness." Thus was hysteria invented. And thus were all the other mental illnesses invented— each identified by the various complaints or functional-behavioral alterations of the persons affected by them. And thus was a compelling parallel constructed between bodily and mental illness: for example, as paresis was considered to be a structural disease of the brain, so hysteria and other mental illnesses were considered to be functional diseases of the same organ. So-called functional illnesses were thus placed in the same category as structural illnesses and were distinguished from imitated or faked illnesses by means of the criterion of voluntary falsification. Accordingly, hysteria, neurasthenia, depression, paranoia, and so forth were regarded as diseases that *happened* to people. Mentally sick persons did not "will" their pathological behavior and were therefore considered "not responsible" for it. These mental diseases were then contrasted with malingering, which was the voluntary imitation of illness. Finally, psychiatrists have asserted that malingering, too, is a form of mental illness. This presents us with the logical absurdity of a disease which, even when it is deliberately counterfeited, is still a disease.

But, clearly, this is the inescapable consequence of confusing discovering diseases with inventing them: the enterprise of trying to discover bodily diseases, constrained by fixed criteria and the requirements of empirical evidence, *cannot* eventuate in the conclusion that every phenomenon observed by the investigator is a disease; but the enterprise of inventing mental diseases, unconstrained by fixed criteria or the requirements of empirical evidence, *must* eventuate in the conclusion that any phenomenon studied by the observer may be defined as a disease.[4]

"Mental illness" is a metaphor—an arbitrary, stigmatizing label—and does not exist as a real entity any more than any other metaphor. Still, metaphors often enhance understanding, but the mental illness metaphor actually *prevents* us from understanding the behaviors called "mental illness" for what they are: problems in living.

[The belief in mental illness] rests on a serious, albeit simple, error: it rests on mistaking or confusing what is real with what is imitation; literal meaning with metaphorical meaning; medicine with morals. In other words, I maintain that mental illness is a metaphorical disease: that bodily illness stands in the same relation to mental illness as a defective television set stands to a bad television program. Of course, the word "sick" is often used metaphorically. We call jokes "sick," economies "sick," sometimes even the whole world "sick"; but only when we call minds "sick" do we systematically mistake and strategically misinterpret metaphor for fact—and send for the doctor to "cure" the "illness." It is as if a television viewer were to send for a television repairman because he dislikes the program he sees on the screen.

Furthermore, just as it is possible for a person to define himself as sick without having a bodily illness, so it is also possible for a physician to define as "sick" a person who feels perfectly well and wants no medical help, and then act as if he were a therapist trying to cure his "patient's" disease. How should we react to such a physician? Should we treat him as if he were a malevolent meddler or a benevolent healer? Today, it is considered quite unscientific and uncivilized to adopt the former posture, everyone—except the victim, and sometimes even he, himself—regarding such a physician as obviously a therapist, that is, a psychiatric therapist. I believe this is a serious error. I hold that psychiatric interventions are directed at moral, not medical, problems; in other words, that psychiatric help sought by the client stands in the same relation to psychiatric intervention imposed on him as religious beliefs voluntarily professed stand to such beliefs imposed by force.

It is widely believed that mental illness is a type of disease, and that psychiatry is a branch of medicine; and yet, whereas people readily think of and call themselves "sick," they rarely think and call themselves "mentally sick." The reason for this, as I shall try to show, is really quite simple: a person might feel sad or elated, insignificant or grandiose, suicidal or homicidal, and so forth; he is, however, not likely to categorize himself as mentally ill or insane; that he is, is more likely to be suggested by someone else. This then, is why bodily diseases are characteristically treated with the consent of the patient, while mental diseases are characteristically treated without his consent. (Individuals who nowadays seek private psychoanalytic or psychotherapeutic help do not, as a rule, consider themselves either "sick" or "mentally sick," but rather view their difficulties as problems in living and the help they receive as a type of counseling.) In short, while medical diagnoses are the names of genuine diseases, psychiatric diagnoses are stigmatizing labels.[5]

• • •

While I maintain that mental illnesses do not exist, I obviously do not imply or mean that the social and psychological occurrences to which this label is attached also do not exist. Like the personal and social troubles that people had in the Middle Ages, contemporary human problems are real enough. It is the labels we give them that concern me, and, having labeled them, what do we do about them. The demonologic concept of problems in living gave rise to therapy along theological lines. Today, a belief in mental illness implies—nay, requires—therapy along medical or psychotherapeutic lines.

I do not here propose to offer a new conception of "psychiatric illness" or a new form of 'therapy." My aim is more modest and yet also more ambitious. It is to suggest that the phenomena now called mental illnesses be looked at afresh and more simply, that they be removed from the category of illnesses, and that they be regarded as the expressions of man's struggles with *the problem of how he should live.* This problem is obviously a vast one, its enormity reflecting not only man's inability to cope with his environment, but even more his increasing self-reflectiveness.

By problems in living, then, I refer to that explosive chain reaction that began with man's fall from divine grace by partaking of the fruit of the tree of knowledge. Man's awareness of himself and of the world about him seems to be a steadily expanding one, bringing in its wake an ever larger *burden of understanding.* This burden is to be expected and must not be misinterpreted. Our only rational means for easing it is more understanding, and appropriate action based on such understanding. The main alternative lies in acting as though the burden were not what in fact we perceive it to be, and taking refuge in an outmoded theological view of man. In such a view, man does not fashion his life and much of his world about him, but merely lives out his fate in a world created by superior beings. This may logically lead to pleading non-responsibility in the face of seemingly unfathomable problems and insurmountable difficulties. Yet, if man fails to take increasing responsibility for his actions, individually as well as collectively it seems unlikely that some higher power or being would assume this task and carry this burden for him. Moreover, this seems hardly a propitious time in human history for obscuring the issue of man's responsibility for his actions by hiding it behind the skirt of an all-explaining conception of mental illness.

The notion of mental illness has outlived whatever usefulness it may have had and it now functions as a myth. As such, it is a true heir to religious myths in general, and to the belief in witchcraft in particular. It was the function of these belief-systems to act as social tranquilizers, fostering hope that mastery of certain problems may be achieved by means of substitutive, symbolic-magical, operations. The concept of mental illness thus serves mainly to obscure the everyday fact that life for most people is a continuous struggle, not for biological survival, but for a "place in the sun," "peace of mind," or some other meaning or value. Once the needs of preserving the body, and perhaps of the race, are satisfied, man faces the problem of personal significance: What should he do with himself? For what should he live? Sustained adherence to the myth of mental illness allows people to avoid facing this problem, believing that mental health, conceived as the absence of mental illness, automatically insures the making of right and safe choices in the conduct of life. But the facts are all the other way. It is the making of wise choices in life that people regard, retrospectively, as evidence of good mental health!

When I assert that mental illness is myth, I am not saying that personal unhappiness and socially deviant behavior do not exist; what I am saying is that we categorize them as diseases at our own peril.

The expression "mental illness" is a metaphor that we have come to mistake for a fact. We call people physically ill when their body-functioning violates certain anatomical and physiological norms; similarly, we call people mentally ill when their personal conduct violates certain ethical, political, and social norms. This explains why many historical figures, from Jesus Christ to Fidel Castro, and from Job to Adolf Hitler, have been diagnosed as suffering from this or that psychiatric malady.

Finally, the myth of mental illness encourages us to believe in its logical corollary: that social intercourse would be harmonious, satisfying, and the secure basis of a good life were it not for the disrupting influences of mental illness, or psychopathology. However, universal human happiness, in this form at least, is but another example of wishful fantasy. I believe that human happiness, or well-being, is possible — not just for a select few, but on a scale hitherto unimaginable. But this can be achieved only if many men, not just a few, are willing and able to confront frankly, and tackle courageously, their ethical, personal, and social conflicts. This means having the courage and integrity to forego waging battles on false fronts, finding solutions for substitute problems — for instance, fighting the battle of stomach acid and chronic fatigue instead of facing up to a marital conflict.

Our adversaries are not demons, witches, fate, or mental illness. We have no enemy that we can fight, exorcise, or dispel by "cure."

What we do have are problems in living—whether these are biologic, economic, political, or sociopsychological. . . . Mental illness is a myth whose function it is to disguise and thus render more palatable the bitter pill of moral conflicts in human relations.[6]

Behaviors, including those called "mental illness," rarely have *predictable* or *specific* chemical-neurological correlates; but even if they did, it would not demonstrate causality or, necessarily, illness.

I do not contend that human relations, or mental events, take place in a neurophysiological vacuum. It is more than likely that if a person, say an Englishman, decides to study French, certain chemical (or other) changes will occur in his brain as he learns the language. Nevertheless, I think it would be a mistake to infer from this assumption that the most significant or useful statements about this learning process must be expressed in the language of physics. This, however, is exactly what the organicist claims.

Notwithstanding the widespread social acceptance of psychoanalysts in contemporary America, there remains a wide circle of physicians and allied scientists whose basic position concerning the problem of mental illness is essentially that expressed in Carl Wernicke's famous dictum: 'Mental diseases are brain diseases." Because, in one sense, this is true of such conditions as paresis and the psychoses associated with systemic intoxications, it is argued that it is also true for all other things *called* mental diseases. It follows that it is only a matter of time until the correct physicochemical, including genetic, "bases" or "causes" of these disorders will be discovered. It is conceivable, of course, that significant physicochemical disturbances will be found in some "mental patients" and in some "conditions" now labeled "mental illnesses." But this does not mean that all so-called mental diseases have biological "causes," for the simple reason that it has become customary to use the term "mental illness" to stigmatize, and thus control, those persons whose behavior offends society—or the psychiatrist making the "diagnosis."[7]

MENTAL ILLNESS AS GAMES, LIES AND COMMUNICATION

Much of "hysteria" or "mental illness" can be understood as lying and playing games.

It is unfashionable nowadays for physicians to speak of lying. Once a person is called a "patient," psychiatrists cease to consider the possibility that he might be deceptive or mendacious; if in fact he is, they regard the lies as symptoms of a mental illness which they call hysteria, hypochondriasis, schizophrenia, or some other "psychopathology." As a result, anyone who continues to speak of lies and deceptions in connection with psychiatric problems is immediately regarded as "antipsychiatric" and "antihumanitarian": in other words, he is dismissed as both mistaken and malevolent.

I have long considered lying as one of the most important phenomena in psychiatry, a view I have formed partly by taking some of Freud's earliest observations seriously. Let us recall here how emphatically Freud condemned certain social and medical hypocrisies, which are, after all, simply lies of a certain kind. Freud was especially critical of the deceitful habits of both physicians and patients with respect to sex and money. This is the gist of Freud's recollection of his encounter, early in his medical career, with the Viennese obstetrician-gynecologist Chrobak. Chrobak had referred a patient to Freud, a woman who, because her husband was impotent, was still a virgin after eighteen years of marriage. The physician's moral obligation in such cases, so Chrobak told Freud, was to shield the husband's reputation by lying about the patient's condition. I mention this case only to show that lying—on the parts of both patients and physicians— was an important issue in psychoanalysis from its very inception. Indeed, I believe that certain psychoanalytic concepts came into being in order to deal with the *idea of lies,* for example, the unconscious and hysterical conversion; and that certain psychoanalytic arrangements came into being in order to deal with the *management of lies,* for example, free association and the psychoanalytic contract.

The medical situation, like the family situation which it often imitates, is, of course, a traditionally rich source of lies. The patients, like children, lie to the doctor. And the physicians, like parents, lie to the patients. The former lie because they are weak and helpless and cannot get their way by direct demands; the latter lie because they want their wards to know only what is "good" for them. Infantilism and paternalism are thus the sources and models for deception in the medical and psychiatric situations.

The following illustration, based on the psychoanalysis of a young woman, may be useful in forming a fuller picture of hysteria as a game. I shall say nothing about why this woman came for help or what sort of person she was, but shall concentrate on only one aspect of her behavior—namely, her lying. That she lied—in the sense that she communicated statement A to someone when she knew perfectly well that statement B was the truth—became apparent early in the analysis and remained a prominent theme throughout it. She felt, and said, that the main reason she lied was because she saw herself as a trapped child, confronted by an oppressive and unreasonable mother. As a child, she discovered that the simplest and most effective way she could cope with her mother was by lying. Her mother's acceptance of her lies encouraged her use of this strategy and firmly established lying as a habitual pattern in her life. When I saw her, many of her friends and especially her husband apparently and ostensibly accepted her lies, much as her mother had done before. Her expectation in regard to her own untruthful communications was revealing. On the one hand, she hoped that her lies would be accepted as truthful statements; on the other hand, she wished that they would be challenged and unmasked. She realized that the price she paid for lying successfully was a persistent psychological dependence on those to whom she lied. I might add that this woman led a socially perfectly normal life and did not lie indiscriminately. She was inclined to lie only to people on whom she felt dependent or toward whom she felt angry. The more she valued a relationship, the more convinced she was that she could not risk any open expression of personal differences; she then felt trapped and lied.

Lying thus became for this patient an indirect communication similar to hysterical conversion or dreaming. As we familiarize ourselves with the type of game she was playing, it became increasingly evident that, much of the time, the people to whom she lied knew she was lying. And, of course, she did too. None of this diminished the usefulness of the maneuver whose main value lay in controlling the behavior or response of the other player(s). In terms of game playing, it was as if she could not afford to take the chance to play honestly. Doing so would have meant that she would have had to make her move and then wait until her partner-opponent made his or hers. The very thought of this made her unbearably anxious, especially when she felt at conflict with someone close to her. Instead of playing honestly and exposing herself to the uncertainties and anxieties this entailed for her, she preferred to play dishonestly; that is, she lied, making communications whose effects she could predict with a high degree of confidence. Her whole marriage was thus a complicated and ceaseless game of lies, her husband ostensibly accepting her falsehoods as truths, only the better to manipulate her with them. This, then, gave her fresh ground for feeling oppressed and for lying to him. The result was a highly predictable series of exchanges between them, and a quite secure marriage for them.

One of the important psychological characteristics of playing games honestly is the absolute freedom of each player to make his moves as he sees fit, and hence the relative unpredictability of the behavior of each by the other. For example, in chess each player is free to make whatever move the game rules allow. Unless the players are extremely unevenly matched—in which case one can hardly speak of a real chess game at all—neither player can foretell with any great certainty what the other's moves will be. This, indeed, is the very point of certain games: the players are presented with risks and uncertainties which they must bear and master. And this, too, is why games are either pleasurably exciting or painfully disturbing.

To play a game, and especially to play it well, it is necessary, therefore, to be able to tolerate a measure—often a very large measure—of uncertainty. This is true no less for the metaphorical games of human relationships than it is for literal games as chess or roulette. In social relations, too, if a person conducts himself honestly, he will often be unable to predict how others will react to him and to his behavior. Suppose, then, that for some reason a person wants to control and predict the behavior of those with whom he interacts: he will then be tempted to lie and cheat. Such a person may even be said to be playing a different game than he would be playing if he were playing honestly, even though, formally, the two games are the same. An example will make this clear: in playing chess honestly, the player's aim is to master the rules of chess; in playing it dishonestly, his aim is to beat his opponent. In one case, winning is secondary to playing well and learning to play better; in the other, winning is primary and all that counts. Honest game playing thus implies that the players value the skills that go into playing the game well; whereas dishonest game playing implies that they do not value these skills. It is evident, then, that honest and dishonest game playing represent two quite different enterprises: in the one, the player's aim is successful mastery of a task—that is, playing the game well; in the other, his aim is control of the other player—that is, coercing or manipulating him to make certain specific moves. The former task requires knowledge and skills; the latter—especially in the metaphorical games of human relations—information about the other player's personality.

These considerations have the most far-reaching implications for social situations in which those in authority are concerned not with their subordinate's performance, but with their personality. Characteristically, in such situations, superiors not only tolerate but often subtly encourage inadequate task performance by their subordinates; what they want is not a competent subordinate but a subordinate they can dominate, control, and "treat." One of the most ironic examples of this is the psychoanalytic training system, in which the trainers are avowedly more concerned with the personality of the trainees than with their competence as psychoanalysts. The workings of countless other bureaucratic and educational organizations, in which superiors seek and secure psychological profiles and psychiatric reports on their subordinates, illustrate and support this interpretation: in these situations, the superiors have replaced the task of doing their job competently with the task of managing their personnel "compassionately."

Lying, as in the marriage described earlier, serves this function of relationship management well, especially if it is mutual. This value of lying derives not so much from its direct, communicative meanings as it does from its indirect, metacommunicative ones. By telling a lie, the liar in effect informs his partner that he fears and depends on him and wishes to please him: this reassures the recipient of the lie that he has some control over the liar and therefore need not fear losing him. At the same time, by accepting the lie without challenging it, the person lied to informs the liar that he, too, needs the relationship and wants to preserve it. In this way, each participant exchanges truth for control, dignity for security. Marriages and other "intimate" human relationships often endure on this basis.

As against such secure though often humiliating arrangements, relationships based on truthful communications tend to be much more vulnerable to dissolution. This accounts for the ironic, but intuitively widely understood fact that bad marriages are often much more stable than good ones. I use the words "good" and "bad" here to refer to such values as dignity, honesty, trustworthiness, and their opposites. The continuation of a marriage or its dissolution by divorce, as mere facts, codifies only the legal status of a complex human relationship; it conveys no information whatever about the true character of the relationship. This is one reason why it is so hopelessly naive and foolish to regard—as psychiatrists often do—contracting or sustaining a marriage as a sign of successful game playing—that is, as a sign of maturity or mental health; and dissolving a marriage by separation or divorce as a sign of unsuccessful game playing—that is, as a sign of immaturity or mental illness.

As an illness, hysteria is characterized by conversion symptoms. As a game, it is characterized by the goal of domination and interpersonal control; the typical strategies by which this goal is pursued are coercion by disability and illness, and by deceitful gambits of various kinds, especially lies.

Diseases may be treated. Game-playing behavior can only be changed. Accordingly, if we wish to address ourselves to the problem of the "treatment" of hysteria (or any other mental illness), we must first come to grips with the patient's life goals and values and with the physician's "therapeutic" goals and values. In what directions, toward what sorts of game-playing behavior, does the patient want to change? In what direction does the therapist want him to change? As against the word "change," the word "treatment" implies that the patient's present behavior is bad—because it is "sick"; and that the direction in which the therapist wants him to change is better or good—because it is "healthier." In this, the traditional psychiatric view, the physician defines what is good or bad, sick or healthy. In the individualistic, autonomous "psychotherapy" which I prefer, the patient himself defines what is good or bad, sick or healthy. With this arrangement, the patient might set himself goals in conflict with the therapist's values: if the therapist does not accept this, he becomes "resistant" to helping the patient—instead of the patient being "resistant" because he fails to submit to the therapist. It seems to me that any sensible description of psychotherapy ought to accomodate both of these possibilities.

In short, accounts of therapeutic interventions with so-called mental patients, and of modifications in their life activities, should be couched in the language of changes in the patient's game orientations rather than in the language of symptoms and cures. Thus, in the case of hysterical patients, changes which might be categorized as "improvements" or "cures" by some might occur in any of the following directions: more effective and ruthless coercion and domination of others; more passive and masochistic submission to others; withdrawal from the struggle over interpersonal control and increasing isolation from human relationships; and finally, learning to play other games and acquiring interest and competence in some of them.

"When one psycho-analyses a patient subject to hysterical attacks," wrote Freud in 1909, "one soon gains the conviction that these attacks are nothing but phantasies projected and translated into motor activity and represented in pantomime." In suggesting that the hysterical symptom is in effect a type of pantomime or dumb-show—the patient expressing a message by means of nonverbal, bodily signs—Freud himself acknowledged that hysteria is not an illness but an idiom or language, not a disease but a dramatization or game. For example, pseudocyesis, or false pregnancy, is the pictorial representation and dramatization of the patient's belief that she is pregnant even though she is not.

In short, hysteria is a type of language in which communication is effected by means of pictures (or iconic signs), instead of by means of words (or conventional signs). Hysterical language thus resembles other picture languages, such as charades. Those who want to deal with so-called hysterical patients must therefore learn not how to diagnose or treat them, but how to understand their special idiom and how to translate it into ordinary language. In a game of charades, one member of a team enacts an idea or proverb, and his teammates try to translate his pantomime into ordinary spoken language. Similarly, in a game of hysteria, the "patient" enacts a belief or complaint—which is what makes him the "patient"; and his teammates—family members, physicians, or psychiatrists—try to translate his pantomime—now called "hysterical conversion"—into ordinary language.[8]

Much of "hysteria" or "mental illness" can be understood as communication; thus, mental illness is idiom, not illness.

In his Introduction to Wittgenstein's *Tractatus,* Russell declares that "the essential business of language is to assert or deny facts." Only a logician, mathematician, or natural scientist, or someone having these enterprises in mind, could make such a statement. In ordinary life, language is used far more often for purposes other than to assert or deny facts than it is for it: in advertising, in friendly conversation, in religion, politics, psychiatry, and the so-called social sciences—in all these fields and situations and in many others language is used to express emotions, influence actions, and make sort of verbal contact with other persons. These distinctions point to still another criterion for classifying languages, namely their *discursiveness.*

Discursiveness is a measure of the degree of arbitrariness in the symbolization. When a mathematician says "Let x stand for a bushel of apples," or "Let g stand for the force of gravity," he is using fully discursive symbols: that is, symbols at once completely arbitrary and completely conventional. Any symbol may be used to denote the force of gravity; its actual use depends on agreement among scientists on that particular symbol.

On the other hand, when a painter uses certain colors or forms to express his despair, or when a housewife uses certain bodily signs to express hers, the symbols they use are not conventional but idiosyncratic. In short, in art, dance, and ritual—and in so-called psychiatric illness—the characteristic symbols are lawful rather than arbitrary, and yet personal rather than social.

Many philosophers have contended, and continue to contend, that when communications do not convey facts, they are mere "noises" expressing the inner feelings of the speaker. In *Philosophy in a New Key,* Suzanne Langer criticizes this view and asserts her belief in the necessity of "a genuine semantic beyond the limits of discursive language." One of my aims is to do just this: namely, to provide a systematic semiotical analysis of a language form hitherto regarded as purely expressive—that is, of the language of certain bodily signs.

In contrast to the arbitrariness of the symbols of discursive languages, one of the most important characteristics of the symbols of nondiscursive languages is their nonarbitrariness. This is best illustrated by means of the picture as a symbol: as Langer points out, the photograph of a man does not describe the person who posed for it but rather presents a replica of him. Nondiscursive symbolism is hence often called *presentational.* Further, while discursive symbols are typically abstract, having general referents, nondiscursive symbols are characteristically concrete, having specific objects or persons as their referents. For example, the word "man" refers to every conceivable man—and even woman!—in the universe, but points to no specific person. On the other hand, the photograph of a man represents and identifies a particular person.

In the earliest forms of written language, representation was achieved by means of iconic signs—that is, by hieroglyphs, which are a form of picture writing. According to Schlauch, the two simplest elements in written language are pictographs and ideographs. Both express their messages by means of pictures that *resemble* the object or idea to be conveyed. They are the earliest prototypes of what we now call the analogic type of codification. Psychoanalysis and "kinesics" are modern attempts to explore and understand the hieroglyphics that a person writes, not on marble tablets, but on and with his own body.

The advantages of discursive symbolism for transmitting information are obvious. The question is whether nondiscursive symbolism has any function besides that of expressing emotions? As I shall now show, it has several such functions.

Since verbal symbols describe the objects they denote in a relatively general, abstract fashion, the identification of a specific object requires much circumlocution (unless it has a name, which is a very special kind of discursive sign). Because of this, Langer notes that

> . . . the correspondence between a word-picture and a visible object can never be as close as that between the object and its photograph. Given all at once to the intelligent eye, an incredible wealth and detail of information is conveyed by the portrait, where we do not have to stop to construe verbal meanings. That is why we use a photograph rather than a description on a passport or in the Rogue's Gallery.

Similarly, so-called hysterical body signs are pictures which bear a much greater similarity to the objects they depict than do words describing the same objects.* To exhibit, by means of bodily signs— say, by paralyses or convulsions—the idea and message that one is sick is at once more impressive and more informative than simply saying: "I am sick." Body signs portray—they literally present and represent—in exactly what way the sufferer considers himself sick. In the symbolism of his symptom, the patient could be said to present his own complaint and—albeit in a highly condensed form—even his autobiography. This

---

*Treating certain forms of behavior as pictures, used to communicate messages, also helps us to comprehend such everyday acts as wearing certain distinctive articles of clothing, such as caps or jackets. Uniforms are used deliberately to bestow a specific identity or role on a person. In all these situations we deal with the social use of iconic signs.

is tacitly recognized by psychoanalysts who often treat the patient's presenting symptom—if he has one—as if it contained the whole history and structure of his "neurosis." When psychoanalysts say that even the simplest symptom can be understood fully only in retrospect, they mean that in order to understand the patient's "symptom" we must be acquainted with all the historically unique aspects of his personal development and social circumstances.

The situation in regard to cases of typical organic disease is quite different. The patient's symptom—say, chest pain due to coronary insufficiency—is not autobiographical. The symbolism is, in other words, not personal and idiosyncratic, but anatomical and physiologic. Chest pains cannot, for example, be the sign of, say, a fractured ankle. Knowledge of pathological anatomy and physiology thus makes it possible to interpret the medical "meaning" of certain bodily symptoms. To interpret iconic symbols, however, it is of no use to be familiar with the language of medicine. What is needed, instead, is familarity with the personality of the sign user, including his personal history, religion, occupation, and so forth.

Because so-called psychiatric problems have to do with difficulties which are, by their very nature, concrete human experiences, presentational symbolism lends itself readily to the expression of such problems. Human beings do not suffer from Oedipus complexes, sexual frustration, or pent-up anger, as abstractions; they suffer from their specific relationships with parents, mates, children, employers, and so forth. The language of psychiatric symptoms fits this situation perfectly: iconic body signs point to particular persons or events.

To better appreciate just why the communicative aspects of hysterical symptoms are incomprehensible in terms of the logic of everyday speech, let us reconsider some of Freud's clinical observations, cited earlier. Remarking on the differences between organic and hysteric pains, Freud states:

> I was struck by the indefiniteness of all the descriptions of the character of her pains given me by the patient, who was nevertheless a highly intelligent person. A patient suffering from organic pains will, unless he is neurotic in addition, describe them definitely and calmly. He will say, for instance, that they are shooting pains, that they occur at certain intervals, that they seem to him to be brought on by one thing or another. Again, when a neurasthenic describes his pains, he gives an impression of being engaged in a difficult intellectual task to which his strength is quite unequal. He is clearly of the opinion that language is too poor to find words for his sensations and that these sensations are something unique and previously unknown, of which it would be quite impossible to give an exhaustive description.

Freud's account shows how exceedingly difficult it is for the patient to find words for his so-called sensations. The same holds true for patients expressing bodily feelings associated with psychiatric syndromes other than hysteria. This loss for words by the psychiatric patient has been attributed either to the patient's having unusual experiences which are difficult to articulate precisely because of their peculiarity, or to the patient's being generally impoverished in the use of words. I would like to suggest still another possible reason for it—namely, that the patient's experience—for example, a bodily feeling—is itself a symbol in, or a part of, a nondiscursive language. The difficulty in expressing such a feeling in verbal language would then be due to the fact that nondiscursive languages do not lend themselves to translation into other idioms, least of all into discursive forms. The referents of nondiscursive symbols have meaning only if the communicants are attuned to each other. This is consistent with the actual operations of psychoanalysis: the analytic procedure rests on the tacit assumption that we cannot know—in fact, must not even expect to know—what troubles our patients until we have become attuned to them.

In what way can nondiscursive languages be used to transmit information? This question has occupied philosophers and students of signs for a long time. The informative function of a particular nondiscursive language, namely, so-called hysterical body signs, has been of special interest to psychiatrists. Although hysteria has been approached as if it were a language, it has never been systematically so codified. Let us therefore consider the informative uses of iconic body signs as a system of nondiscursive language. The following remarks will, of course, apply not only to hysteria, but also hypochondriasis, schizophrenia, and many other "mental illnesses," insofar as the patient exhibiting them makes use of body signs. Where traditional psychiatric nosology emphasizes "diagnosis," I emphasize here the use of iconic symbols in a medical or psychiatric context.

The informative use of language depends generally on the referents of its symbols. The radical positivist view, rarely held any more, maintains that nondiscursive languages have no referents at all; messages framed in this idiom are considered to be meaningless. A more balanced and today more widely accepted philosophical position regards the difference between discursive and nondiscursive languages as a matter of degree rather than kind: nondiscursive languages, too, are considered to have referents and cognitive meaning.

Anatol Rapoport has suggested that referents of nondiscursive symbols are the "inner states" of the communicants. While acknowledging that nondiscursive languages have referents, he continued to adhere to a traditional "out there-in here" distinction between them. Although nondiscursive communications tend to be simple and concrete, they are often not just expressions of the sender's inner experience. Let us consider, in this connection, the example of people fleeing a burning theater. The panicky behavior of some members of the audience may signify — even someone who neither sees flames nor hears anyone shout "Fire!" — more than mere panic. At first, perhaps, one may respond to the purely affective function of body language: "People around me are panicky: I, too, feel panicky." But closely connected with this, there is also a communication of a quasi-cognitive message: "I am in danger! I must flee to save myself!"

I cite this case to show that the referent inside a communicant — say, his affect — cannot be completely severed from the experiencing person's relationship to the world about him. This is because affects are at once private — "inner referents" — and public — indices of relationships between ego and object(s), self and others. Affects are thus the primary link between inner, private experiences and outer, publicly verifiable occurrences. Herein lies the ground for assigning more than only subjective, idiosyncratic meanings to the referents of nondiscursive languages. Accordingly, the limitation of iconic body signs does not lie only in the subjectiveness of the experience and its expression — that is, in the fact that no one can feel another's pain; it lies, also, in the fact that such signs present a picture — say, of a person writhing in pain — which, standing alone, has a very limited cognitive content.

The role of gestural communication is pertinent in this connection. Gesture is the earliest faculty of communication, the "elder brother of speech," which is consistent with the relatively primitive cognitive use to which it may be put and with the equally primitive learning — by imitation or identification — which it subserves. In semiotical terms, gesture is a highly iconic system of signs, verbal speech is only slightly iconic, while mathematics is completely noniconic.

When hysterical body signs are used to transmit information, they exhibit the same limitations as do nondiscursive languages generally. Weakly discursive languages cannot be readily translated into more strongly discursive ones. When such translation is attempted, the possibilities for error are enormous, since virtually any discursive rendition of the original message will, in a sense, be false. There are two basic reasons, then, why hysterical symptoms so often misinform: one is the linguistic difficulty, just noted, of rendering nondiscursive symbolism into discursive form; the other is that the message may actually be intended for an internal object and not for the recipient who actually receives and interprets it.

To be sure, misinformation — whether it be a mistake or a lie — may be communicated by means of ordinary language as well as by iconic body signs. We speak of a lie when the misinformation serves the speaker's interests and when we believe that he has sent the false message deliberately. And we speak of mistake when the misinformation appears to be indifferent and when we believe that the speaker has not sent the false message deliberately. Hence, there can be no such thing as a "deliberate mistake," but mistakes out of accident, ignorance, or lack of skill are possible.

In formulating this distinction between lies and mistakes I have deliberately avoided the concept of consciousness. The traditional psychoanalytic idea that so-called conscious imitation of illness is "malingering" and hence "not illness," whereas its allegedly unconscious simulation is itself "illness," that is, "hysteria," creates more problems than it solves. I think it is more useful to distinguish between goal-directed and rule-following behavior on the one hand, and indifferent mistakes on the other. In psychoanalytic theory there is no room for indifferent mistakes—because it is tacitly assumed that all action is goal-directed. It then follows that a person's failure to perform adequately cannot be due to his ignorance of the rules of the game or to his lack of skills in playing it. Instead, the failure itself is regarded as a goal, albeit, an unconscious one. This perspective is useful for the therapeutic attitude it inspires. But it is obvious that not all human error is of this purposive kind. To insist on this view is to deny the very possibility of genuine error.

Furthermore, when discovered, people caught in a lie usually utter more lies or say they were merely mistaken (which itself may be a lie), whereas people caught in a mistake usually apologize for it. From a cognitive point of view, of course, both lies and mistakes are simply falsehoods; from a pragmatic point of view, lies are acts for which we hold persons responsible, whereas mistakes are occurrences for which we do not hold them responsible. Accordingly, whether a particular communication is considered to be a lie or a mistake depends in part on the observer's attitude toward the speaker and his judgement of the speaker's character and conduct. In short, we have a choice between regarding hysteria as a lie or as a mistake. I believe it is cognitively more accurate, and morally more dignified, to regard it as a lie rather than a mistake: empirical evidence favors this view as description or theory; and the desirability of treating persons as responsible agents rather than as inert things favors this view as prescription or strategy.

The study of hysteria, and of psychiatric problems generally, places Donne's famous utterance "No man is an island, entire of itself" in a fresh perspective. Human beings need other human beings. This need cannot be reduced to other, more elementary needs. Freud went far in elucidating the young child's immense need for and dependence upon his parents; especially his mother or mother surrogate. The theory of object relationships—so central to contemporary psychoanalytic theory—presupposes the need for objects. The essential task of psychoanalysis may even be said to be the study and clarification of the kinds of objects people need, and the exact ways in which they need them. Indeed, much of recent psychoanalytic literature deals with the various mechanisms for seeking and maintaining object relationships. This perspective has made it possible to interpret such things as touching, caressing, cuddling, and, sexual intercourse as various means of making contact with objects.

There is no reason to assume that what is true for gestural communications is not also true for verbal language. Since all communicative behavior is addressed to someone, it has, among other functions, also the aim of making contact with another human being. We may call this the object-seeking and relationship-maintaining function of language. The significance and success of this function varies with the discursiveness of the language used. If the principal aim of the communication is to establish human contact, the language used to achieve it will be relatively nondiscursive—for example, small talk, dancing, "schizophrenic" bodily symptoms. Because of this, we are justified in treating relatively slightly discursive communications mainly as methods of making contact with people rather than as methods of communicating information to them.

This viewpoint is especially relevant to the interpretation of such things as the dance, music, religious ritual, and the representative arts. In all of these, one person can enter into a significant relationship with another by means of a nondiscursive sign system. Using a pharmaceutical analogy, it is as if the language—dance, art, etc.—were the vehicle in which the active ingredient—human contact—is suspended and contained. Many things that people do together have mainly this function, whether it be playing tennis, going hunting with a friend, or attending a scientific meeting.

The object-contacting function of language is most important during the early years of life. With psychological development, its significance is replaced by the informative function of communication. The foremost aim of the child's earliest communications is often to seek objects and to maintain contact with them. Gradually, this "grasping" function of language diminishes. Children then learn to use language abstractly. Serious psychological commitment to reading and writing implies an orientation to persons not physically present. While verbal language, as well as the special languages of science, retain an object-seeking aspect, this becomes increasingly less personal.

Abstract symbol systems, such as mathematics, are especially valuable for object-seeking for schizoid personalities. By means of such symbolizations, object contact may be sought and obtained, while at the same time a psychological distance may be maintained between self and other; it is virtually impossible to have a personal relationship and at the same time to maintain such distance.

Highly discursive languages, such as mathematics, permit only direct communications. Mathematical signs have clearly defined referents, accepted by the mutual agreement of all who engage in "conversation" in this idiom. Ambiguity and misunderstanding are thus reduced to a minimum.

The principal linguistic cause of misunderstanding is ambiguity. In ordinary language many signs are employed in several different senses, a circumstance that allows for much ambiguity and hence misunderstanding. At the same time, referential ambiguity allows one to make indirect communications intentionally, by employing expressions known to be interpretable in more than one way.

The difference between indirectness and nondiscursiveness may now be stated. A language is called nondiscursive not because its signs have a multiplicity of well-defined referents, but rather because the referents are idiosyncratic and, hence, poorly defined. Directness and discursiveness overlap at one end, in that highly discursive expressions are also direct. They do not overlap at the other end, for nondiscursiveness itself is no guarantee that the language is useful for indirect communications. For this purpose a language of some discursiveness, such as ordinary language, is more useful than one that is completely nondiscursive, such as music.

There are many terms for various kinds of indirect communications—such as hinting, alluding, speaking in metaphor, double talk, insinuation, implication, punning, and so forth. Significantly, while hinting is neutral in regard to what is being alluded to, insinuation refers only to depreciatory allusions. Moreover, insinuation has no antonym: there is no expression to describe insinuating something "good" about someone. Although flattery might at times be communicated by allusion, the fact that no special word exists for it provides linguistic support for the thesis that hinting serves mainly to protect a speaker who is afraid of offending.

When the relationship between two people is emotionally significant but uncertain—or when either one feels dependent on or threatened by the other—then the stage is set for the exchange of indirect messages between them. There is good reason for this—namely, that indirect messages serve two important functions—to transmit information and to explore and modify the relationship between the communicants. The exploratory function may include the aim of attempting, however subtly, to change the other person's attitude to make him more receptive to the speaker's needs and desires.

Dating and courtship provide many examples of indirect communications. The young man may want sexual intercourse. The young woman may want marriage. In the intitial stages of the dating game, neither knows just what the other wants. Hence, they do not know precisely what game they are going to play. Moreover, in our culture direct communications about sexual interests and activities are still felt to be discouraged, even prohibited. Hinting and alluding thus become indispensable methods of communication.

Indirect messages permit communicative contacts when, without them, the alternatives would be total inhibition, silence, and solitude on the one hand, or, on the other, communicative behavior that is direct, offensive, and hence forbidden. This is a painful choice. In actual practice, neither alternative is likely to result in the gratification of personal or sexual needs. In this dilemma, indirect communications provide a useful compromise. As an early move in the dating game, the young man might invite the young woman to dinner or to the movies. These communications are polyvalent: both the invitation and the response to it have several "levels" of meaning. One is the level of the overt message—that is, whether they will have dinner together, go to a movie, and so forth. Another, more covert, level pertains to the question of sexual activity: acceptance of the dinner invitation implies that sexual overtures might perhaps follow. Conversely, rejection of the invitation means not only refusal of companionship for dinner, but also of the possibility of further sexual exploration. There may still be other levels of meaning. For example, acceptance of the dinner invitation may be interpreted as a sign of personal or sexual worth and hence grounds for increased self-esteem, whereas its rejection may mean the opposite and generate feelings of worthlessness.

Freud was a master of elucidating the psychological function of indirect communications. Speaking of the patient's associations to neurotic symptoms, he writes: "The idea occurring to the patient must be in the nature of an *allusion* to the repressed element, like a representation of it in indirect speech." The concept of indirect communication occupies a central position in Freud's theory of dream work and neurotic symptom formation. He compared dream formation to the difficulty which confronts "the political writer who has disagreeable truths to tell those in authority." The political writer, like the dreamer, cannot speak directly. The censor will not allow it. Each must avail himself of "indirect representations."

Indirect communication is also a frequent source of jokes, cartoons and humor of all sorts. Why is the story of the rich playboy asking the aspiring actress to come to his apartment to view his etchings funny? It is evident that the man is not interested in showing his etchings, nor the woman in looking at them, but that both are interested in sex. The man is interested because it will give him pleasure, the woman perhaps because she will be rewarded in some material way. The same message conveyed in direct language—that is, telling of a man offering a woman, say, fifty dollars to go to bed with him—would be informative but not humorous.

A linguistic interpretation of humor would thus attribute its pleasurable effects to the successful mastery of a communicative task. If a joke is taken literally—as it often is by children, persons who do not speak the language well, or so-called schizophrenics—it is no longer funny.[9]

The idiomatic communications of the "mentally ill" are strategic or purposive, often serving to insulate its user from the responsibility or blame for its expression; this use of communication characterizes, but is not peculiar to, the "mentally ill."

The protective function of indirect communications is especially important when they convey embarrassing or prohibited ideas or wishes, such as sexual and dependency needs and problems about money. Faced with such "delicate" matters, indirect communications permit the expression of a need and its simultaneous denial or disavowal. A classic example from medical practice is the physician's avoidance of discussing fees with patients and his assigning this task to a secretary or nurse. The physician communicating through his employee is simultaneously asking for money and not asking for it. The first message is contained *explicitly* in the secretary's request; the second is contained *implicitly* in the doctor's avoidance of the subject. Since the secretary acts as the physician's agent, the physician is, in effect, asking for money. However, by not discussing financial matters openly, the physician is implying that money is of no importance in his relationship with the patient. Much of what is called hypocrisy is this sort of indirect communication, serving, as a rule, the interests of the speaker and infringing correspondingly on the interests of the listener.

Whether a person considers bodily diseases and personal problems acceptable or unacceptable will depend on his particular problems as well as on his system of values. In today's health-conscious atmosphere, most bodily diseases are acceptable, but most problems in living—lip service to the contrary notwithstanding—are not. Indeed, they are especially unacceptable in a medical setting. Both patients and physicians are thus inclined to deny personal problems and to communicate in terms of bodily illnesses: for example, a man worried about his job or marriage may seek medical attention for hyperacidity and insomnia; and his physician is likely to treat him with antacids and tranquilizers.

The main advantage of hinting over more direct forms of communication is the protection it affords the speaker by enabling him to communicate without committing himself to what he says. Should the message be ill received, hinting leaves an escape route open. Indirect communications ensure the speaker that he will be held responsible only for the explicit meaning in his message. The overt message is thus a sort of vehicle for the covert message whose effect is feared.

Any reported dream may be regarded as an indirect communication or hint. The manifest dream story is the overt message, while the latent dream thoughts constitute the covert message to which the dreamer alludes. This function of dreaming—and of dream communication—is best observed in the psychoanalytic situation, since in it the recounting of dreams is a fully acceptable form of social behavior. Analytic patients often produce dreams that refer to the analyst. Frequently, such dreams reveal that the analysand has some feelings or knowledge about the analyst which he finds distressing and is afraid to mention lest the analyst become angry. For example, the analyst might have been late or might have greeted the patient absent-mindedly. The patient now finds himself in the difficult position of wanting to talk about this, to restore a more harmonious relationship with the analyst, yet being afraid to do so, lest by mentioning it he alienate the analyst still more. In this dilemma, the patient may resort to a dream communication. He might then report a dream alluding to the distressing occurrence, omitting perhaps the person of the analyst from it. This makes it possible for the patient to make the dangerous communication while keeping himself protected, since the analyst can interpret the dream in many different ways.

If the analyst is able and willing to accept the patient's reproach, he can so interpret the dream. Its covert communicative aim will then have been achieved: the embarrassing message was dispatched, the relationship to the analyst was not further endangered, and a more harmonious relationship between patient and analyst was established. On the other hand, if the analyst is upset, defensive, or otherwise unresponsive to the dream's hidden message, he might interpret the communication in some other way. Although this is clearly less desirable for the course of the analysis, it is preferable for the patient to making an overt accusation and being reprimanded for it. The misunderstanding at least does not place an additional burden on an already disharmonious relationship.

The idea that dreams are allusions is not new, Freud himself having suggested it. However, he paid less attention to dream communications as interpersonal events than he did to the mental or intrapsychic aspects of dreaming. Ferenczi went further: in a short paper provocatively titled "To Whom Does One Relate One's Dreams?" he dealt with dreams explicitly as indirect communications.

Just as any reported dream may be regarded as a hint, so may any reported hysterical symptom. Freud attributed the multiplicity of meanings characteristic of hysterical and other psychiatric symptoms and of dreams to a "motivational overdetermination"—that is, to the multiplicity of instinctual needs which the symptom satisfied. I approach the same phenomena here from a semiotical rather than from a motivational point of view: accordingly, instead of an "overdetermination of symptoms," I speak of a diversity of communicational meanings.

The hinting function of hysterical symptoms may be illustrated by the following example. Freud's patient Frau Cäcilie M. suffered from hysterical facial pain, which had at least two distinct meanings.

1. Its overt meaning, directed to the self, significant objects, physician, and others, might be stated as follows: "I am sick. You must help me! You must be good to me!"

2. Its covert meaning, directed principally to a specific person (who may have been either an actual person, or an internal object, or both), might be paraphrased as follows: "You have hurt me as if you had slapped my face. You should be sorry and make amends."

Such communicational interactions, common between husbands and wives and between parents and children, are fostered by situations which make people closely interdependent, requiring that each person curb some of his desires in order to satisfy any of them. Moreover, having curbed some of his needs, the person then demands that his partner(s) do likewise. Thus, the open, undistorted expression of needs is discouraged, and various types of indirect communications and need-satisfactions are encouraged. This sort of arrangement must be contrasted with those situations in which one person supplies the needs of another because of his special knowledge or skills, rather than because of a special relationship between them.

Institutionally based, restrictive relationships, such as those among family members or professional colleagues, must thus be contrasted with instrumentally based, nonrestrictive relationships serving the aims of practical pursuits, such as those between freely practicing experts and their clients or between sellers and buyers. In instrumentally structured situations it is not necessary for the participants to curb their needs, because the mere expression of needs in no way compels others to gratify them, as it tends to do in the family. Indeed, not only is the frank expression of needs not inhibited, but it is often encouraged, since it helps to identify a problem or need for which someone might have a solution or satisfaction.

Two proverbs illustrate these principles. "Honesty is the best policy" is a familiar English saying. In Hungarian, an equally familiar saying is "Tell the truth and get your head bashed in." The contradictions between these two proverbs is more apparent than real. In fact, each refers to a different social situation; and each is valid in its own context. Honesty is the best policy in instrumentally oriented relationships, but is dangerous in institutional settings. Einstein was rewarded for telling the truth in the open society of science; Galileo was punished for it in the closed society of the Church.

Although the idea that psychiatry deals with the analysis of communications is not new, the view that so-called mental illnesses are idioms rather than illnesses has not been adequately articulated, nor have its implications been fully appreciated.

I submit that hysteria—meaning communications by means of complaints about the body and bodily signs—constitutes a special form of sign-using behavior. This idiom has a twofold origin: first, the human body—subject to disease and disability, manifested by means of bodily signs (for example, paralysis, convulsions, etc.) and bodily feelings (for example, pain, fatigue, etc.); second, culture and society—in particular the seemingly universal custom of making life easier, at least temporarily, for those who are ill. These two basic factors account for the development and use of the special language of hysteria—which is nothing other than the "language of illness." People use this language because they have not learned to use any other, or because it is especially useful for them in their situation.

The implications of viewing and treating hysteria—and mental disorders generally—as confronting us with problems like those presented by persons speaking foreign languages rather than like those presented by persons suffering from bodily diseases are briefly as follows. We think and speak of diseases as having "causes," "treatments," and "cures." However, if a person speaks a language other than our own, we do not look for the "cause" of his peculiar linguistic behavior. It would be foolish—and fruitless—to search for the "etiology" of speaking French. To understand such behavior, we must think in terms of learning and meaning. Accordingly, we might conclude that speaking French is the result of living among people who speak French.

It follows, then, that if hysteria is an idiom rather than an illness, it is senseless to inquire into its "causes." As with languages, we shall be able to ask only how hysteria was learned and what it means. It also follows that we cannot meaningfully talk about the "treatment" of hysteria. Although it is obvious that under certain circumstances it may be desirable for a person to change from one language to another—for example, to discontinue speaking French and begin speaking English—we do not call this change a "cure." Thus, speaking, in terms of learning rather than in terms of etiology permits one to acknowledge that among a diversity of communicative forms each has its own *raison d'être,* and that, because of the particular circumstances of the communicants, each may be as "valid" as any other.

Finally, while in treating a disease the physician does something to a patient, in teaching a language the instructor helps the student to do something for himself. One may get cured of a disease, but one must learn a (foreign) language. The perennial frustration of psychiatrists and psychotherapists thus comes down to the simple fact that they often try to teach new languages to persons who have not the least interest in learning them. When his patients refused to profit from his "interpretations," Freud declared them to be "resistant" to "treatment." But when immigrants refuse to speak the language of the country in which they live and stick to their old habits of speech, we understand their behavior without recourse to such mysterious pseudomedical explanations.[10]

SCHIZOPHRENIA AS THE CENTRAL MYTH

Historically, schizophrenia has served, and continues to serve, as the cornerstone and central paradigm of the myth of mental illness.

Every group or organization whose numbers are held together by shared ideas and ideals has its distinguishing symbols and rituals. For Christians the most sacred symbol is the cross and the revered ritual is the Mass; for physicians they are the M.D. degree and the diagnosis of disease.

Persons, both as individuals and as group members, experience such symbols and rituals as their most treasured possessions which they must zealously protect from usurpation by others, especially nonmembers. In effect, they regard them as holy things whose purity they must vigilantly safeguard against pollution by insiders and outsiders alike.

Psychiatrists constitute a group. Since they are physicians, their guild is a subgroup of the medical profession as a whole. The two groups thus share, as their major symbol and ritual, the M.D. degree and the diagnosis of disease. They also share many of the other symbols and rituals of medicine, such as the white coat, the prescription blank, and the use of hospitals, clinics, nurses, and drugs. If these are the symbols and rituals that regular physicians and psychiatrists share, which are the symbols and rituals that distinguish them?

The symbol that most specifically characterizes psychiatrists as members of a distinct group of doctors is the concept of schizophrenia; and the ritual that does so most clearly is their diagnosing this disease in persons who do not want to be their patients.

When a priest blesses water, it turns into holy water—and thus becomes the carrier of the most beneficent powers. Similarly, when a psychiatrist curses a person, he turns into a schizophrenic—and thus becomes the carrier of the most maleficent powers. Like "divine" and "demonic," "schizophrenic" is a concept wonderfully vague in its content and terrifyingly awesome in its implications.

Schizophrenia has become the Christ on the cross that psychiatrists worship, and in whose name they march in the battle to reconquer reason from unreason, sanity from insanity; reverence toward it has become the mark of psychiatric orthodoxy, and irreverence toward it the mark of psychiatric heresy.[11]

• • •

Because of the dominating role and importance of schizophrenia in modern psychiatry, it is easy to fall into the trap of believing that schizophrenia has always been an important problem in this field, and in the world. This is simply not so.

Actually, the concept of dementia praecox, as we now know it, was invented by Emil Kraepelin (1855-1926) in 1898. He has since been hailed as a great medical scientist, as if he had discovered a new disease or developed a new treatment; in fact, he did neither. What he did, according to Arieti—who is very respectful toward his achievements— was this: "Kraepelin's insight consisted in including three conditions under one syndrome." The three "conditions" were "catatonia," or stupors, originally described by Karl Ludwig Kahlbaum (1828-1899); "hebephrenia," or silly and stilted behavior, partially described by Ewald Hecker (1843-1909); and "vesania typica," or hallucinations and delusions, also previously described by Kahlbaum. The point I want to emphasize here is that each of these terms refers to behavior, not disease; to disapproved conduct, not histopathological change; hence, they may loosely be called "conditions," but they are not, strictly speaking, medical conditions. If none of these three items is a disease, putting them together still does not add up to a disease. Nevertheless, the unpleasantness of the persons who displayed such "psychotic" behavior, the actual or seeming social incapacity of the "patients," and the professional prestige of physicians such as Kraepelin sufficed to establish dementia praecox as a disease whose histopathology, etiology, and treatment now awaited only the further advances of medical science.

Without waiting for such developments to occur, the disease was etymologically enhanced. Its name was changed from Latin to Greek—that is, from dementia praecox to schizophrenia. And its incidence—that is, its epidemiological significance—was increased with the stroke of a pen. All this was done by Eugen Bleuler (1857-1939) who, again, according to Arieti, accepted the fundamental nosologic concept of Kraepelin but enlarged it to a great extent, because he considered as related to dementia praecox many other conditions such as psychosis with psychopathic personalities, alcoholic hallucinoses, etc. Furthermore, he thought that the largest number of patients are never hospitalized because their symptoms are not severe enough; that is, they are latent cases.

The imagery and vocabulary of syphilology are unmistakable here: "severe cases" requiring confinement, and "latent cases" lurking about without the patient realizing that he is ill. (According to Freud, homosexuality and virtually every other kind of "psychopathology" could also be either overt or latent.) Since Bleuler, too, neither discovered a new disease nor developed a new treatment, his fame rests, in my opinion, on having invented a new disease—and, through it, a new justification for regarding the psychiatrist as a physician, the schizophrenic as a patient, and the prison where the former confines the latter as a hospital.

Still the question remained: Just what was schizophrenia? Bleuler answered this question—at least to the satisfaction of most psychiatrists past and present.

Prior to 1900, psychiatrists believed that paresis was due to bad heredity, alcoholism, smoking, and masturbation. These beliefs are now of only historical interest, like the belief in demonic possession or exorcism. We celebrate and credit with discoveries the physicians— Alzheimer, Schaudinn, Wassermann, Noguchi, and Moore—whose work demonstrated irrefutably that paresis was due to, and was a manifestation of, syphilis.

Similarly, today psychiatrists believe that schizophrenia is due to, and is a manifestation of, an organic disease of the brain. Batchelor's phrasing is illustrative: "Both Kraepelin and Bleuler believed that schizophrenia was the outcome of a pathological, anatomical, or chemical disturbance of the brain." But why should we care about what Kraepelin and Bleuler *believed?* Bleuler also believed in abstaining from alcohol and in the metaphoric rather than the literal interpretation of the Eucharist. These beliefs of Bleuler's are of no more consequence for the histopathology of schizophrenia than are Fleming's religious beliefs for the therapeutic powers of penicillin. Why, then, do psychiatrists continue to record Kraepelin's and Bleuler's *beliefs* regarding the nature of schizophrenia? Why do they not emphasize instead Kraepelin's and Bleuler's utter inability to support their beliefs with a shred of relevant *evidence?* Actually, Kraepelin and Bleuler were psychiatric clinicians, not medical investigators. Hence, they were not in a favorable position to generate any truly relevant evidence in support of their beliefs regarding the etiology or pathology of schizophrenia.

Instead, what they did was subtly to redefine the criterion of disease, from histopathology to psychopathology—that is, from abnormal bodily structure to abnormal personal behavior. Since it was unquestionably true that most people confined in mental hospitals "misbehaved," this opened the road toward charting the maps of psychopathology, thus identifying "existing" mental diseases and "discovering" new ones. It will repay us to review exactly how Bleuler achieved this scientific sleight of hand. The following quotations are from Bleuler's *Dementia Praecox or the Group of Schizophrenias,* published in 1911:

> By the term "dementia praecox" or "schizophrenia" we designate a group of psychoses whose course is at times chronic, at times marked by intermittent attacks, and which can stop or retrograde at any stage, but does not permit a full restitatio ad integrum. The disease is characterized by a specific type of alteration of thinking. . . .

But "alteration of thinking" is irrelevant from a strictly medical or physicochemical point of view. The fact that paresis is a brain disease could never have been established by studying the paretic's thinking. Then why study the schizophrenic's? Not, it seems to me, in order to prove that he is sick: that has already been established by the *presumption* of psychiatric authority whose power neither patient nor layman can match, and which no colleague dare challenge. The schizophrenic's thinking is thus anatomized and pathologized in order to create a science of psychopathology, and then of psychoanalysis and psychodynamics, all of which in turn serve to legitimize the madman as a medical (psychiatric) patient, and the mad-doctor as a medical (psychiatric) healer.

Throughout his book Bleuler emphasizes that the schizophrenic patient suffers from a "thinking disorder" manifested by a "language disorder." His book is full of illustrations of the remarks, pleas, letters, and other linguistic productions of so-called schizophrenic patients. He offers many comments about language, of which the following is typical:

> Blocking, poverty of ideas, incoherence, clouding, delusions, and emotional anomalies are expressed in the language of the patients. However, the abnormality does not lie in the language itself, but rather in its content.

Here and elsewhere, Bleuler goes to great effort to protect himself against creating the impression that in describing a schizophrenic patient he is merely describing someone who speaks oddly or differently than he does, and with whom he, Bleuler, disagrees. He never ceases to emphasize that this is not the case, that, on the contrary, the "patient" is sick and his linguistic behavior is only a "symptom" of his "illness." Here is one of Bleuler's statements epitomizing this line of argument:

> The form of linguistic expression may show every imaginable abnormality, or be absolutely correct. We often find very convincing ways of speaking in intelligent individuals. At times, I was unable to convince all of my audiences attending clinical demonstrations of the pathology of such severely schizophrenic logic.

Bleuler's premise and posture here preclude—and seem intended to preclude—questioning that the so-called schizophrenic is "sick," that he is a bona fide "patient." We are allowed to question only in what way he is sick—what sort of illness he has, what sort of "pathology" his "thinking" exhibits. To assent to this is, of course, to give away the game before beginning to play it.

Actually, often the only thing "wrong" (as it were) with the so-called schizophrenic is that he speaks in metaphors unacceptable to his audience, in particular to his psychiatrist. Sometimes Bleuler comes close to acknowledging this. For example he writes that,

> a patient says that he is being "subjected to rape," although his confinement in a mental hospital constitutes a different kind of violation of his person. To a large extent, *inappropriate figures of speech* are employed, particularly the word "murder," which recurs constantly for all forms of torment and in the most varied combinations (italics added).

Here I submit, we have a rare opportunity to see how language displays what is quintessentially human, and at the same time, to see how language may be used to deprive individuals of their humanity. When persons imprisoned in mental hospitals speak of "rape" and "murder," they use inappropriate figures of speech which signify that they suffer from thought disorders; when psychiatrists call their prisons "hospitals," their prisoners "patients," and their "patients" desire for liberty "disease," the psychiatrists are not using figures of speech, but are stating facts.

The remarkable thing about all of this is that Bleuler understood perfectly well, probably much better than do many psychiatrists today, that much of what appears strange or objectionable in schizophrenic language is the way such persons use metaphor. Nevertheless, he felt justified, on the ground of this fact alone—as the following vignette illustrates—in regarding such persons as suffering from a disease in the literal rather than metaphorical sense:

When one patient declares that she is Switzerland, or when another wants to take a bunch of flowers to bed with her so that she will not awaken any more—these utterances seem to be quite incomprehensible at first glance. But we obtain a key to the explanation by virtue of the knowledge that these patients readily substitute similarities for identities and think in symbols infinitely more frequently than the healthy: that is, they employ symbols without any regard for their appropriateness in the given situation.

Bleuler's explanation of these "symptoms" creates still further problems for the psychiatrist, logician, and civil libertarian. For this now-classic psychiatric perspective presses these questions upon us: If what makes "schizophrenic" utterances "symptoms" is that they are incomprehensible, do they still remain "symptoms" after they are no longer incomprehensible? If the utterances are comprehensible, why confine those who utter them in madhouses? Indeed, why confine persons even if their utterances are incomprehensible? These are the questions Bleuler never asks. Moreover, these questions cannot be raised in psychiatry even today, for such queries expose the empires of psychiatry as being as devoid of visible diseases as the legendary emperor was of visible clothes.

Consider in this connection the woman patient who, Bleuler writes, "'possesses' Switzerland; and in the same sense she says, 'I am Switzerland.' She may also say, 'I am freedom,' since for her Switzerland meant nothing else than freedom." What makes this woman a "schizophrenic" rather than a "poet?" Bleuler explains:

> The difference between the use of such phrases in the healthy and in the schizophrenics rests in the fact that in the former, it is a mere metaphor whereas for the patients the dividing line between direct and indirect representation has been obscured. The result is that they frequently think of these metaphors in a literal sense.

The source of Bleuler's egocentric and ethnocentric fallacy is dramatically evident here. Would a Catholic psychiatrist writing in a Catholic country have expressed himself so cavalierly about the literalization of metaphor constituting the cardinal symptom of schizophrenia, the most malignant form of madness known to medical science? For what, from a Protestant point of view, is the Catholic doctrine of transubstantiation if not the literalization of a metaphor? *Mutatis mutandis,* I hold that the psychiatric conception of mental illness is also a literalized metaphor. The main difference, in my view, between these cardinal Catholic and psychiatric metaphors and the metaphors of so-called schizophrenic patients lies not in any linguistic or logical peculiarity of the symbols but in their special legitimacy— the former being legitimate metaphors and the latter being illegitimate.

Thus, slowly and subtly but surely indeed, Bleuler—and, of course, Freud, Jung, and the other pioneer psychopathologists and psychoanalysts—managed to bring about the great epistemological transformation of our medical age: from histopathology to psychopathology. It is now unappreciated how closely these three men worked together in the crucial years before the outbreak of World War I, and how intimately intertwined were the earliest developments of psychoanalysis and psychopathology. The first psychoanalytic journal, published in 1909, was entitled *Jahrbuch für Psychoanalytische und Psychopathologische Forschungen (Yearbook for Psychoanalytic and Psychopathologic Investigations)*. Its publishers were Eugen Bleuler and Sigmund Freud, and its editor was Carl Jung. Bleuler was then the professor of psychiatry, and Jung a Privatedozent, at the University of Zürich Medical School.

Freud's fondness for pathologizing psychology—that is, life itself—was, of course, fully disclosed eight years earlier, in his popular work *The Psychopathology of Everyday Life* (1901). It was in this book that he most fully developed "his belief in the universal application of determinism to mental events." Concepts such as "idea," "choice'" and "decision," all become, in Freud's hands, "events," and all are "determined." "I believe," he writes, "in external (real) chance, it is true, but not in internal (psychical) accidental events." Thus have Bleuler, Freud, and their followers transformed our image and idea of illness, and our vocabulary for describing and defining it; thus have they displaced lesion by language, disease by disagreement, pathophysiology by psychohistory—and, generally, histopathology by psychopathology.[12]

Contemporary notions of schizophrenia represent a category error demonstrating the fundamental invalidity of the "mental illness" concept generally and, more specifically, the claim that neurological discoveries have validated, will validate, or could validate current perspectives on schizophrenia. Moreover, were some "schizophrenics" found to actually suffer from biological abnormalities, such a discovery would make current legal and moral policies toward them indefensible. The major function of the concept "schizophrenia" is epithetic, a discrediting function.

This idea has been rediscovered during the past few decades with increasing numbers of psychiatrists claiming, as if it were a novel proposition, that schizophrenia is a brain disease caused by genetic abnormalities and/or specific neurochemical defects. It is of course possible that some persons now identified as schizophrenic suffer from a biological brain abnormality; that such an abnormality affects their behavior, making them the victims of an "organic psychosis"; and that although such a specific biological defect is at present not yet demonstrable, it may, with the development of more sophisticated biomedical technology, become demonstrable in the future.

I concede the possibility that some persons now diagnosed as schizophrenic might suffer from such a disease. Indeed, research into the pathological anatomy and physiology of schizophrenia, and hence the development of a rational therapy for it, demand such an assumption. But this concession only strengthens my arguments regarding the moral and legal problems posed by so-called schizophrenic patients. It is imperative that we understand why this is so.

The proposition that schizophrenia is a brain disease is another way of saying that it is a delirium or an organic psychosis. Assuming that it is such a condition—that it is, say, like the mental state associated with diabetic ketosis—then, like diabetes, schizophrenia would be a biological condition of the organism. It would be incurable, but many of its pathological consequences—among them its mental symptoms—could be controlled by appropriate chemical agents. In that event, it would be possible to ascertain, by means of objective tests, whether a person suffers from schizophrenia. The term "schizophrenia" would then no longer designate a mental condition or a form of behavior; it would become the name of biological abnormality of the human body.

We are already familiar with a score of such diseases—Parkinsonism, epilepsy, pheochromocytoma, hypothyroidism, Cushing's syndrome (endogenous and exogenous), as well as diabetes. All of these diseases "cause" mental symptoms. Nevertheless, not one of these diseases is treated against the patient's will; none serve as the legal basis for depriving the patient of his liberty or civil rights; and no specialist in these diseases ever testifies in court that the persons afflicted with these ailments commit crimes *because* of them and are therefore not responsible for their illegal acts.

If an objective, biomedical defintion of, and test for, schizophrenia existed, then its diagnosis and treatment would of necessity conform to the diagnosis and treatment of other (real) diseases. Thus, some persons now diagnosed schizophrenic, as well as some *not* now so diagnosed, might be discovered to have schizophrenia; whereas others now diagnosed as schizophrenic might be discovered not to have schizophrenia. Obviously, involuntary psychiatric interventions, both diagnostic and therapeutic, would have to be abolished. There would be no more justification for compulsory psychiatric measures imposed on persons suffering from schizophrenia than there are for compulsory medical measures imposed on persons suffering from other (real) diseases. Likewise, the insanity defense would have to be abolished. There would be no more justification for compulsory psychiatric measures imposed on persons suffering from schizophrenia than there are for compulsory medical measures imposed on persons suffering from other (real) disease. Likewise, the insanity defense would have to be abolished. There would be no more justification for excusing schizophrenic persons for their illegal acts than there is now for excusing other sick persons for such acts.

The diagnosis and treatment of schizophrenia would thus become assimilated to the diagnosis and treatment of other (metabolic or central nervous system) diseases. The part of psychiatry devoted to identifying and treating persons so afflicted would be indistinguishable from certain other branches of medicine. To that extent, psychiatry, as we know it, would disappear. That, I fear, is neither the hope nor the expectation of the psychiatrists who claim that schizophrenia is a disease of the brain; and who, on the contrary, seem to base their professional legitimacy on the premise, and the promise, that schizophrenia is such a disease.

Conventional psychiatry treats the mind as if it were an organ like the brain. "Psychiatrists," declares Malcolm Lader, "deal with disorders of the mind and hence of the human brain, the most complex of all organs. Such an assertion rests on a fundamental categorical error. The relation of brain to mind, conventional psychiatry notwithstanding, is of a different order from the relation of kidney to urine.

Although categorized as a "mental" illness, schizophrenia is defined in behavioral terms. But, *prima facie,* the diagnosis of so-called abnormalities of behavior rests on cultural, legal, moral, and political criteria or standards. Among these, the pivotal "symptom" of the "patient's" inability to adjust to reality is particularly vexing. Clearly, the ability to make such an adjustment depends not only on the subject's (mental) capacities, but also on his economic resources and political power. Persons wielding despotic powers can always adjust to reality by making reality adjust to them. This explains why men like Hitler and Stalin were never diagnosed as schizophrenic by those who were in their grasp, but were often so diagnosed by those who were not.

The very rich may escape being diagnosed as schizophrenic for the same reason. For example, in the course of the litigation over Howard Hughes's will, one of his aides testified that Hughes "issued detailed instructions to the aides that . . . when the telephone rang in their room, and that if the call was from Mr. Hughes, they were to turn off the (T.V.) set. The reason . . . was that Mr. Hughes feared that radiation generated by a television set could travel to his ear across the telephone line." Although Hughes displayed many other "bizarre delusions" he was never diagnosed as schizophrenic.

On the other hand, poor persons may be diagnosed as schizophrenic if they upset or threaten members of their families or have no place to live. Also, now that "de-hospitalization" has become the latest psychiatric strategy in the struggle against schizophrenia, poor persons may produce "schizophrenic" symptoms to coerce psychiatrists to give them a roof over their heads. A recent newspaper article, fittingly entitled "People Without a Place," records the plight of mental patients who instead of being incarcerated in the mental hospital against their will, are discharged from it against their will. "Eddie likes his new life 'outside'," notes the reporter, "but a young schizophrenic drank hair tonic to get back in."

I have long maintained that the issue of power—economic, social, or political—is the crucial determination as to whether a person is diagnosed and detained as schizophrenic. Standard accounts of "schizophrenia" are, however, cast in a language that conceals the most elementary human conflicts about occupation, money, and family relations behind a smokescreen of so-called delusions, hallucinations, and other psychotic symptoms. Any case history of a schizophrenic patient, in any psychiatric text, supports this contention.

Today, this sort of use of the term "schizophrenia" is perhaps most familiar in its Russian version where it consists, typically, of a so-called dissident intellectual being declared schizophrenic and incarcerated in a madhouse. Faced with this phenomenon, Western psychiatrists assume (they do not usually know the "patient") and assert that the diagnosis is false and the dissident patient is, in fact, mentally healthy. In this context, they regard the term "schizophrenia" as a deliberately contrived verbal weapon used by the Soviet authorities to defame dissidents and to justify their forcible detention as mentally deranged. Accordingly, Western psychiatrists call such practices "psychiatric abuses" to contrast them with the correct uses of psychiatric diagnoses and detentions.

In fact, however, the epithetic and injunctive uses of the term "schizophrenia" are not limited to the Soviet Union: nor are they limited in the Soviet Union to political critics of the system. Indeed, in proportion as one considers coercive contemporary Western psychiatric practices unacceptable, one will recognize that the "correct" Western use of the diagnosis of schizophrenia possesses the same function of epithetic derogation and injuctive disposition as does its "abusive" Soviet version. This is not only in such obvious cases as the "schizophrenization" of Hitler, Stalin or Barry Goldwater—but also in the seemingly less obvious instances reported almost daily in the newspapers where the diagnosis of schizophrenia is attached to a person after he has committed, or has been accused of committing, a dramatic crime.

More abstractly, the epithetic sense in which the term "schizophrenia" functions may be illustrated as follows. When we say that a politician or some other public figure is a "bum" or a "crook," it is clear that we are expressing our personal opinion of his or her moral and personal worth. Anyone acquainted with the person may thus reasonably reply by saying: "I don't agree with you." But suppose that, instead of these ordinary epithets, the person is called "schizophrenic" by a psychiatrist or by a whole group of psychiatrists; suppose, further, that this "diagnosis" is offered by psychiatrists who have actually "examined" his writings or other "evidence" upon which such a diagnosis may supposedly be based. It is now no longer possible for any ordinary person acquainted with the subject to offer the rejoinder: "I don't agree with you." Why not? Because the discourse has been shifted from common sense to "psychiatric science," and because the supposed "evidence" which justifies the use of the diagnostic epithet is available only to psychiatrists and among them especially to those who have "examined" the individual.

The injunctive sense in which the term "schizophrenia" functions may be illustrated as follows. When we say that a door is white, we are making a statement about it. But when we say to someone: "Close the door!" we are not making a statement about a door at all, we are requesting a person do something to or with the door. Similarily, when we say that "Mr. Jones is a diabetic," we are making a statement about Mr. Jones. However, when we say that "Mr. Jones is a schizophrenic," we are (in all likelihood) not making a statement about Mr. Jones at all; instead, we are requesting that someone do something to or with Mr. Jones. Typically we are requesting that Mr. Jones either be inculpated as mad and hence a fit subject for psychiatric confinement, or that he be exculpated as not guilty of some crime by reason of insanity and hence not a fit subject for penal confinement. In short, "schizophrenia" is usually treated as if it were a description, when in fact it is an epithet and an injunction.

According to conventional psychiatry, the schizophrenic is a "patient" helplessly in the grip of an "illness" that "causes" him to display abnormal social behavior, much as a patient with diabetes displays abnormal carbohydrate metabolism. In fact, however, schizophrenic behavior is conduct, not "symptom." Persons called "schizophrenic" do not lack the capacity to make moral decisions; on the contrary, they exaggerate the moral dimensions of ordinary acts, displaying a caricature of decision-making behavior. "The last thing that can be said of a lunatic," writes Gilbert K. Chesterton, "is that his actions are causeless. If any human acts may loosely be called causeless, they are the minor acts of a healthy man; whistling as he walks; slashing the grass with a stick; kicking his heels or rubbing his hands." Chesterton then delivers this stunning aphorism about madness: "The madman is not the man who has lost his reason. The madman is the man who has lost everything except his reason."

I agree. I believe that whatever small truth might lurk in the biological and psychological "explanations" of schizophrenia, such accounts are largely false—for the same reason that the schizophrenic's "delusive" explanations of the world about him are false; both accounts serve to disguise certain unbearably painful truths about human existence. In my opinion, being schizophrenic (in the sense of schizophrenia as mental disease) is a career, just as being a psychiatrist is a career. We are now prevented from seeing this because officially "schizophrenia" is the name of a psychosis and "psychiatry" is the name of a profession. But names are only labels. Conventional psychiatry refuses to scrutinize schizophrenia as a name and insists that because it is the name of a disease, the thing it names is a disease. That reasoning is not worthy of further criticism.

Except when used in the highly restricted sense of a name for an as yet undiscovered brain disease, schizophrenia is not a medical but a moral problem. Bleuler's great predecessor, that famous physician of the soul, has warned: "For what shall it profit a man, if he shall gain the whole world, and lose his own soul?" Jesus understood that the man who loses his soul loses everything—except his reason! That is why the poets used to call madmen "lost souls" or the "living dead." Accordingly, such persons need spiritual regeneration (or generation)—something that theologians no longer respect and therapists refuse to recognize.

The void between the spiritual and material realms has plagued mankind for millennia. In the past, men tried to fill that void with theological fables. Today they try to fill it with therapeutic fables. Among these fables, the theories and treatments of schizophrenia are among the most popular.[13]

4

Mental Therapy Is a Myth

> Psychotherapy is a myth. Psychotherapeutic interventions are
> metaphorical treatments that stand in the same sort of relation to
> medical treatments as criticizing and editing television programs
> stand to repairing television receivers.[1]

THERAPY AS PSEUDO-MEDICINE

Psychotherapies are pseudo-medical, metaphorical treatments. With rhetorical skills and mystification, a psychotherapist may define as "therapy"
any act he or she advocates.

It is widely believed today that just as some diseases and patients are,
and ought to be, treated by means of chemotherapy or radiation therapy, others are, and ought to be, treated by means of psychotherapy.
Our language, the mirror of our mind, reflects this equation of the
medical and the mental. Fears and foibles are "psychiatric symptoms";
persons exhibiting these and countless other manifestations of "psychiatric diseases" are "psychiatric patients"; and the interventions sought
by or imposed on them are "psychiatric treatments" among which
"psychotherapies" occupy a prominent rank.

    In several books, I have argued that this entire system of inter-
locking concepts, beliefs, and practices is incorrect and immoral. In

The Myth of Mental Illness I showed why the concept of mental illness is erroneous and misleading; in *Law, Liberty, and Psychiatry,* why many of the legal uses to which psychiatric ideas and interventions are put are immoral and inimical to the ideals of individual freedom and responsibility; in *The Manufacture of Madness,* why the moral beliefs and social practices based on the concept of mental illness constitute an ideology of intolerance, with belief in mental illness and the persecution of mental patients having replaced belief in witchcraft and the persecution of witches. Here, I extend this critical perspective to the principles and practices of mental healing, in an effort to show that psychotherapeutic interventions are not medical but moral in character and are, therefore, not literal but metaphorical treatments.

There are three fundamental reasons for holding that psychotherapies are metaphorical treatments. First, if the conditions psychotherapists seek to cure are not diseases, then the procedures they use are not genuine treatments. Second, if such procedures are imposed on persons against their will, then they are tortures rather than treatments. And third, if the psychotherapeutic procedures consist of nothing but listening and talking, then they constitute a type of conversation which can be therapeutic only in a metaphorical sense.

In the eighteenth and nineteenth centuries, when people spoke of the "cure of souls," everyone knew that the diseases such cures were supposed to heal were spiritual, that the therapists were clerical, and that the cures were metaphorical. Whereas today—with the soul securely displaced by the mind and the mind securely subsumed as a function of the brain—people speak of the "cure of minds," and everyone knows that the diseases psychiatrists treat are basically similar to ordinary medical diseases, that the therapists who administer such treatment are physicians, and that the cures are the results of literal treatments.

This is neither the first nor most likely the last time in history that people have mistaken the metaphorical meaning of a word for its literal meaning and have then used the literalized metaphor for their own personal and political purposes. Coercion and conversation have become analogized to medical treatment. The results are now all around us: dance therapy and sex therapy, art therapy and aversion therapy, behavior therapy and reality therapy, individual psychotherapy and group psychotherapy. Virtually anything anyone might do in the company of another person may now be defined as psychotherapeutic. If the definer has the proper credentials, and if his audience is sufficiently gullible, any such act will be publicly accepted and accredited as a form of psychotherapy.

Mental illness and mental treatment are symmetrical and indeed symbiotic ideas. The extension of somatic therapy into psychotherapy and the metaphorization of personal influence as psychotherapeutic coincide with the extension of pathology into psychopathology and the metaphorization of personal problems as mental diseases. Since the Freudian revolution, and especially since the Second World War, the secret formula has been this: If you want to debase what a person is doing, call his act psychopathological and call him mentally ill; if you want to exalt what a person is doing, call his act psychotherapeutic and call him a mental healer. Examples of this sort of speaking and writing abound.

It used to be that the forcible abduction of one person by another constituted kidnapping. The captor's efforts to change the moral beliefs of his captive constituted coerced religious conversion. Now these acts are called "deprogramming" and "reality therapy."

"Moonies' parents given custody; 'Deprogramming' sessions begin today," reads the headline of a typical newspaper story. From an Associated Press dispatch, we learn that "five young followers of the Rev. Sun Myung Moon today begin 'deprogramming' sessions their parents hope will change their lives. 'This is very scary,' said John Hovard, 23, of Danville, California, after a court decision Thursday returned him and four others to the custody of their parents for 30 days. 'This is like the mental institutions they put dissidents in in Russia.' . . . Wayne Howard, an attorney for the parents, told reporters that 'reality therapy'— procedures commonly called deprogramming—'will begin immediately!'"

Although an appeals court stayed the judicial order for "deprogramming," it upheld the order placing the "children" in their parents' custody. "'This is a case about the very essence of life—mother, father, and children,' said Judge Vavuris in his decision. 'There is nothing closer in our society than the family. A child is a child, even though the parent might be 90 and the child 60.'" Judge Vavuris was mistaken in asserting that there is, in our society, nothing "closer" (presumably meaning "more important") than the family: in modern American society psychiatry is even more important, just as in medieval European society Christianity was even more important. These, after all, are the institutions that legitimize the family and thus support society.

Of course, before there was deprogramming or reality therapy, there was incarceration in the good old-fashioned insane asylum. In the best seller *Haywire,* Brooke Hayward describes how that method of psychiatric treatment was used by her father and by the famed Menninger Clinic on her brother Bill. It is an episode that proved strangely unsettling to several reviewers of her book. John Leonard, for example, is dismayed that "[Leland] Hayward's [an important theatrical agent and producer] idea of being a father was to send his son to a mental institution in Topeka, Kansas, when 16-year-old Bill wanted to quit school." Peter Prescott writes even more indignantly—indeed, libelously, were it not true—that "Bill, the youngest [child], angered his father, who had him thrown into the Menninger psychiatric clinic for two years. Sane when he entered, he quickly deteriorated." For decades, the Menninger Clinic has been looked upon as the psychiatric equivalent of the Mayo Clinic, a veritable Lourdes for lunatics. Nevertheless, in the context of their book reviews, these noted commentators allow themselves, and their readers, a momentary glimpse behind the psychotherapeutic rhetoric. They do not say, as Leland Hayward probably would have said, that Bill Hayward was confined in a psychiatric hospital because he was mentally ill; nor do they say, as the mad-doctors at the Menninger Clinic probably would have said, that the psychiatrists accepted Bill as a patient because he needed mental treatment. (After all, Hayward could not have "thrown" his son into a mental hospital if the psychiatists had not agreed that he was a fit subject for psychotherapy). The point, of course, is that when a person views the proceedings approvingly, he calls imprisonment in institutions such as the Menninger Clinic "psychotherapeutic."

Not only is confinement in a mental hospital therapeutic, but so is temporary leave from it. In 1976, New York State Department of Health Regulation #76-128 redefined "trial visits" as "therapeutic leaves." If being paroled from a mental hospital is a form of treatment, then of course Medicaid and insurance companies will pay for it. The justification for this piece of psychiatric legerdemain was articulated by an apologist for the American Psychiatric Association as follows: "Therapeutic leaves of increasing length as well as overnight leaves must be introduced as early as possible into the treatment plan. These leaves must be professionally monitored, regulated, and modified as clinical conditions require. . . . One has to conclude that not only are therapeutic leaves therapeutic, but that they are crucial to any rational treatment plan, and from a practical point of view they must be reimbursable." The Hospital Association of New York State has endorsed this view and has advised area hospitals that "day passes would be reimbursed if they were a part of a therapeutic plan and fully documented." Moreover, only so-called acute patients are limited to day passes; chronic patients can, apparently, have unlimited passes and their nonhospitalization may still be regarded as treatment and reimbursed by Medicaid. "Passes of greater than 24 hours duration were not possible under the present federal guidelines," according to the association, "except for chronic (hospitalization for more than 60 days) patients." The therapeutic possibilities of psychiatric semantics are clearly boundless.

A more amusing recent example of psychotherapy is the use of profanity. Traditionally, foul language has been regarded as a sign of poor manners. Since the psychiatric enlightenment, it is no doubt also a symptom of the passive-aggressive personality, and perhaps of other as yet undiscovered and unnamed mental maladies. During the declining days of the Nixon presidency, it was elevated to the ranks of psychotherapy — by, of all people, a Jesuit priest! On May 9, 1974, the *New York Times* reported that Dr. John McLaughlin, a Jesuit priest who was a special assistant to President Nixon, held a news conference in which he defended the president against growing charges that "Watergate transcripts portrayed 'deplorable, disgusting, shabby, immoral performances' by the President and his aides." Referring specifically to the "liberal use of profanity" in the Watergate transcripts, Father McLaughlin declared that "that language had 'no meaning, no moral meaning,' but served as a 'form of emotional drainage. This form of therapy is not only understandable,' Father McLaughlin said, 'but, I think, if looked at closely, good, valid, sound.'"

The most dramatic — and, at the same time, historically, the most transparent — examples of how the language of psychopathology and psychotherapy is used to vilify and glorify various human acts lie in the area of sexual behavior. Three examples will suffice.

Throughout the nineteenth century masturbation was regarded as a cause and symptom of insanity. Today, it is a psychotherapeutic technique used by sex therapists. For example, Helen Kaplan emphasizes that even though "a patient can avoid talking about masturbation guilt in psychotherapy, she must come to terms with this issue if, in sex therapy, she is instructed to experiment with self-stimulation." "Sexual tasks" play an important role in Kaplan's therapeutic armamentarium. For retarded ejaculation she prescibes the following treatment: "The patient is instructed to ejaculate in situations which in the past had evoked progressively more intense anxiety. Initially, he may masturbate to orgasm in the presence of his partner. Then she may bring him to orgasm manually." In a similar vein, Jack Annon asserts that "masturbation may be therapeutically helpful in treating a wide variety of sexual problems and, therefore, it is important for the clinician to become knowledgeable and comfortable in the area if he or she wishes to take advantage of such a treatment modality." It is indeed unfortunate that masturbation is a tax-deductible activity only if it is prescribed by a physician.

For decades, nudism was considered a form of exhibitionism and voyeurism — that is, a perversion and hence a mental illness. Today, it is an accepted form of medical treatment. In reply to an inquiry from a reader, an editorial note in the authoritative journal, *Modern Medicine*, explains that "according to the Internal Revenue Service, such [*i.e.,* nude] therapy is a deductible medical expense if the patient is referred to the group by his physician and a written statement to that effect by the physician accompanies the patient's tax return.

One of the oldest tactics in the battle between the sexes must surely be the refusal of women to gratify the sexual desires of men. With the dawn of psychiatric enlightment this behavior too has been attributed to mental illnesses, such as hysteria and frigidity; today, however, it is also enlisted in the struggle against mental illness, specifically as a cure for alcoholism. An item in *Parade* magazine begins with the following question: "How does a wife get a husband to stop drinking?" In Sydney, Australia, we learn, some wives do it by "withholding sex from their husbands." Lest the reader unscientifically conclude that these women do this because they do not like, or are angry with, their husbands, we learn that the wives' conduct is in fact a form of psychotherapy: "It's all part of a program directed by Professor S. H. Lovibond, a psychologist at the University of New South Wales. 'We don't tell the wives,' explains Professor Lovibond, 'that withholding sex is the only aversion technique, but each is left to devise her own method. Quite a few have devised sex withholding to help an alcoholically addicted husband conquer his weakness.'" Professor Lovibond's use of language is revealing: he calls alcoholism a weakness, and sex withholding an aversion technique. The article in *Parade* goes on to assure the reader that for husbands who might be happy with their wives' sexual withholding, Professor Lovibond has more persuasive therapeutic tools at his command: "Professor Lovibond also uses electroshock therapy on his problem drinkers to dissuade heavy drinkers from the bottle."

I cite these examples here not to argue that all so-called psychotherapies are coercive, fraudulent, or otherwise evil. That view is as false and foolish an oversimplification as is the view that all such interventions are healing, helpful, or otherwise good, merely because they are called "therapeutic." My point is rather that many, perhaps most, so-called psychotherapeutic procedures are harmful for the so-called patients; that this simple fact is now obscured by the expanded, loose, metaphorical—in short, jargonized—contemporary use of the term *psychotherapy;* and that all such interventions and proposals should therefore be regarded as evil until they are proven otherwise.[2]

At best, "psychotherapies" are nonmedical attempts to influence, for ethical or unethical purposes; at worst, they camouflage brutal coercion in the name of medicine.

When I suggest that psychotherapy is a myth I do not mean to deny the reality of the phenomena to which that term is applied. People do suffer from all sorts of aches and pangs, fears and guilts, depressions and futilities; many such persons do consult, or are compelled to consult, experts called psychotherapists; and one or more of the participants in the resulting transaction may consider it helpful, useful, or "therapeutic." The coming together of these two parties and the results of their coming together are conventionally called psychotherapy. All that exists and is very much a part of our social reality. But therein, precisely, lies the mythology of psychotherapy: for these comings together have nothing whatever to do with psyches and are not therapeutic.

Definitions, especially the power to construct definitions and to impose them on others, are of great importance in all aspects of human life. In psychiatry and psychotherapy, because these disciplines deal with human relations and with the influence of persons and groups on one another, how words are used is extremely important. It seems appropriate, therefore, to begin with a discussion of some definitions of psychotherapy.

Noyes' Modern Clinical Psychiatry, perhaps the single most generally accepted and widely used American psychiatric text, defines psychotherapy as:

> The treatment of emotional or personality disorders by psychological means. Although many different psychological techniques may be employed in an effort to relieve problems and disorders and make the patient a mature, satisfied, and independent person, an important therapeutic factor common to them all is the therapist-patient relationship, with its interpersonal experiences. Through this relationship the patient comes to know that he can share his feelings, attitudes, and experiences with the physician and that the latter, with his warmth, understanding, empathy, acceptance, and support, will not depreciate, censure, or judge him no matter what he may reveal, but will respect his dignity or worth.

Perhaps the best that can be said about this definition—which offers a "technique" that will make its object mature, satisfied, and independent—is that it is naïvely self-congratulatory: it characterizes the psychotherapist as warm, understanding, empathic, accepting, and supporting, and indeed as all of this regardless of what his patient tells him! Perhaps the worst that can be said about this definition—which asserts that the therapists will not depreciate, censure, or judge the patient—is that it is deliberately mendacious: it not only conceals the complex moral and political character of psychotherapy behind a series of quasi-medical pronouncements, but actually flies in the face of the very real fact that the psychotherapist often belittles, censures, and judges his patient, and that he may, indeed, go much further than this by stigmatizing him with socially destructive psychiatric-diagnostic labels and imposing involuntary hospitalization and treatment on him.

According to the Canadian Psychiatric Association, psychotherapy is "a medical act by which a physician, through sessions of verbal or other communications, explores and attempts to influence the behavior of a psychiatrically disordered patient with the objective of reducing his disability." That, of course, is a purely institutional defintion: it does not identify x in terms of y, as does, for example, the definition of the centigrade scale of temperature; instead, it simply claims and defends a sphere of economic and political interest, as does, for example, the definition of a modern state's "national interest."

What conclusions can we draw from these and the other usual definitions of psychotherapy? We can conclude that they are purely verbal exercises, having incantatory, ritualistic, and strategic functions rather than identifying, as they ostensibly do, discrete forms of medical treatments. In trying to understand psychotherapy (or psychopathology), we are confronted with masses of confusions and problems that result from the stubborn and strategic misuse of words, or, as Wittgenstein put it: "Your concept is wrong. However, I cannot illumine the matter by fighting against your words, but only by trying to turn your attention away from certain expressions, illustrations, images, and *towards* the *employment* of the words." Let us heed Wittgenstein's advice and focus on the actual use of the vocabulary of psychotherapy. To do so, we must first consider the ways in which genuine medical treatments are described and classified.

Since I argue that psychotherapeutic interventions are metaphorical treatments, it is necessary that I indicate what I consider literal treatments. By literal treatments I mean medical or surgical treatments—that is, material or physicochemical interventions on a person's body with the aim of ameliorating or curing the disorder of that body.

This definiton is an essentially instrumental one: medical treatment is identified by *what is done,* not by *who does it.* Thus, when a person suffering from pneumonia or syphilis takes penicillin, he is receiving chemotherapy whether the drug is prescribed by a duly licensed physician, is dispensed by a quack, or is ingested by the patient on his own intiative. In some cases of medical treatment—as in chemotherapy, radiation therapy, inhalation therapy—the treatment is identified by the method employed; again, regardless of who gives it and regardless of who gets it, such treatment is clearly identified by *what is done.* In still other cases of treatment—especially those employing surgery—the procedure is usually identified by a combination of words that point both to the *method* of therapy and to the *organ* or part of the body treated. Thus, neurosurgery is surgery on the nervous system, abdominal surgery is surgery on intra-abdominal organs, and so forth.

Where, then, are the parallels between medical treatments and psychotherapies? To best demonstrate the illusory, fake, or metaphorical character of psychotherapy, we might begin by employing the broadest definition of this term—that is, the one which designates as psychotherapy all efforts to relieve or cure "mental illness." One such effort is psychosurgery.

Psychosurgery is a wonderfully revealing term. Perhaps because its developer received the Nobel prize in medicine rather than in literature, it has received more neurologic than semantic attention. Clearly, *psychosurgery* is a term fashioned after such other terms as *neurosurgery* or *urologic surgery*. But the qualifiers in the latter terms obviously refer to organ systems or body parts, whereas the term *psyche* refers to no such thing. I need not consider here what the psyche is or is not to assert that the very term *psychosurgery* is political rhetoric of the most dangerous kind: by creating and legitimizing a scientific-sounding term, physicians are in effect given permission to operate on perfectly healthy brains! After all, if a person's brain is diseased and if a surgeon operates on such a patient, he is said to be doing neurosurgery. Hence, the very invention of the word *psychosurgery* is deeply revealing of its character as fake therapy on a metaphorical organ.

To be sure, psychosurgery is real surgery, just as Clifford Irving's manuscript on Howard Huges was a real manuscript. But the claim that such surgery is therapeutic for the patient rests solely on the fact that it *resembles* therapeutic surgery, just as the claim that Irving's book was a biography of Hughes rested solely on the fact that it resembled a genuine biography of Hughes. In the one case, a person claims to have recorded interviews with someone he never saw; in the other, a person claims to have operated on organs or tissues no one ever saw. The literary impostor is recognized as a confidence man, and his production as a fabric of lies fashioned to sound like the truth. The psyhchiatric impostor, on the other hand, is not so exposed; on the contrary—because he supports a common, culturally shared desire to equate and confuse brain and mind, nerves and nervousness—he is hailed as the discoverer of a new "treatment" for "mental illness."

In contrast to the foregoing defintions of medical treatment, the definitions of psychotherapy are quite imprecise. Does the term *psychotherapy* refer to the method used or to the organ or body part affected by disease and hence the target of remedial influence? Actually, it refers to both. Thus, in one of its uses, the term *psychotherapy* is analogous to the term *chemotherapy:* just as in the latter chemicals are used to treat disease, so in the former psyches are thus used. Indeed, we have come to accept as psychotherapy all conceivable practices and situations in which the soul, spirit, mind, or personality of an individual who claims to be a healer is employed to bring about some sort of change, called "therapeutic," in the soul, spirit, mind, or personality of another individual who is called the patient. The only thing these diverse

enterprises have in common is that the method used is psychological—
that is, nonphysical.

The proposition that *psychotherapy* is a metaphor, an expansion
of the customary use of the word *therapy* to cover things hitherto not
meant by it, is evident if one takes the trouble to examine what psychotherapists actually do. A dramatic example of the origin of one such
metaphorical treatment—what some American therapists now brazenly
call "love therapy"—may be found in Freud's account of the history of
the psychoanalytic movement. When Freud was a young practitioner,
Rudolf Chrobak, a famous Viennese obstetrician and gynecologist,
referred a woman to him. Let us see what was wrong with this "patient,"
what Chrobak regarded as the appropriate "therapy" for her, and what
Freud thought about the problem. In "On the History of the Psycho-
Analytic Movement," Freud reminisces:

> Although the patient had been married for eighteen years [she] was still
> *virgo intacta*. The husband was absolutely impotent. In such cases, he
> [Chrobak] said, there was nothing medical for such a man to do but to
> shield this domestic misfortune with his own reputation, and put up with it
> if people shrugged their shoulders and said of him: "He's no good if he can't
> cure her after so many years." The sole prescription for such a malady, he
> added, is familiar enough to us, but we cannot order it. It runs:
>   'Rx
>   Penis normalis
>   dosim
>   repetatur!'
> I have never heard of such a prescription, and felt inclined to shake my
> head over my kind friend's cynicism.   .

The imagery and vocabulary of treatment are used here in an obviously metaphorical, even humorous way. But in the nearly one hundred
years that have elapsed since that episode, what was said in jest came to
be taken in earnest; what had been metaphor was systematically redefined
as literal.

To be sure, Freud never defined sexual intercourse as therapy. But
he did something that was, in a way, more far-reaching and harmful:
he defined listening and talking—that is, conversation—as therapy.
Furthermore, he defined the people to whom he talked in his office—
and, soon everyone at whom he looked in terms of his personal philosophy which he called "psychoanalysis" and whom he described in the
pseudomedical vocabulary of that philosophy which he called "psychoanalytic theory"—as "patients" suffering from various types of "mental
diseases." Instead of conquering what had been presented to him as mental
diseases by curing these diseases, he conquered what is in effect the human
condition by annexing it in its entirety to the medical profession.

In summary, then, psychotherapy is the name we give to a particular kind of personal influence: by means of communication, one person identified as the psychotherapist exerts an ostensibly therapeutic influence on another person identified as the patient. This process is, of course, but a special member of a much larger class – indeed, a class so vast that virtually all human interactions fall within it. In countless other situations people influence one another. But who is to say whether or when such interactions are helpful or harmful, and to whom? The concept of psychotherapy betrays us by prejudging the interaction as "therapeutic" for the patient, in intent or effect or both.

People try to influence one another constantly. The question that concerns those interested in psychotherapy is: What kind of influence do psychotherapists exert on their clients? People influence one another to support some values and to oppose others. In the past, they promoted such overt values as chastity, obedience, thrift. Today, they advocate such covert values as the common good, mental health, welfare – blanks that may be filled in with any meaning the speaker or listener desires. Herein lies the great value of these vague terms for the demagogue, whether political or professional. Just as a presidential candidate may talk about restoring the nation's economy to a "healthy" condition, without specifying whether he is promoting a balanced budget or deficit financing, so a psychiatrist may talk about "mental health," without revealing whether he is promoting individualism or collectivism, autonomy or heteronomy.

Psychotherapists do many things; the professed goal is always to provide therapy. Often, however, attempts to treat a patient are really efforts to alter his conduct from one mode to another. Thus, there are psychiatrists who try to convert unhappily married couples into happily married ones; homosexuals into heterosexuals; criminals into noncriminals; or, in general, mentally sick patients into mentally healthy former patients. In short, psychotherapy is secular ethics. It is the religion of the formally irreligious – with its language, which is not Latin but medical jargon; with its codes of conduct, which are not ethical but legalistic; with its theology, which is not Christianity but positivism.[3]

THERAPY AS CONVERSATION

Most commonly, psychotherapy is simple conversation, in which the therapist engages in rhetoric (persuasive discourse), not healing. The great debt psychiatry has to the field of rhetoric often goes unrecognized.

Trying to demonstrate that psychotherapy is rhetoric is like trying to demonstrate that the cow is a mammal. Why do it then? For two reasons: because it is now the official opinion of the dominant institutions of society that psychotherapy is a form of medical treatment, and because an appreciation of rhetoric has all but disappeared from contemporary consciousness. Seeing psychotherapy as conversation rather than cure thus requires that we not only consider the error of classifying it as medical intervention, but that we also look anew at the subject of rhetoric and assess its relevance to mental healing.

In plain language, what do patient and psychotherapist actually do? They speak and listen to each other. What do they speak about? Narrowly put, the patient speaks about himself, and the therapist speaks about the patient. In a broader sense, however, both also speak about other persons and about various matters of concern to their lives. The point is that each tries to move the other to see or do things in a certain way. That is what qualifies their actions as fundamentally rhetorical. If the psychotherapist and his patient were not rhetoricians, they could not engage in the activity we now conventionally call *psychotherapy*—just as if cows did not suckle their young, we could not call them mammals.

One of the most important influences on Freud's development of psychoanalysis was the Socratic dialogues. Socrates engaged his perplexed interlocutors in a certain kind of conversation which the Greeks called *rhetoric*. And Socrates was hailed as a great *rhetorician*. Why, then, are Sigmund Freud, Carl Jung, and the other pioneer psychotherapists not also called rhetoricians, and why is their art not called rhetoric?

The sharp distinction in Western thought between body and mind, between bodily and mental diseases, goes back to Plato. It is to Plato, moreover, that we owe the view that the task of the physician of the body is to heal by biological or scientific means, whereas the task of the physician of the soul is to heal by verbal or rhetorical means. In the *Phaedrus,* Plato puts it, through Socrates, as follows: "It may be that the art of rhetoric follows the same methods as does the art of medicine. . . . In both cases you must analyze a nature, in the one that of the body, in the other that of the soul, if you are going to proceed scientifically, not merely by empirical routine, to apply medicine and diet to create health and strength in the one case—while in the other to apply proper words and rules of conduct to communicate such convictions and virtues as you may desire." The nature of that division of labor could hardly be better expressed.

The Romans rearticulated not only the classic Platonic division between the cure of bodies and the cure of souls, but also reemphasized that whereas the methods of the former were "mute," those of the latter were "verbal." For Vergil, medicine is *muta ars,* the silent art; and Vegetius, a fourth-century Roman writer, specifically enjoins that "animals and men must not be treated with vain words but by the sure art of medicine." Indeed, the importance of the distinction between the silent art of the body-doctor and the semantic art of the soul-doctor cannot be overemphasized in connection with our effort to clarify the historical origins of modern psychotherapy.

In his fine study, *The Therapy of the Word in Classical Antiquity,* Pedro Lain Entralgo traces those origins to the rhetoricians of Greece and Rome. The art of speaking well was then, of course, a matter of supreme importance, placing the orator or rhetorician foremost among men. Indeed, for the Greeks there was something divine about the art of persuasive speech; they had a goddess of persuasion, called Peitho. Although Lain Entralgo's own views lead him to attempt to recombine the cure of bodies and the cure of souls, medicine and psychiatry, he notes nevertheless, that in the classical Greek conception of rhetoric, the persuasive word could heal or harm depending on the intentions of the user. "But we have also heard," he writes, "that the persuasive word is a *pharmakon,* in the double sense, a medicament and poison, of that Greek term."

Lain Entralgo also shows that Plato recognized the crucial role of *katharsis,* in the dual sense of purgation and purification, in the cure of souls: "For Plato, the cathartic agent that the 'malady of the soul' specifically requires is the apt and effective word." This idea is expressed most succinctly in *Charmides,* where Plato has Socrates saying: "The cure of the soul . . . has to be effected by the use of certain charms, and these charms are fair words." Lain Entralgo thus concludes that we are obliged "to see Plato as the inventor of scientific, or *kata technen,* verbal psychotherapy. . . . Beyond the shadow of a doubt, Plato thus becomes the inventor of a rigorously technical verbal psychotherapy." Although Lain Entralgo's evidence is right, I think he is quite wrong in concluding that Plato's invention is "scientific."

Aristotle has cautioned against confusing rhetoric with science. If we want to grasp the true nature of psychotherapy, we must revive Aristotle's ideas on rhetoric and relate them to the practices of modern mental healers.

Aristotle begins his book on *Rhetoric* with this observation: "Rhetoric is the counterpart of Dialectic. Both alike are concerned with such things as come, more or less, within the general ken of all men and belong to no definite science. Accordingly, all men make use, more or less, of both." Aristotle here uses rhetoric and dialectic to refer to the arts of public speaking and logical discussion. Having identified rhetoric as persuasive speech, Aristotle distinguishes three varieties of it—political, forensic, and ceremonial:

> Political speaking urges us either to do or not to do something: one of these two courses is always taken by private counsellors, as well as by men who

address public assemblies. Forensic speaking either attacks or defends somebody: one or the other of these two things must always be done by the parties in a case. The ceremonial oratory of display either praises or censures somebody. These three kinds of rhetoric refer to three different kinds of time. The political orator is concerned with the future: it is about things to be done hereafter that he advises, for or against. The party in a case at law is concerned with the past; one man accuses the other, and the other defends himself, with reference to things already done. The ceremonial orator is, properly speaking, concerned with the present, since all men praise or blame in view of the state of things existing at the time, though they often find it useful also to recall the past and to make guesses at the future.

Psychotherapists engage in all three types of rhetorical discourse; and, as a rule, so do their clients. Indeed, Aristotle casually remarks, as if it were quite obvious—which, in classical Greece it no doubt was—that private counselors do the same thing as men who address public assemblies. Here is the category error of modern psychiatry writ large: no one now believes that what politicians do constitutes a form of medical treatment, but many believe that what psychiatrists do does.

Aristotle describes the various ways in which the rhetorician does his job, which is to persuade his interlocutor or audience. Among his methods, the use of enthymemes—which Aristotle considers the "substance of rhetorical persuasion"—ranks very high. An enthymeme is a type of sollogism or argument in which one of the propositions, usually the premise, is understood but is not stated. The enthymeme is thus closely related to the metaphor. For example, the argument that the psychotherapist is a type of medical healer and should be a qualified physician is an enthymeme: the unstated premise is that a person who makes a seemingly sick individual feel better by a seemingly medical method is performing a treatment and is therefore practicing medicine. Having stated the premise, one can debate it. For example, one could maintain that just as not everything that makes people feel bad constitutes an illness, so not everything that makes them feel well constitutes treatment.

Aristotle also considers the relation of rhetoric to science. "The truth is," he writes, "that rhetoric is a combination of the science of logic and of the ethical branch of politics; and it l be refashioning them and shall be passing into the region of sciences dealing with definite subjects rather than simply with words and forms of reasoning."

Since rhetoric is the art of persuasive discourse, considerations of rhetoric necessarily raise the issue of the rhetorician's aims. The ends of political rhetoric, Aristotle explains, vary just as do those of government. "The end of democracy," he writes, "is freedom; of oligarchy, wealth; of aristocracy, the maintenance of education and national institutions; of tyranny, the protection of the tyrant." Similarly, the end of medicine is health; and of psychotherapy, mental health. This latter statement, however, is itself an enthymeme, concealing the premise that mental health is as readily identifiable as freedom or wealth.

Indeed, immediately after the passage quoted above, Aristotle explicitly rejects such a nominalist approach to human affairs, opting instead for a refreshingly empirical position. "We shall learn the qualities of governments," he declares, "in the same way as we learn the qualities of individuals, since they are revealed in their deliberate acts of choice; and these are determined by the ends that inspire them." Just so for mental patients and mental healers: the symptoms of the former and the treatments of the latter are, themselves, acts of choice made by moral agents. Of course, they may not be deliberate acts in quite the same sense in which we choose to put on one tie rather than another; but they are "deliberate acts of choice," nevertheless, and they reveal, as indeed nothing else does, the actors' aims. That simple idea is the key Freud and Jung used for unlocking the meaning of mental symptoms; and it is the key that we can use to unlock the meaning of mental treatments as well. We cannot assimilate mental illnesses and treatments to a medical model; through their symptoms, mental patients seek to attain certain ends, as do mental healers, through their treatments. Insofar as these two parties join forces, it is necessary to reinspect their acts toward each other and to infer from them what ends each is pursuing separately, and what end both are pursuing together. In actuality, these ends vary just as do the ends pursued by politicians and people generally.

Aristotle has thus provided us with firm foundations for seeing and studying human beings as moral agents. He even anticipated some of the modern positivistic-reductionistic "explanations" of the "causes" of human actions, which were, even in his day, evidently not lacking for supporters. "Nor, again, is action due to wealth or poverty," declares Aristotle, as if he were answering the modern mental-health rhetorician making excuses on behalf of "disadvantaged" muggers and murderers. "It is of course true that poor men, being short of money, do have an appetite for it, and that rich men, being able to command needless pleasures, do have an appetite for such pleasures: but here, again, their actions will be *due* not to wealth or poverty but to appetite.⁴

5

Deviant Behavior Is Freedom of Choice

> Under the guise of diagnosing disease, the psychiatrist disqualifies deviance.[1]

DRUGS AND ADDICTION

The prohibition of drug consumption reflects political and ethical norms rather than medical ones, an outrage made acceptable through rhetorical subterfuge. The notion of "drug addiction" used in lay language is a myth, one also perpetuated through rhetorical camouflage.

There is only one political sin: independence; and only one political virtue: obedience. To put it differently, there is only one offense against authority: self-control; and only one obeisance to it: submission to control by authority.

Why is self-control, autonomy, such a threat to authority? Because the person who controls himself, who is his own master, has no need for an authority to be his master. This, then, renders authority unemployed. What is he to do if he cannot control others? To be sure, he could mind his own business. But this is a fatuous answer, for those who are satisfied to mind own business do not aspire to become authorities. In short, the authority needs subjects, persons not in command

115

of themselves—just as parents need children and physicians need patients.

Autonomy is the death knell of authority, and authority knows it: hence the ceaseless warfare of authority against the exercise, both real and symbolic, of autonomy—that is, against suicide, against masturbation, against self-medication, against the proper use of language itself.

The parable of the Fall illustrates this fight to the death between control and self-control. Did Eve, tempted by the Serpent, seduce Adam, who then lost control of himself and succumbed to evil? Or did Adam, facing a choice between obedience to the authority of God and his own destiny, choose self-control?

How, then, shall we view the situation of the so-called drug abuser or drug addict? As a stupid, sick, and helpless child, who, tempted by pushers, peers, and the pleasures of drugs, succumbs to the lure and loses control of himself? Or, as a person in control of himself, who, like Adam, chooses the forbidden fruit as the elemental and elementary way of pitting himself against authority?

There is no empirical or scientific way of choosing between these two answers, of deciding which is right and which is wrong. The questions frame two different moral perspectives, and the answers define two different moral strategies; if we side with authority and wish to repress the individual, we shall treat him *as if* he were helpless, the innocent victim of overwhelming temptation; and we shall then "protect" him from further temptation by treating him as a child, slave, or madman. If we side with the individual and wish to refute the legitimacy and reject the power of authority to infantilize him, we shall treat him *as if* he were in command of himself, the executor of responsible decisions; and we shall then demand that he respect others as he respects himself by treating him as an adult, a free individual, or a "rational" person.

Either of these positions makes sense. What makes less sense— what is confusing in principle and chaotic in practice—is to treat people as adults *and* children, as free and unfree, as sane and insane.

Nevertheless, this is just what social authorities throughout history have done: in ancient Greece, in medieval Europe, in the contemporary world, we find various mixtures in the attitudes of the authorities toward the people; in some societies, the individual is treated as more free than unfree, and we call these societies "free"; in others, he is treated as more determined than self-determining, and we call these societies "totalitarian." In none is the individual treated as completely free. Perhaps this would be impossible: many persons insist that no society could survive on such a premise consistently carried through. Perhaps this is something that lies in the future of mankind. In any case, we should take satisfaction in the evident impossibility of the opposite situation: no society has ever treated the individual, nor perhaps could it treat him, as completely determined. The apparent freedom of the authority, controlling both himself and subject, provides an irresistible model: if God can control, if pope and prince can control, if politician and psychiatrist can control—then perhaps the person can also control, at least himself.

The conflicts between those who have power and those who want to take it away from them fall into three distinct categories. In moral, political, and social affairs (and I of course include psychiatric affairs among these), these categories must be clearly distinguished; if we do not distinguish among them we are likely to mistake opposition to absolute or arbitrary power with what may, actually, be an attempt to gain such power for oneself or for the groups or leaders one admires.

First, there are those who want to take power away from the oppressor and give it to the oppressed, as a class—as exemplified by Marx, Lenin, and the Communists. Revealingly, they dream of the "dictatorship" of the proletariat or some other group.

Second, there are those who want to take power away from the oppressor and give it to themselves as the protectors of the oppressed—as exemplified by Robespierre in politics; Rush in medicine; and by their liberal, radical, and medical followers. Revealingly, they dream of the incorruptibly honest or incontrovertibly sane ruler leading his happy or healthy flock.

And third, there are those who want to take power away from the oppressor and give it to the oppressed as individuals, for each to do with as he pleases, but hopefully for his own self-control—as exemplified by Mill, von Mises, the free-market economists, and their libertarian followers. Revealingly, they dream of people so self-governing that their need for and tolerance of rules is minimal or nil.

While countless men say they love liberty, clearly only those who, by virtue of their actions, fall into the third category, mean it. The others merely want to replace a hated oppressor by a loved one—having usually themselves in mind for the job.

As we have seen, psychiatrists (and some other physicians, notably public health administrators) have traditionally opted for "reforms" of the second type; that is, their opposition to existing powers, ecclesiastic or secular, has had as its conscious and avowed aim the paternalistic care of the citizen-patient, and not the freedom of the autonomous individual. Hence, medical methods of social control tended not only to replace religious methods, but sometimes to exceed them in stringency and severity. In short, the usual response of medical authority to the controls exercised by non-medical authority has been to try to take over and then escalate the controls, rather than to endorse the principle and promote the practice of removing the controls by which the oppressed are victimized.

As a result, until recently, most psychiatrists, psychologists, and other behavioral scientists had nothing but praise for the "behavioral controls" of medicine and psychiatry. We are now beginning to witness, however, a seeming backlash against this position, many behavioral scientists jumping on what they evidently consider to be the next "correct" and "liberal" position, namely, a criticism of behavioral controls. But since most of these "scientists" remain as hostile to individual freedom and responsibility, to choice and dignity, as they have always been, their criticism conforms to the pattern I have described above: they demand more "controls"—that is, professional and governmental controls—over "behavior controls." This is like first urging a person to drive over icy roads at breakneck speed to get over them as fast as possible, and then, when his car goes into a skid, advising him to apply his brakes. Whether because they are stupid or wicked or both, such persons invariably recommend fewer controls where more are needed, for example in relation to punishing offenders—and more controls where fewer are needed, for example in relation to contracts between consenting adults. Truly, the supporters of the Therapeutic State are countless and tireless—now proposing more therpeutic controls in the name of "controlling behavior controls."

Clearly, the seeds of this fundamental human propensity—to react to the loss of control, or to the threat of such loss, with an intensification of control, thus generating a spiraling symbiosis of escalating controls and counter-controls—have fallen on fertile soil in contemporary medicine and psychiatry and have yielded a luxuriant harvest of "therapeutic" coercions, The alcoholic and Alcoholics Anonymous, the glutton and Weight Watchers, the drug abuser and the drug-abuseologist—each is an image at war with its mirror image, each creating and defining, dignifying and defaming the other, and each trying to negate his own reflection, which he can accomplish only by negating himself.

There is only one way to split apart and unlock such pairings, to resolve such dilemmas—namely, by trying to control the other less, not more; and by replacing control of the other with self-control.

The person who uses drugs—legal or illegal drugs, with or without a physician's prescription—may be submitting to authority, may be revolting against it, or may be exercising his own power of making a free decision. It is quite impossible to know—without knowing a great deal about such a person, his family and friends, and his whole cultural setting—just what such an individual is doing and why. But it is quite possible, indeed it is easy, to know what those persons who try to repress certain kinds of drug uses and drug users are doing and why.

As the war against heresy was in reality a war for "true" faith, so the war against drug abuse is in reality a war for "faithful" drug use: concealed behind the war against marijuana and heroin is the war for tobacco and alcohol; and, more generally, concealed behind the war against the use of politically and medically disapproved drugs, is the war for the use of politically and medically approved drugs.

Let us recall, again, one of the principles implicit in the psychiatric perspective on man, and some of the practices that follow from it: the madman is a person lacking adequate internal controls over his behavior; hence, he requires — for his own protection as well as for the protection of society — external restraints upon it. This, then, justifies the incarceration of "mental patients" in "mental hospitals" — and much else besides.

The drug abuser is a person lacking adequate internal controls over his drug use; hence, he requires — for his own protection as well as the protection of society — external restraints upon it. This, then, justifies the prohibition of "dangerous drugs," the incarceration and involuntary treatment of "addicts," the eradication of "pushers" — and much else besides.

Confronted with the phenomena of "drug abuse" and "drug addiction," how else could psychiatry and a society imbued with it have reacted? They could respond only as they did — namely, by defining the moderate use of legal drugs as the result of the sane control of resistible impulses; and by defining the immoderate use of any drug, and any use of illegal drugs, as the insane surrender to irresistible impulses. Hence the circular psychiatric definitions of drug habits, such as the claim that illicit drug use (for example, smoking marijuana) causes mental illness and also constitutes a symptom of it; and the seemingly contradictory claim that the wholly similar use of licit drugs (for example, smoking tobacco) is neither a cause nor a symptom of mental illness.

Formerly, opium was a panacea; now it is the cause and symptom of countless maladies, medical and social, the world over. Formerly, masturbation was the cause and symptom of mental illness; now it is the cure for social inhibition and the practice ground for training in heterosexual athleticism. It is clear, then, that if we want to understand and accept drugtaking behavior, we must take a larger view of the so-called drug problem. (Of course, if we want to persecute "pushers" and "treat addicts," then information inconvenient to our doing these things will only get in our way. Drug-abuseologists can no more be "educated" out of their coercive tactics than can drug addicts.)

What does this larger view show us? How can it help us? It shows us that our present attitudes toward the whole subject of drug use, drug abuse, and drug control are nothing but the reflections, in the mirror of "social reality," of our own expectations toward drugs and toward those who use them; and that our ideas about and interventions in drugtaking behavior have only the most tenuous connection with the actual pharmacological properties of "dangerous drugs." The "danger" of masturbation disappeared when we ceased to believe in it: we then ceased to attribute danger to the practice and to its practitioners; and ceased to call it "self-abuse."

Of course, some people still behave in disagreeable and even dangerous ways, but we no longer attribute their behavior to masturbation or self-abuse: we now attribute their behavior to self-medication or drug abuse. We thus play a game of musical chairs with medical alibis for human desire, determination, and depravity. Though this sort of intolerance is easy, it is also expensive: it seems clear that only in accepting human beings for what they are can we accept the chemical substances they use for what they are. In short, only insofar as we are able and willing to accept men, women, and children as neither angels nor devils, but as persons with certain inalienable rights and irrepudiable duties, shall we be able and willing to accept heroin, cocaine, and marijuana as neither panaceas nor panapathogens, but as drugs with certain chemical properties and ceremonial possibilities. . . .[2]

Just as culturally approved drugs have generally been promoted as symbols of maturity, and their habitual use as proof of competence in life's games—so culturally disapproved drugs have generally been prohibited as the symbols of immaturity, and their habitual use as proof of incompetence in life's games and hence the symptom of mental disease or moral debauchment or both. Thus, in the literature of official psychiatry, the dogma that drug addiction is a mental illness is never questioned; nor is the belief that a person becomes an addict because of an "underlying defect" in his personality. In short, the psychiatric mythology concerning drug abuse is an exact replica of the psychiatric mythology concerning self-abuse (masturbation).

This sort of psychiatric interpretation is, of course, circular. Traditional psychiatry has accepted the conventional definition of a certain kind of behavior—masturbation, the use of illegal drugs, and so forth—as a type of disease falling specifically within the province of the "psychiatric physician." Having done so, all that remained for psychiatry was to establish its "etiology": a defect in the depth of the psyche; describe the course of the "untreated disease"; steady deterioration leading straight to the insane asylum; and prescribe its "treatment": psychiatric coercion with or without the use of additional, "therapeutic" drugs (heroin for morphine; methadone for heroin; antabuse for alcohol).

Thus, a critique of the languages of drug use and drug avoidance cannot proceed very far before one is compelled to observe that there is, in fact, no such thing as "drug addiction." To be sure, some people do take drugs that the authorities do not want them to take; and some people do become used to taking certain substances, or become habituated to them; and the various substances which people take may be legal or illegal, relatively harmless or quite harmful. But the difference between someone "using a drug" and his being "addicted" to it is not a matter of fact, but a matter of our moral attitude and political strategy toward him. Indeed, we might, and must, go further than this, and the note that the very identification of a substance as a drug or not a drug is not a matter of fact but a matter of moral attitude and political strategy: tobacco, in common parlance, is not considered to be a drug, but marijuana is; gin is not, but Valium is. . . .

In our day, nowhere is the language of scapegoating more clearly displayed than in the way we write and talk about drug use and drug avoidance. The proximal scapegoat is the "dangerous drug"; a slightly more distal one is "the addict" who "infects" others with his "disease"; and the ultimate one is the "pusher." This addiction-mongering rhetoric has now been escalated to an invocation of a "doomsday'" of "infection," and to the demand that all other human interests and values be subordinated to a fanatical quest for freedom from the poppy. Many of the foremost political, scientific, and literary figures throughout the world have joined this frenzied chorus.[3]

The taking of drugs by adults is a fundamental right akin to other fundamental rights. The advocacy of this right, however, does not imply approval.

Clearly, the argument that marijuana — or heroin, methadone, or morphine — is prohibited because it is addictive or dangerous, cannot be supported by facts. For one thing, there are many drugs, from insulin to penicillin, that are neither addictive nor dangerous but are nevertheless also prohibited; they can be obtained only through a physician's prescription. For another, there are many things, from dynamite to guns, that are much more dangerous than narcotics (especially to others) but are not prohibited. As everyone knows, it is still possible in the United States to walk into a store and walk out with a shotgun. We enjoy this right not because we believe that guns are safe but because we believe even more strongly that civil liberties are precious. At the same time, it is not possible in the United States to walk into a store and walk out with a bottle of barbiturates, codeine, or other drugs.

I believe that just as we regard freedom of speech and religion as fundamental rights, so should we regard freedom of self-medication as a fundamental right. Like most rights, the right of self-medication should apply only to adults; and it should not be an unqualified right. Since these are important qualifications, it is necessary to specify their precise range.

John Stuart Mill said (approximately) that a person's right to swing his arm ends where his neighbor's nose begins. And Oliver Wendell Holmes said that no one has a right to shout "Fire!" in a crowded theater. Similarly, the limiting condition with respect to self-medication should be the inflicting of actual (as against symbolic) harm on others.

Our present practices with respect to alcohol embody and reflect this individualistic ethic. We have the right to buy, possess, and consume alcoholic beverages. Regardless of how offensive drunkenness might be to a person, he cannot interfere with another person's "right" to become inebriated so long as that person drinks in the privacy of his own home or at some other appropriate location, and so long as he conducts himself in an otherwise law-abiding manner. In short, we have a right to be intoxicated—in private. Public intoxication is considered an offense to others and is therefore a violation of the criminal law. It makes sense that what is a "right" in one place may become, by virtue of its disruptive or disturbing effect on others, an offense somewhere else.

The right to self-medication should be hedged in by similar limits. Public intoxication, not only with alcohol but with any drug, should be an offense punishable by the criminal law. Furthermore, acts that may injure others—such as driving a car—should, when carried out in a drug-intoxicated state, be punished especially strictly and severely. The right to self-medication must thus entail unqualified responsibility for the effects of one's drug-intoxicated behavior on others. For unless we are willing to hold ourselves responsible for our own behavior, and hold others responsible for theirs, the liberty to use drugs (or to engage in other acts) degenerates into a license to hurt others.

Such, then, would be the situation of adults, if we regarded the freedom to take drugs as a fundamental right similar to the freedom to read and worship. What would be the situation of children? Since many people who are now said to be drug addicts or drug abusers are minors, it is especially important that we think clearly about this aspect of the problem.

I do not believe, and I do not advocate, that children should have a right to ingest, inject, or otherwise use any drug or substance they want. Children do not have the right to drive, drink, vote, marry, or make binding contracts. They acquire these rights at various ages, coming into their full possession at maturity, usually between the ages of eighteen and twenty-one. The right to self-medication should similarly be withheld until maturity.

In short, I suggest that "dangerous" drugs be treated, more or less, as alcohol is treated now. Neither the use of narcotics, nor their possession, should be prohibited, but only their sale to minors. Of course, this would result in the ready availability of all kinds of drugs among minors—though perhaps their availability would be no greater than it is now, but would only be more visible and hence more easily subject to proper controls. This arrangement would place responsibility for the use of all drugs by children where it belongs: on parents and their children. This is where the major responsibility rests for the use of alcohol. It is a tragic symptom of our refusal to take personal liberty and responsibility seriously that there appears to be no public desire to assume a similar stance toward other "dangerous" drugs.

Consider what would happen should a child bring a bottle of gin to school and get drunk there. Would the school authorities blame the local liquor stores as pushers? Or would they blame the parents and the child himself? There is liquor in practically every home in America and yet children rarely bring liquor to school. Whereas marijuana, Dexedrine, and heroin—substances children usually do not find at home and whose very possession is a criminal offense—frequently find their way into the school.

Our attitude toward sexual activity provides another model for our attitude toward drugs. Although we generally discourage children below a certain age from engaging in sexual activities with others, we do not prohibit such activities by law. What we do prohibit by law is the sexual seduction of children by adults. The "pharmacological seduction" of children by adults should be similarly punishable. In other words, adults who give or sell drugs to children should be regarded as offenders. Such a specific and limited prohibition—as against the kinds of generalized prohibitions that we had under the Volstead Act or have now with respect to countless drugs—would be relatively easy to enforce. Moreover, it would probably be rarely violated, for there would be little psychological interest and no economic profit in doing so.

•   •   •

Sooner or later we shall have to confront the basic moral dilemmas underlying this problem: does a person have the right to take a drug, any drug—not because he needs it to cure an illness, but because he wants to take it?

The Declaration of Independence speaks of our inalienable right to "life, liberty, and the pursuit of happiness." How are we to interpret this? By asserting that we ought to be free to pursue happiness by play-ing golf or watching television, but not by drinking alcohol, or smoking marijuana, or ingesting pep pills?

The Constitution and the Bill of Rights are silent on the subject of drugs. This would seem to imply that the adult citizen has, or ought to have, the right to medicate his own body as he sees fit. Were this not the case, why should there have been a need for a Constitutional Amendment to outlaw drinking? But if ingesting alcohol was, and is now again, a Constitutional right, is ingesting opium, or heroin, or barbiturates, or anything else, not also such a right? . . .

After all is said and done, the issue comes down to whether we ac-cept or reject the ethical principle John Stuart Mill so clearly enunciated:

> The only purpose [he wrote in *On Liberty*] for which power can be right-fully exercised over any member of a civilized community, against his will, is to prevent harm to others. His own good, either physical or moral, is not a sufficient warrant. He cannot rightfully be compelled to do or forbear because it will make him happier, because in the opinion of others, to do so would be wise, or even right. . . . In the part [of his conduct] which merely concerns himself, his independence is, of right, absolute. Over himself, over his own body, the individual is sovereign.

By recognizing the problem of drug abuse for what it is—a moral and political question rather than a medical or therapeutic one—we can choose to maximize the sphere of action of the state at the expense of the individual, of the individual at the expense of the state. In other words, we could commit ourselves to the view that the state, the repre-sentative of many, is more important than the individual; that it therefore has the right, indeed the duty, to regulate the life of the individ-ual in the best interests of the group. Or we could commit ourselves to the view that individual dignity and liberty are the supreme values of life, and that the foremost duty of the state is to protect and promote these values.

In short, we must choose between the ethic of collectivism and individualism, and pay the price of either—or of both. . . .[4]

* * *

Criticism of anti-drug laws and so-called narcotics controls is often misinterpreted as approval or endorsement of drug use or drug addiction. Those who so interpret my position—or any position of laissez faire and tolerance with respect to drug use—do so because they implicitly subscribe to the principle that anyone who does not support their position supports their adversary's. Nothing could be further from the truth. I regard tolerance with respect to drugs as wholly analogous to tolerance with respect to religion. To be sure, a Christian advocating religious tolerance at the height of the Inquisition would himself have been accused of heresy. Today, however, no one would misinterpret his position as an endorsement or advocacy of a non-Christian religion or of atheism. The fact that a contemporary American's, and especially physician's, advocacy of tolerance with respect to drugs is generally viewed as an endorsement or support of undisciplined licentiousness in the use of "dangerous drugs" signifies that we are now at the height of an "anti-narcotic" inquisition.[5]

ALCOHOLISM

"Alcoholism" is a bad habit; bad habits are not diseases; and people should be free to exercise bad habits, but they should be held responsible for the consequences of these habits.

Morris E. Chafetz, M.D., director of the National Institute on Alcohol Abuse and Alcoholism, has announced the promulgation of a "Bill of Rights for Alcoholic People," drafted for them by the Commissioners on Uniform State Laws at their annual meeting in August, 1971. This Bill, Dr. Chafetz explains, removes "the crime of public-intoxication and the illness of alcoholism from the criminal codes and places them in the public health area where they rightfully belong." Since some people who drink do not consider themselves alcoholics and hence decline medical care, Dr. Chafetz adds that the Uniform Alcoholism and Intoxication Treatment Act adopted by the Commission "guarantees, in those few instances where civil commitment is necessary, a right to treatment 'which is likely to be beneficial'."

A subsequent editorial warmly endorsed the creation of the Institute headed by Dr. Chafetz, and concluded with this ringing exhortation:

> It is to be hoped that through government incentives, the support of medical students throughout the country, and the efforts of local medical societies together with the American Medical Association and other professional organizations, the medical schools will become much more aware of the need to equip tomorrow's physicians with the ability and imagination to cope with two of the most pressing problems of medical care facing the nation—alcoholism and drug dependence.

I submit that the foregoing views consist of an approximately equal mixture of mendacity and nonsense. As a teacher in a medical school, I believe it is my duty to teach facts and theories as I see them, and not as the State, the American Medical Association, Alcoholics Anonymous, the Women's Christian Temperance Union, the liquor industry, or any other group of special interests see them. In my judgment, the view that alcoholism is a disease is false; and the programmes sponsored by the State and supported by tax moneys to "cure" it are immoral and inconsistent with our political commitment to individual freedom and responsibility.

It is impossible, of course, to discuss what is and is not illness, without agreement on how we shall use the word "illness." First, then, we must distinguish—as do both physicians and patients, and as our language does—between bodily and mental illness.

When a person asserts that he is ill, he usually means two things: first, that he suffers, or that he believes he suffers, from an abnormality or malfunctioning of his body; and, second, that he wants, or is at least willing to accept, medical help for it. Should the first of these conditions be absent, we would not consider the person to be physically ill; should the second be absent we would not consider him to be a medical patient. This is because the practice of modern Western medicine rests on the scientific premise that the physician's task is to diagnose and treat disorders of the human body; and the moral premise that he can carry out these services only with the consent of his patient. Strictly speaking, then, disease or illness can affect only the body.

Accordingly, there can be no such thing as mental illness. The term "mental illness" is a metaphor. Bodily illness stands in the same relation to mental illness as a defective television set stands to a bad television programme. Of course, the word "sick," is often used metaphorically. We call jokes "sick," economies "sick," sometimes even the whole world "sick"; but only when we call minds "sick" do we systematically mistake and strategically misinterpret metaphor for fact—and send for the doctor to "cure" the "illness"! It is as if a television viewer were to send for a TV repairman because he dislikes the programme he sees on the screen.

With the foregoing definitions in mind, I offer the following observations about alcoholism and its relation to the medical profession.

(1) Drinking to excess may cause illness, but in itself is not a disease—in the ordinary sense of the world "disease." Excessive drinking is a habit. According to the person's values, he may consider it a good or bad habit. If we choose to call bad habits "diseases," there is no limit to what we may define as "disease"—and "treat" involuntarily. The misuse of alcohol—whatever the reason for it—is no more an illness than is the misuse

of any other product of human inventiveness, from language to nuclear energy.

(2) Every individual, the alcoholic included, is capable of injuring or killing himself. This potentiality is a fundamental expression of man's freedom of action. Such conduct may be regarded as immoral or sinful or undisciplined, and penalized by means of informal sanctions. But it should not, in a free society, be regarded as either a crime or a disease, warranting the use of the police powers of the State for its control or suppression.

(3) Every individual, the alcoholic included, is also capable of injuring or killing others—both while under the influence of alcohol and while not under its influence. This potentiality, too, is a fundamental expression of man's freedom. Such conduct not only justifies self-defense by those attacked, but also often requires the formalized protection of society from the harmful individual by means of criminal laws and sanctions. In other words, the alcoholic should be left free to injure himself; those who wish to help him should be left free to offer their services to him, but should not be allowed to use force or fraud in their efforts to "help"; at the same time, the alcoholic should not be left free to injure others; nor should his alcoholism be accepted as an excuse for any criminal act he may have committed.

(4) It is one thing to maintain that a person is not responsible for being an alcoholic; it is quite another to maintain that he is not responsible for the interpersonal, occupational, economic, and legal consequences of his actions. The former proposition implies only an unwillingness to punish a person for excessive drinking; the latter implies either giving the alcoholic an excuse for injuring others, or justifying legislation for controlling his alcoholism rather than his illegal behavior.

(5) If we regard alcoholism as a bona fide disease—"like any other"—then we ought to let the alcoholic accept or reject treatment for it. Venereal diseases are now said to be of epidemic proportions. They are, moreover, genuine, bodily diseases [for most of which] we now possess efficacious and safe methods of treatment—yet such treatment is not compulsory. Advocating the compulsory "treatment" of alcoholics (and other "addicts") through what is euphemistically called "civil commitment," and calling such involuntary interventions a "Bill of Rights for Alcoholic People," are, in my opinion, manifestations of a state of affairs in American medicine and government far more alarming than the "diseases" against which such "cures" and their sordid justifications are invoked.

By a curious coincidence, in one of his most important short pieces, George Orwell compared the abuse of language with the abuse of alcohol. "A man may take to drink," he wrote, "because he feels himself to be a failure, and then fail all the more completely because he drinks. It is rather the same thing that is happening to the English language. It becomes ugly and inaccurate because our thoughts are foolish, but the slovenliness of our language makes it easier for us to have foolish thoughts."

When Dr. Chafetz asserts that alcoholism is an illness—without telling us what is "alcoholism" and what is "illness"; that "It is the task of the practicing physician to take the initiative in acting to provide adequate medical and follow-up care for alcoholic persons . . . ," when in fact his task is to offer care only to those persons who want it; when he calls giving physicians the power to imprison alcoholics a "Bill of Rights" for the victims; and when the American Medical Association uncritically and unqualifiedly endorses such humbug—we then stand before the phenomenon Orwell described.

But, of course, Orwell did more than describe; he warned that ". . . if thought corrupts language, language can also corrupt thought." And he concluded that political language—and to this we may here add medical language—"is designed to make lies sound truthful and murder respectable, and to give an appearance of solidity to pure wind."

As an academician and a teacher, I believe our duty now is to stand up against the Lyshenkoism that is sweeping the country. Whether we may want to dub it "Jaffeism," or "Chafetzism," or the "Crusade Against Alcoholism and Addiction," or by some other catchy phrase hardly matters; what matters is that as physicians and teachers we resist politically motivated and mandated redefinitions of (bad) habits as diseases; that we condemn and eschew involuntary medical and psychiatric interventions; and that, instead of joining and supporting the "holy war" on alcoholism and drug abuse, we actively repudiate this contemporary version of "popular delusion and crowd madness."

In the past half-century, the medical sciences have advanced as never before in history; yet, morally, the medical profession has fallen upon bad times. Everywhere, it has allowed itself to be enslaved by the State; at the same time, it has encroached on the liberties of the patients, making them, in turn, the slaves of the doctors. But, as Montaigne, quoting Apollonius, observed: "It is for slaves to lie, and for free men to speak the truth." Where are the free men of medicine?[6]

DEVIANT SEX

Beyond diseases of, or relating to, the sexual organs, sexual behavior is an interpersonal, not a medical concern. Deviant sexual behavior, therefore, is a matter of individual and moral choice, not a province of the medical community. Sexologists and other "doctors" of sex use rhetoric and mystification to make sexual matters appear to be medical matters.

Before the present century, when people spoke of "doctors" they were more likely to have in mind clerics than clinicians. Now it is the other way around. That metamorphosis, together with a reversal of values as blind as it is stubborn, epitomizes the basic change in the Western perspective on sex—from the days of the Church Fathers to those of the sex therapists.

"I was," wrote St. Augustine, "bound down by this disease of the flesh . . . that only you [God] can cure." To the Great Doctor of Christianity in the fourth century, sexual desire was a disease; to the great doctors of coitus today, lack of sexual desire is a disease. "Inadequate sexual desire," asserts Helen Singer Kaplan, a professor of psychiatry at Cornell Medical Center and a prominent sex therapist, "is probably the most prevalent of the sexual dysfunctions." Surely, among the achievements of modern education must be reckoned the fact that men and women who do not know the meaning of the word "concupiscence," *know,* nevertheless, that it is the unmistakable sign of freedom from the dread "diseases of desire" dear to the hearts of modern doctors of sexology.

Doctors of theology and doctors of medicine, clerics, and clinicians, have much in common, especially when it comes to sex. What they share, above all else, is an arrogant certainty that they and they alone know how God or Nature intends us to enjoy ourselves—sexually and otherwise. Hence, they have always been, and apparently always will be, not great teachers, as their name "doctor" implies, but great meddlers. From time to time, clerics as well as clinicians have changed their minds about what we must do to be in harmony with the designs of God or Nature—but this has never caused them to entertain the least doubt that they were the proper interpreter and enforcers of those designs. Sexual self-satisfaction (now usually called masturbation) is a good case in point.

Men and women—and, of course, children too—must have always known that rubbing the genitals causes pleasureable relief of sexual tension. Even some mammals and primates have, through experience, discovered this elementary piece of sex educational information. "I wish to heaven," remarked the Greek philosopher Diogenes (in the fourth century B.C.), "that I could satisfy my hunger when my stomach barks for food by rubbing it." During the period ironically called the Englightenment, that piece of sexological insight was replaced by the medical dogma known as the "doctrine of masturbatory insanity." For more than two hundred years—well into the twentieth century—the leaders of Western science and thought maintained that masturbation caused a host of diseases and was itself a disease. Now they maintain that it cures a host of diseases and that abstinence from it is a disease. Diogenes and his contemporaries knew better: they understood that desire, whether for food or sex, is not a disease; and that the satisfaction of desire, whether it involves alimentary or erotic acts, is not a treatment.

Eating and copulating have always been of interest to people and are likely to remain so. Each of these behaviors satisfies a basic biological need—eating, the survival of the individual; copulating, the survival of the species. Each may be a rich source of pleasure through the gratification of desire—or a rich source of pain, for many reasons, among them being diseases or conditions believed to be diseases. Nutritional and sexual behaviors thus exhibit three faces: spiritual, sumptuary, and hygienic. If we want to know what God permits or prohibits us from ingesting, we turn to rabbis and priests; if we want to enhance our enjoyment of eating, we turn to gourmet cooks; if we want relief from diseases of the digestive system, we turn to doctors. Similarly, the religious-ritual aspects of sex are the concern of the clergyman and the theologian; the aesthetic-hedonic aspects of it are the concern of the poet and the pornographer; the medical aspects of it—that is, the diseases of the sexual organs and their treatment—are the concern of the physician.

Whether, when, with whom, and how a person should engage in sexual acts depends on whether he wants to please God, enhance his erotic enjoyment, or promote his health. Hence, a question such as how many orgasms a woman should have is like the question of how many children she should have. In the past, people in the Christian West believed that women should have as many children and as few orgasms as possible; now they believe just the opposite. These beliefs are important—but what, if anything, have they to do with medicine? To put it differently, what relationship, if any, is there between gourmet cooking and medicine, epicurean dining and diseases of the digestive system, pleasure in drinking and eating and psychiatry? The question is plainly absurd. Every educated person knows that if he wants to learn about good eating, he must consult Craig Claiborne, not his gastroenterologist; that doctors teach people how to abstain from eating and drinking, not how to enjoy these "indulgences."

When it comes to sex, however, such common sense vanishes. Everyone now *knows* that physicians, especially gynecologists and psychiatrists, are experts on sex. When people want to enjoy copulation or masturbation or some other erotic act, they turn to doctors to advise them. This folly rests on the belief that because physicians are knowledgeable about the physiology and pathology of the genital organs, they are experts on the experiencing and enjoying of the erotic passions as well.

Eating is a basic bodily function. We do not consider eating itself to be a disease or medical problem. We only consider certain disturbances in eating—such as occur, say, in cancer of the esophagus—to be the manifestation of a disease. And we do not assume that, because physicians are experts on esophageal cancer, they are also experts on questions such as whether people should eat with knives and forks or with chopsticks, sitting on chairs or reclining on sofas or carpets.

Like other bodily organs, the sexual organs are subject to disease. In addition, even in the absence of diseases, affecting the genitals, the act of sexual intercourse gives rise to two conditions that people have often found undesirable and hence sought to prevent—namely, pregnancy and venereal disease. Since the prevention of conception and infectious disease requires medical knowledge, the physician must, indeed, be intimately involved in matters sexual. This is why contraception and the prevention and treatment of venereal diseases have formed two of the portals through which the physician entered the area of human sexuality. A third portal—perhaps the most important one for modern sexology—was formed by so-called disturbances of the sexual function, such as impotence and frigidity.

What, exactly, are impotence and frigidity? How shall we view them, understand them, "treat" them? Impotence—the inability to have or sustain an erection—can be the manifestation of a disease, say of multiple sclerosis; or it can be the manifestation of a man's conscience, say of his belief that certain (or all) sexual acts are wrong and forbidden. Frigidity—the woman's inability to enjoy certain (or all) sexual acts—can likewise be a manifestation of either a medical or a moral condition. In other words, the presence or absence of appetite, whether for food or sexual satisfaction, depends both on the condition of the *body* and the character of the *person*. We are expected to develop an aversion to eating the flesh of cats or dogs or human beings and hence would not consider a lack of salivary or gastric arousal for such foods, even if we were hungry, the manifestation of a disorder of the digestive system. Lack of sexual arousal in certain situations is usually a similar affair, signifying the person's true feelings about the matter. The penis, some wag has observed, never lies. But sexologists do—principally because they are determined to conceal moral values and social policies as medical diagnoses and treatments.[7]

•   •   •

Our language informs and even defines our perceptions. When we talk about sexual dysfunctions the implication is that the labels for such alleged disorders name abnormal sexual conditions that exist— in the same sense in which, say, cancer of the colon exists. This is simply not true.

Illustrative of the blinders that our language places on our view of human sexuality is the fact that we have only a single term for the pleasurable experience associated with the relief of sexual tension. Because of this verbal constraint, sexologists write as if there were an orgasm or orgastic experience that is always the same—even for men and women. But this is contrary to common sense and experience. A person does not have the same pleasure every time he eats the same food or drinks the same drink—regardless of how much he likes these substances. Moreover, although our body is primed to feel sexual pleasure, we must nevertheless acquire the experience through learning. Just as we do not all react to music or food in the same way, we do not react to sex in the same way. The varieties of human sexual experience are, indeed, as rich and varied as the varieties of human religious experience.

Some parallels between eating and sex may help us see contemporary sexological claims in a clearer light. Let us look upon eating as if it were an oro-gastric performance—that is, a set of actions performed by our mouth, salivary and gastric glands, esophagus, and stomach. What are the various oro-gastric performances that might be displayed by a hungry person confronted with the possibility of eating a certain food—say, oysters? We need to know neither gastroenterology (that is, about diseases of the digestive tract) nor gastronomy (that is, about the art of good eating) to recognize that such a person's reaction is likely to fall into one or another of the following four categories; he may refuse to eat oysters and be perfectly happy about it; he may seemingly accept the oysters, but, unable to "stomach" them, he may gag on them; he may accept the oysters and get them down, but without any pleasure; or he may eagerly desire oysters, savor them slowly and delight in eating them. None of these is considered to be a medical matter: we have no Greco-Latin diagnostic names to attach to such attitudes toward food.

Let us look upon heterosexual intercourse in the male similarly—as if it were a performance by the penis. What are the various sexual performances that might be displayed by a sexually hungry man confronted with the possibility of engaging in a certain sexual act—say, intercourse with a beautiful, sexually experienced, and willing woman? Again, we need not be experts on sex to recognize that such a man's reactions are likely to fall into one or another of some familiar categories: he may reject the sexual opportunity as morally unacceptable and be perfectly happy about it; he may try to engage in intercourse but find himself unable to achieve an erection; he may have an erection, but ejaculate promptly after penetration or even prior to it; he may have an erection, penetrate, but feel as if his penis were anaesthetized and be unable to ejaculate; finally, he may engage in a highly stimulating and satisfying act of sexual intercourse. While all this is rather obvious, by cataloguing these sexual patterns we see that whereas our language attaches no labels of illness-and-health to the various reactions a man has toward an object of food, it does attach such labels to the various reactions he has toward a "sex object." Thus, for more than a century, terms such as "impotence," "premature ejaculation," and "retarded ejaculation" have been accepted as the names of certain abnormal or pathological conditions affecting the so-called male sexual apparatus or male sexual functions. This is sheer nonsense. I am not saying, of course, that the sexual performances I have described do not actually occur or are not real. I deny only that these phenomena are *ipso facto* medical diseases or problems.

However, *some* of these phenomena *may* be due to organic diseases or the effects of drugs. Impotence, in particular, may be due to congenital malformation of the penis (which is rare); to injury to the nerves supplying the genitals (which may be a complication, or unavoidable side effect, of pelvic or urogenital surgery); to certain systemic diseases (for example, diabetes, severe arteriosclerosis, leukemia); and to certain drugs (for example, alcohol, anti-hypertensives, psychoactive agents). Frigidity may have similar causes. The traditional distinction between organic and psychogenic sexual disorders remains of paramount importance. I am addressing myself here only to the latter group of phenomena—that is, to so-called sexual dysfunctions displayed by persons with healthy bodies, or with diseases that do not impair their sexual abilities.

Failure of the heart, the lung, or the liver to perform its function is always considered a disease, in men as well as women. This is not always true for failure of the sexual organs to perform theirs: some such nonfunctions do not count as a disease at all, while others may count as a disease for one sex but not the other. A quick review of currently accepted sexual (coital) disorders will illustrate this point.

1. The person wants to perform sexually—or believes and declares that he or she wants to—but is unable to do so: in men this is called impotence; in women, vaginismus. The term "frigidity" should not be applied to this condition, though sometimes it is, because women can engage in an essentially passive kind of sexual performance (that is, without genital activity). This is why in the woman, unconscious rejection of the sexual act is manifested by a *stiffening* of the vaginal muscles—whereas in the man, who must be genitally active to perform sexually, it is manifested by a *softening* of the penile shaft.

2. The person's sexual performance is deemed to be too quick: in men this is called premature ejaculation (ejaculatio praecox); in women it is not considered to be an illness and is not named.

3. The person's sexual performance is deemed to be too slow: in men this is called retarded ejaculation (ejaculatio retardata); in women this is

usually not considered to be an illness and is not named — or it may be called frigidity.

4. The sexual performance is normal, but the performer experiences no pleasure: in women this is called frigidity or anorgasmia; in men this was, until recently, not considered an illness, but is now called anorgasmia.

5. Sexual acts are deliberately avoided and the subject regards his or nonperformance as meritorious; this is called chastity in both men and women (and it may or may not be considered an illness).[8]

CRIMINALITY AND DELINQUENCY

All physically uncoerced criminal behavior, however mysterious or unusual, represents the perpetrator's freely chosen actions, not illness, for which he is fully responsible. Brainwashing as a cause of behavior is a sub-myth of the "mental illness" mythology.

Like all persons accused of a dramatic crime, Patty Hearst managed, for however brief a period, to make people pay attention to her. Although the play in which she appeared was likely to have a short run, she was its undisputed star in the victim of mind-rape. Truly, life imitates art. We have had *The Manchurian Candidate* and *A Clockwork Orange*. Then we had *The Brainwashed Heiress*.

Gone are the days when people asked "Did she or didn't she?" Who cares any more what people do — legally or sexually? What people now want to know is what's in other people's brains. So they ask: "Was she or wasn't she brainwashed?" Having asked it they demand an answer with the same impatience with which a spoiled child demands an ice cream cone. And the experts on brainwashing will give them an answer as eagerly as doting parents give ice cream cones to their whining children. In fact, although people are asking for only one answer, they shall inevitably get two: yes, she was brainwashed; no, she was not.

But the question is meaningless. Asking it is an intellectual and moral copout; answering it is psychiatric prostitution; and believing the answer is self-deception.

Nietzsche was right when he said that "a criminal is frequently not equal to his deed: he makes it smaller and slanders it." Patty Hearst, the victorious SLA soldier, with gun slung snappily over her shoulder, seemed proud and self-assured. Her lawyers claimed that she was then "brainwashed." Patty Hearst, the victim of kidnapping, with a decorous dress draped over her slender frame, seemed shrunken and bewildered. Was this what Nietzsche had in mind when he remarked that "lawyers defending a criminal are rarely artists enough to turn the beautiful terrible mess of the criminal's deed to his advantage"?

Was there any significant change in Patty Hearst's behavior? Before her arrest, she demeaned and denounced those who "helped" her as a child; after her arrest, she demeaned and denounced those who "helped" her as a fugitive. For whatever reason, she seemed to be inclined to make her life exciting at the expense of the dignity, liberty and property of others.

The basic facts in the Hearst trial were simple and uncontested. The defendant engaged in numerous acts which, unless legally excusable and excused, constitute serious crimes. What legal excuses mitigate or negate "criminal responsibility" for such acts? There are only a few. One is actual, physical duress. If a person forces another to commit an illegal act—say, literally at gunpoint—then the coerced actor is not legally responsible for his act. Another excuse is insanity. The illegal act, according to this claim, is not something that the defendant has done; it is something that has happened to him. The defendant is therefore no more responsible for his illegal act than a patient with myocardial insufficiency is responsible for his abnormal electrocardiogram. Patty Hearst did not claim this defense.

What excuse is left? Only what used to be called "temporary insanity," a concept that has become unfashionable in forensic psychiatry; hence, "temporary insanity" has been refashioned into "brainwashing." The defendant, according to this claim, was not "really" himself when he committed the illegal acts; he was "really" someone else, that is, his "brainwashed" self; hence his "unbrainwashed" self cannot be held responsible for these acts. This was Patty Hearst's defense.

The crucial question thus becomes: What is "brainwashing"? Are there, as the term implies, two kinds of brains: washed and unwashed? How do we know which is which?

Actually, it's all quite simple. Like many dramatic terms, "brainwashing" is a metaphor. A person can no more wash another's brain with coercion or conversation than he can make him bleed with a cutting remark.

If there is no such thing as brainwashing, what does this metaphor stand for? It stands for one of the most universal human experiences and events, namely for one person influencing another. However, we do not call all types of personal or psychological influences "brainwashing." We reserve this term for influences of which we disapprove.

In other words, "brainwashing" is like "perversion": as the latter term refers only to those sexual activities that one disdains, so the former refers only to those educational or psychological influences one abhors. While she was with the SLA, Patty Hearst was no doubt influenced by her captors and associates; Hearst, Bailey, the press and nearly everyone else calls this "brainwashing." Between the time of her arrest, when she identified herself as an "urban guerrilla," and her appearance in court as a demure and dutiful daughter, Patty Hearst was no doubt influenced by her new captors and associates: no one calls this "brainwashing."

In short, trying to ascertain whether Patty Hearst had been brainwashed by having her examined by psychiatrists was like trying to ascertain whether holy water is holy by having it examined by priests. Terms like "brainwashing" and "holy water" (and others like them) are invented and deployed strategically by these very "experts" for their own purposes. If we really want to understand what holy water is, we must examine priests, not water; if we really want to understand what brainwashing is, we must examine psychiatrists, not brains (or criminal defendants).

What, then, were the psychiatrists doing in the Hearst trial? They were "testifying" for whoever paid them. More than 300 years ago, an English aristocrat defined an ambassador as an honest man sent abroad to lie for his country. I would define a forensic psychiatrist as an honest doctor sent into court to lie for his masters.

We have done away with canon law and no longer look to priests to tell us about the purity or pollution of the soul. But we have substituted for it mental hygiene law and look to psychiatrists to tell us about the purity or pollution of the brain.[9]

6

Forensic Psychiatry Is Fraudulent

The insanity defense and the insanity verdict are joined in unholy matrimony in the insanity trial. The defendent claims the nonexistent condition of insanity as an excuse for what he did to his victim; the court claims the same nonexistent condition as a justification for what it does to the defendent.[1]

Mises, Hayek, and Banfield: Political philosophers across the spectrum agree on the legitimacy of psychiatric social control.

Psychiatric interference with the rule of law in the name of individualized justice and therapy is precisely the sort of thing that, as we might expect, would appeal to statists of all persuasions—as the contemporary literature on "psychiatric justice" in fact reveals. However, the fact that psychiatric justice is also embraced by antistatists—by classical liberals, conservatives, and even libertarians—is, on the face of it, rather surprising. It illustrates, as I shall try to show, that, like nearly everyone in modern society, the antistatists too are sometimes the unwitting victims of a psychiatric-therapeutic world view.

Because Ludwig von Mises is justly considered to be a pioneer recreator, in its contemporary version, of free market economics and of the moral philosophy on which it rests, I shall begin my review of the capitulation of antistatists before the onslaught of modern psychiatry by remarking briefly on his comments relevant to our subject.

137

The crux of Mises's mistake about psychiatry is simple: he accepts that there exists a class of persons whom certain medical experts called "psychiatrists," can reliably identify as insane, and that such persons cannot be treated as moral agents. "The anarchists," writes Mises, "overlook the undeniable fact that some people are either too narrow-minded or too weak to adjust themselves spontaneously to the conditions of social life. Even if we admit that every sane adult is endowed with the faculty of realizing the good of social cooperation and of acting accordingly, there still remains the problem of the infants, the aged, and the insane."

Mises here places the very young, the very old, and the very odd in the same class—all characterized by their supposed inability to cooperate with their fellow human beings. What is wrong with this? Everything. I will show this by examples, rather than by exposition. The argument I shall construct may be a little simplified, but it is, I believe, entirely accurate.

A month old infant cannot cooperate. It cannot contract for care, but can only feel hunger, or pain, scream, and thus coerce relief. The same goes for a senile person, especially if he is a bed-ridden invalid, who is, save for one big difference, much like an infant. The difference is that whereas the helpless infant "waits" to live and others wait for him to live, the helpless old person "waits" to die and others wait for him to die.

How does an insane person resemble them? The answer depends on what one means by an "insane person." If one means an individual whose brain has been destroyed by syphilis, who is demented with paresis, then what is true for the old invalid is also true for the insane. But it is inconceivable that in 1949 that is what Mises meant by "insanity." It is more likely that by "insanity" he meant the sort of (mis)behavior that psychiatrists call schizophrenia, exemplified by the "patient" declaring that he is Jesus. Such a person, I contend, is not incapable of cooperating and contracting; he chooses, instead, to coerce by means of dramatic, deceptive, and self-aggrandizing claims about himself. He is more like a counterfeiter than like a child. He is defiant, rather than defective. Mises completely ignores that possibility, treating the "insane" person as if he were utterly incapable of cooperating.

"We may agree," continues Mises, "that he who acts antisocially should be considered mentally sick and in need of care." Mises here compounds the confusion between bodily defect and personal defiance, medical disease and moral deviance. It is distressing, too, to see someone like Mises use a vague and potentially vicious term like "antisocial" so cavalierly. How could he so casually psychiatrize the protestor as psychotic and consign him into the crushing embrace of the psychiatrist?

There can only be one answer: by accepting the principles and practices of psychiatry as intellectually valid and morally sound. This conclusion is borne out by his next statement: "But as long as not all are cured [of insanity], and as long as there are infants and the senile, some provision must be taken lest they jeopardize society."

Mises keeps persisting with his catastrophic classification of infants, invalids, and the insane as members of the same class. Of course, I agree with Mises that infants, children, very old persons, and those disabled by incapacitating illness require special protection and represent special problems that threaten the well-being of those members of society that support the very existence of that society. That is why, on the one hand, such persons receive special protections from society, and on the other hand, are excluded—either by law, as are children, or by biology, as are invalids—from any of the rights and privileges granted to the healthy, adult members of society. However, I disagree strongly with Mises about his placing insane persons in the same class with infants and invalids, and about the sort of societal response that would, in a free society, be most appropriate for dealing with them.

Infants, incapable of caring for themselves, are also incapable of rejecting the protections offered them. Whether so-called insane persons are capable of caring for themselves is, sometimes, debatable; that they are capable of rejecting the help offered them—indeed, that they often go to extreme lengths to reject it—is, however, painfully obvious. Mises suggests that in the face of such behavior, psychiatric coercion is a legitimate and necessary societal option. I believe it is neither legitimate nor necessary. If so-called insane persons refuse the protection that is offered them, a right that no society can deny them, and remain free, then I believe we should adopt a moral perspective and a social policy toward such persons that is more consistent with the principles of the rule of law than as recourse to psychiatric coercion. I propose that we regard "insane" individuals as deviant or defiant persons rather than as diseased or demented patients; and that we treat them the same way we treat the so-called normal members of society—that is, by leaving them alone so long as they obey the law, and by prosecuting and punishing them if they break it.

Friedrich von Hayek has articulated the political philosophy of individual liberty and responsibility more fully than anyone else. Nevertheless, he has the same blindspot when it comes to psychiatry that we encountered in Mises. I shall try to show that Hayek's views on individual liberty are inconsistent and incompatible with his own views on the legitimacy of its psychiatric curtailment.

Psychiatric diversion comes into being mainly in response to the need for social protection from all sorts of difficulties that are conveniently attributed to madness or to madmen. Because such diversion arises out of a conflict between liberty and security, it is logical to begin with Hayek's own candid acknowledgment of this phenomenon as a general social problem. "It is very probable," he writes, "that there are people who do not value the liberty with which we are concerned, who cannot see that they derive great benefit from it, and who will be ready to give it up to gain other advantages; it may even be true that the necessity to act according to one's own plans and decisions may be felt by them to be more of a burden than an advantage."

This is an essential point for our understanding of the problems so-called psychiatric illness pose for the political philosopher, the lawmaker, and the judge. That is because a great many people who, in effect, define themselves as mad—by acting crazy, by inviting (overtly or covertly) psychiatric interference in their lives—do so because they loathe liberty. These are persons who, so to speak, do not know what to do with themselves and with their lives. They are incompetent, helpless, aimless, and dependent on others; they try to unload their problems of making a life for themselves on the shoulders of others. Unless they manage to find a husband or wife willing to assume this burden for them, such persons often get defined as psychiatric patients. As a result, a sort of psychiatric matrimony comes into being, in which liberty is sacrificed for another, higher, good: the patient sacrifices his own liberty for security; and the psychiatrist sacrifices the patient's liberty (and often some of his own as well) for the domination he gains over him.

As a rule, institutionalized mental patients rank liberty low on their scale of values. Such persons pose a difficult problem for the philosopher of freedom, as indeed do all those who loathe liberty. How should he treat the person who instead of wanting to be free, wants to be enslaved? Who instead of wanting to be an adult, wants to be a child? Both Mises and Hayek treat such a person as if he were, in fact, incapable of being free because, like the infant or the imbecile, he lacks responsibility. But responsibility is not something like a spleen that a person may literally possess or fail to possess. Instead, it is something that a person assumes or fails to assume, or something that we ascribe or do not ascribe to him. The point is that individuals who complain of mental symptoms or irresistible impulses feel or claim to feel unfree with respect to certain experiences or desires; whereas individuals confined in mental institutions actually lose some of their liberty. In both cases— more obviously in the latter—the "victim" is, however, "compensated" for his loss by a commensurate relief from the responsibility of having to lead his own life.

It is in confronting this obvious and universal social-psychological phenomenon and the problems it poses for political philosophy that Hayek's analysis, too, exhibits a serious weakness. It lies, essentially, in his treating insanity as if it were a biosocial condition, like infancy, rather than an individual-ethical strategy, like imitation. It is worth noting that psychiatry's assault on the philosophy of liberty has traditionally been concentrated at this very point—at that philosophy's veritable Achilles' heel—that is, on the notion of personal responsibility. For centuries alienists, mad-doctors, and psychiatrists have claimed that, like infants and imbeciles, insane persons are not responsible for their behavior; and people in all walks of life—professionals and laymen alike—have increasingly accepted that claim. Therein lie the ideological foundations for the widespread acceptance—among liberals, conservatives, and even libertarians—of the legitimacy of psychiatric diversion from liberty. Thus, Hayek writes:

> The complementarity of liberty and responsibility means that the argument for liberty can apply only to those who can be held responsible. It cannot apply to infants, idiots, or the insane. It presupposes that a person is capable of learning from experience and of guiding his actions by knowledge thus acquired; it is invalid for those who have not yet learned enough or are incapable of learning. A person whose actions are fully determined by the same unchangeable impulses uncontrolled by knowledge of the consequences or a genuine split personality, a schizophrenic, could in this sense not be held responsible, because his knowledge that he will be held responsible could not alter his actions. The same would apply to persons suffering from really uncontrollable urges, kleptomaniacs and dipsomaniacs, whom experience has proved not to be responsive to normal motives.

The proposition that so-called kleptomaniacs and dipsomaniacs "suffer from uncontrollable urges" is, however, conceptually faulty and unsupported (and indeed unsupportable) by evidence. Conceptually, Hayek here falls into the linguistic trap of psychiatry: he seems to think that because a word ends with the Greek suffix "maniac," it designates a medical (psychiatric) illness, presumably characterized by irresistible impulses to commit a particular act. Thus, the person who likes to steal becomes a "kleptomaniac," the person who likes to drink becomes a "dipsomaniac," the person who likes to commit arson becomes a "pyromaniac," and the person who likes his own single-minded obsession becomes a "monomaniac." However, there are obvious dangers in that direction. Would calling cigarette smokers "nicotinomaniacs" make them into mental patients suffering from an uncontrollable urge to smoke? Just how grievously short-sighted and self-serving such ostensible diagnoses are is illustrated by the term "drapetomania" which, a little over a century ago, was considered to be a mental disease characterized by the slave's uncontrollable urge to escape from bondage and seek liberty.

The language of psychiatry serves the purpose of making men seem like madmen, exhibiting behaviors they do not "will" and for which they are not "responsible." Hayek adopts this language when he speaks of "schizophrenics . . . whose actions are fully determined." The trouble with this sort of statement is, first, that there is no objective way of knowing who is and who is not schizophrenic; and second, that if an action were fully determined, it would cease to be an action and would become a movement or reflex. Both of these considerations are crucial, especially in the context of Hayek's own argument, since Hayek himself insists that freedom under law requires the impartial application of rules applicable equally to all, and that responsibility is not an attribute but an ascription. Let me briefly elaborate on each of these points.

When Hayek speaks of a "schizophrenic" as a person whose actions are not altered by his knowledge that he will be held responsible for them, he is simply mistaken. I say this partly because the conduct of schizophrenics is susceptible to influence, albeit perhaps of a different sort from that which would be effective with others; partly because there is, as I noted already, no satisfactory way of dividing people into two groups, schizophrenics and nonschizophrenics; and partly because his argument about schizophrenics contradicts one of his most important caveats—namely, that "in public life freedom requires that we be regarded as types, not as unique individuals, and treated on the presumption that normal motives and deterrents will be effective, whether this be true in the particular instance or not." I assume that by types Hayek here means categories such as "persons accused of speeding" or "persons convicted of murder," and not categories such as "Jews" or "Catholics," "fat persons" or "thin persons." Since in its official psychiatric use, the term "schizophrenia" denotes a personal characteristic, like Jewishness or obesity, rather than an illegal act, it is not clear how Hayek would reconcile his recommendation to treat people as types in precisely that public life in which psychiatrists and their supporters insist that schizophrenics (as indeed all mental patients) ought to be treated as unique individuals.

Actually, Hayek's well-reasoned insistence that, in a free society, laws should promulgate abstract or general rules is itself enough to invalidate all psychiatric coercions. "Because the rule is laid down in ignorance of the particular case," explains Hayek in a passage that could have been written specifically to refute the justifications for psychiatric methods of social control, "and no man's will decides the coercion used to enforce it, the law is not arbitrary. This, however, is true only if by 'law' we mean the general rules that apply equally to everybody. . . . As a true law should not name any particulars, so it should especially not single out any specific persons or groups of persons." Commitment laws and other regulations mandating psychiatric diversion do precisely what Hayek here says genuine laws should not do — namely, they single out specific persons or groups of persons whose behavior is to be judged differently from that of other members of society.

Moreover, Hayek explicitly — and I believe correctly — excludes nonpunitive sanctions from among the legitimate powers of the government in a free society. "Under the rule of law," he writes, "government can infringe a person's protected private sphere only as punishment for breaking an announced general rule." This proposition actually contains two parts, only one of which Hayek emphasizes. The part he emphasizes has to do with "breaking an announced general rule": that is, if a person breaks no announced general rule, he ought to be left unmolested by the government. But his proposition contains another important part: that is, the "government can infringe a person's protected private sphere only as punishment." In other words, it cannot do so as diagnosis or treatment. Since jurists and psychiatrists never tire of asserting that psychiatric coercions are not punitive but therapeutic, such interventions have, by Hayek's own criteria, no legitimate place in a free society.

Edward Banfield — who may be included among the contemporary critics of statism but whose position on political philosophy otherwise defies categorization — is so unreserved in his support of psychiatric methods of social control that in this regard his position is indistinguishable from that of the psychiatric statists who created psychiatry at the beginning of the nineteenth century and have dominated it ever since. Although I am familiar with the characteristic cant of institutional psychiatry, I find it somewhat astonishing to hear it re-echoed, without the slightest doubt or criticism, by a person of Banfield's acumen. By psychiatric cant I mean statements such as the following: "However, much of the violence in lower class life is probably more an expression of mental illness than of class culture. The incidence of serious mental illness is greater in the lower class than in any of the others." And further:

> In the chapters that follow, the term *normal* will be used to refer to class culture that is not lower class. The implication that lower class culture is pathological seems fully warranted both because of the relatively high incidence of mental illness in the lower class and also because human nature seems loath to accept a style of life that is so radically present-oriented.

I am surprised that Banfield has not yet been awarded the order of merit by the American Psychiatric Association. Perhaps he has not because his statements about mental illness are more extreme than even the APA would now dare to offer. Banfield's assigning all persons who share in the lower class culture to the category of the mentally ill is reminiscent of the Spanish Inquisition's declaring, in the second half of the sixteenth century, the entire population of the Netherlands to be heretics and sentencing it, en masse, to death.

Such ideas and opinions are, however, not matters for merriment. They are serious in the extreme, since—as I have tried to show in my work—mental illness is today one of the main justifications for the scapegoating and persecution of individuals and groups. Banfield's own further remarks about mental illness support this contention. Although he writes as if madness were a descriptive term, he actually deploys it as the dispositional weapon it is:

> There are individuals whose propensity to crime is so high that no set of incentives that it is feasible to offer to the whole population would influence their behavior. They may be compelled, but they cannot be deterred. The only effective way of *compelling* someone not to commit crimes is to lock him up—in the most extreme case, in solitary confinement. Society does this even if the individual has not committed a crime when it is considered almost certain that he cannot be prevented in any other way from committing very serious crimes. No one would doubt the wisdom or justice of confining indefinitely a madman who, if released, would rush to attack anyone he saw—and this even if he had not yet seriously injured anyone.

I would doubt the wisdom and justice of such a course of action, so would many other people. It is important to note that Banfield here endorses psychiatric diversion both as a general principle that is allegedly unchallenged and unchallengeable intellectually and as a social practice without any rules or guarantees for protecting persons from being placed in the class of madman mistakenly or maliciously. The casual assurance with which Banfield supports psychiatric coercion is a stark reminder of how profoundly this method of social control has subverted the classic principles of the rule of law.

The sort of psychiatric diversion from the criminal justice system that characterizes our present American situation constitutes a genuinely fresh danger to individual liberty in the history of man and society. It therefore calls for appropriate new correctives.

Traditionally, societies have been tyrannical. Those who wished to secure liberty or to enlarge its scope were thus occupied with efforts to curb the powers of the rulers, whether they be theocratic, aristocratic, or democratic. From Montesquieu and Jefferson to Mises and Hayek, the magic formula has been limited government. That made sense in the context of its underlying premise: the rulers wanted to do too much (especially in the way of coercing others); hence the thing to do was to make it difficult or impossible for them to do certain things (especially coercing others not guilty of lawbreaking). Thus was constitutional government born.

Today, however, we are confronted with some societies, in particular with American society, in which that classic premise is no longer valid, or rather is not valid in its original form. The American government is now a threat to the freedom of its own people not because it punishes the innocent, nor because its punishments are too harsh, but rather because it does not punish the guilty. One result is an ever-increasing army of thieves and thugs, muggers and murderers, abroad in the land, preying on a people unprotected by their own police and judiciary. Another result is an ever-increasing tendency not to punish those who are evil and who commit evil acts but instead to treat them for nonexistent illness.

I only state the obvious when I now say that our personal liberty is as easily threatened by a desperado as by a despot, by a mugger as by a monarch. We all know that. Why, then, do we keep asking stupid questions, such as: Why is crime increasing? Why do so many people rob and kill?

One answer to these questions lies in inverting the patently false adage that "crime does pay." Crime indeed pays, and in more ways than one—that is, it pays not only for the criminals but also for the criminologists (by which term I refer here to all those who make a living confining, diagnosing, treating, rehabilitating, and otherwise managing and studying offenders). And it pays each of them both economically and existentially—that is, by putting money in their pockets and meaning into their lives. We cannot reduce crime until we recognize these facts. And even when we do recognize them, we shall be able to reduce crime only in proportion as we either make noncriminal pursuits more attractive for would-be criminals, or make criminal activities less attractive for them, or both. We are not likely to do any of these things as long as we look to professional criminologists (and other statist reformers) to solve a problem of which they themselves are so important a part.

In summary, it seems to me that however complex the nature of our present crime problem in America might be, it has at least one obvious cause, for which there is at least one obvious remedy. That cause is the unwillingness of the American people—as individual citizens and as members of the government at every level—to shoulder the responsibility for punishing men, women, and children who deprive other individuals of their life, liberty, or property. And that remedy is to reject the ethic of fake psychiatric therapeutism masquerading as the rehabilitation of offenders, and to re-embrace the ethic of a truly dignified system of criminal sanctions consisting of minimal but fitting punishments meted out as inexorably and as fairly as possible. I believe that such a system of criminal justice is no more utopian than is a system of constitutional government. In proportion as limited government has been realized, people have been safe from tyranny. In proportion as a decent punitive penology would be realized, people would be safe from crime.[2]

Legal Insanity

Lawbreakers are natural adversaries of society; society should see the insanity plea as a fraudulent strategy to evade criminal responsibility, and the plea, therefore, should be abolished.

Not only do I believe that mental illness should never be accepted as a release from criminal responsibility, but also that it should never be the ground for a refusal to try a person charged with an offense. Everyone accused of breaking the law should be tried. This sweeping statement requires clarification.

I believe that we should continue to adhere to the principle that a person should not be tried unless he can understand the charges against him and can assist in his own defense. It might be argued that if a person is in a catatonic state—mute, immobile, and perhaps unable even to feed himself—he should not be put on trial. The point of my argument is this: the reason for not trying such a person is that he is unable to assist in his own defense—not that he is schizophrenic.

My thesis is that psychiatric considerations *as such* are irrelevant to the conduct of a trial. The psychiatric expert may be allowed to testify on certain facts or observations, but not on psychiatric disease or criminal responsibility. Because such a modification would, in effect, abolish the special psychiatric plea (the insanity plea), and the special psychiatric disposition (not guilty by reason of insanity), there would be little need for psychiatric testimony. Extreme psychiatric conditions, such as a catatonic stupor, make it obvious that a person is unfit to stand trial; hence no psychiatrist is needed to make that determination. On the other hand, such conditions are usually temporary and lead either to death or a remission of symptoms. Trial would thus be postponed only until gross behavioral incapacity disappeared. A person with "mental illness" of less than extreme proportions should not be declared unfit to stand trial. No two people are equally capable of defending themselves against criminal charges. Hence, even if some so-called mental illnesses should impair a person's capacity to defend himself—others, however, might improve it—it would be no more logical not to try a person for this reason than for relative lack of education. (Surely a cleaning woman, accused of political subversion, cannot defend herself as well as a professor of political science. This, however, does not prevent us from trying her. Thus, even if so-called mental illnesses were to impair a person's ability to defend himself, we could not, on this basis alone, declare him unfit to be tried, unless we were to limit the privilege of standing trial to the most highly educated members of society.

In sum, then, all persons charged with offenses—except those grossly disabled—should be tried. The emphasis here is on gross disability: it should be readily apparent or easily explicable to a group of lay persons, like a jury. The claim that trial may endanger a defendant's physical or mental health seems to me preposterous. Such a claim can *always* be made, and therefore, except for gross disability, should never be allowed. If found innocent, the defendent should be set free, even though considered mentally ill. If he is found guilty, he should be sentenced, according to the law. Finally, if the accused is declared both guilty and "mentally ill" he could be cared for in institutions suitably equipped and staffed.

The scheme I have outlined would eliminate the confusion between mental sickness, defined as an illness-like phenomenon, and criminality, defined as lawbreaking. Obviously, these concepts and phenomena are not mutually exclusive. However, we must distinguish between mental illness and crime, not because our theories of human conduct demand it, but because the ethic of a free society requires it. The hybridization of mental hospitals with jails undermines the security of every person's constitutional rights. The undoing of this hybridization, with the consequent separation of institutions for voluntary care from prisons, will guarantee that if a man keeps within the law, he cannot be deprived of his liberty. And it will guarantee, also, that if he does break the law, he will lose his liberty for a limited period only.

•   •   •

Judicial sentencing of lawbreakers does not deprive us of the opportunity of also trying to help them. Even if we accept the argument that many criminals are mentally sick, it does not follow that they should be in mental hospitals rather than in prisons. Mental hospitalization of offenders should not be, and cannot be, a substitute for prison reform.

•   •   •

The desire to treat decently those who break our laws does not require or justify turning prisons into mental hospitals. Mental hospitalization of offenders, however sincerely advocated, can only aggravate an already bad situation in both our penal and psychiatric institutions.[3]

Outrageous crimes such as assassinations are just that: crimes, not illnesses.

With the dramatic unfolding of events after the attempted assassination of President Reagan, even his bitterest critics were forced to concede that his behavior under fire was courageous and inspiring. Veritably, Reagan seemed to possess all of the virtues of the Western hero he had portrayed so often and so well on the screen. Unfortunately, on April 22, 1891, in the first interview he gave the press since the shooting, he fell off his horse and didn't even seem to know it. Quite unwittingly, Reagan offered some comments about John W. Hinckley, Jr. that were, in my opinion, unfounded and misguided and that gravely prejudiced his trial.

What President Reagan said was this: "I hope, indeed I pray, that he can find an answer to his problem. He seems to be a very disturbed young man. He comes from a fine family. They must be devastated by this. And I hope he'll get well, too."

I believe that these remarks are important enough to justify my taking them on one sentence at a time.

"I hope, indeed I pray, that he can find an answer to his problem." In the old Westerns, if memory doesn't deceive me, the good men first hanged the bad men and only then did they pray for their souls. Elsewhere in the same interview Reagan also said that he prays daily for Brady's recovery. As I do not pray, I grant that my views on prayer may be impious and "incorrect." Nevertheless, I believe that the dignity of prayer is cheapened when it is bestowed as indiscriminately as this. Is there anyone for whom Reagan would not pray? Did he pray for Brezhnev's health? For Stalin's soul? If not, then why for Hinckley? Surely, Solzhenitsyn is no less pious than Reagan, but I do not recall Solzhenitsyn's ever mentioning that he prays for communist murderers. Perhaps capitalist would-be murderers who fail to kill anyone and succeed only in lobotomizing a press secretary are more deserving.

One more comment on this brief but psychiatrically significant sentence needs to be added here. President Reagan's statement implies that Hinckley has a "problem" and is looking to "find an answer" to it. But I think Reagan (and the conventional psychiatric mind-set he so naively displays) may have got this backward. Hinckley had a *problem* before the assassination attempt. The criminal act was his *solution* to it. Now other people, especially poor Jim Brady and his family, have got a problem. I, for one, find the compassion for Hinckley premature. Like the men Reagan used to impersonate, I believe that Hinckley deserves punishment first, compassion and forgiveness later, if ever.

"He [Hinckley] seems to be a very disturbed young man." Anyone with any respect for language—and without respect there can be neither truth nor justice—must realize that while this may be a piece of received psychiatric truth, it is a big lie nevertheless. Hinckley is not disturbed, he is disturbing. He is not sick, he is sickening.

"He [Hinckley] comes from a fine family." How does Reagan know this? All we were told so far is that Hinckley comes from a wealthy family.

There is one more thing we know, and I cannot emphasize its importance enough: namely, that Hinckley has not been allowed to speak for himself. In effect, he has been muzzled, he has been silenced [except for a few post-trial interviews and letters], while everyone, including the president of the United States, is busy explaining that he is "disturbed." For all we know, Hinckley may now feel quite undisturbed.

"They [Hinckley's family] must be devastated by this." That is likely and is probably one of the reasons for Hinckley's dastardly deed. But this is a speculation. And so is the possibility that the Hinckley family might have preferred George Bush for president. But that is heresy. We treasure our received psychiatric truths about mentally ill assassins precisely in order to banish such thoughts from our collective consciousness. In America, political motives for the murder of the high and mighty exist only in the half-forgotten pages of Shakespeare's tragedies.

"And I hope he'll get well, too." By thus acknowledging that Hinckley is ill, Reagan here implicitly supported an insanity defense for him. When Hinckley pleaded insanity his lawyers could have been able to appeal to the "expert testimony" of the president of the United States to support the contention that Hinckley was innocent because he was insane when he wounded Reagan instead of killing him.

President Reagan made a mistake in answering any questions about Hinckley at all. Respect for the law should have made him say, quite simply, that Hinckley's fate—and in particular the question of whether he is disturbed or depraved—would be for the jury to determine. The fact is that the distinction between disturbance and depravity—between madness and badness, between mental illness and criminality, call it what you will—is not a specialized or technical judgment doctors can make because they possess an MD degree or psychiatrists can make because they possess training in diagnosing and treating mental illness; or the president of the United States can make because he occupies a lofty office. That distinction is a *moral judgment,* which is why a jury, and no one else, is supposed to make it. If we forget that, we might as well forget about America.[4]

CIVIL COMMITMENT

The primary justification for civil commitment concerns a psychiatric/medical prediction of dangerousness to self and to others. But dangerousness is a vague, inconsistent, and nonmedical criterion.

Let us now analyze the justifications for commitment. Usually one or more of the following reasons are mentioned: (1) the person is psychotic or insane; (2) he is dangerous to himself; (3) he is dangerous to others; (4) he is mentally sick and needs hospital care and treatment, but does not understand his condition and the need for treatment.

As a rule, no single reason can account for the commitment of a particular person at a given time. Even all four, taken together, fail to explain some of the most essential features of this social phenomenon.

The so-called psychotic state of an individual is neither a necessary nor a sufficient cause for his commitment. Impecunious elderly persons, addicts, and offenders are committed; yet, they are not usually considered to be psychotic. Conversely, many persons whom psychiatrists regard as psychotic remain at liberty.

A person's dangerousness, to himself or others, is a more relevant consideration. However, dangerousness is undefined. Hence, this criterion also fails to offer a reliable guide for explaining the commitment of one person and the noncommitment of another equally as dangerous.

In the "Draft Act Governing Hospitalization of the Mentally Ill" (Federal Security Agency, 1952), involuntary hospitalization is considered to be justified if the following conditions are met:

(A) He [the patient] is mentally ill, and

(B) because of his illness is likely to injure himself or others if allowed to remain at liberty or

(C) is in need of care or treatment in a mental hospital, and because of his illness, lacks sufficient insight or capacity to make responsible application, therefore:

What constitutes dangerousness is left unspecified, perhaps intentionally, to allow for administrative decisions by lawyers and psychiatrists.

In my opinion, whether or not a person is dangerous is not the real issue. It is rather *who* he is, and *in what way* he is dangerous. Some persons are allowed to be dangerous to others with impunity. Also, most of us are allowed to be dangerous in some ways, but not in others.

Drunken drivers are dangerous both to themselves and to others. They injure and kill many more people than, for example, persons with paranoid delusions of persecution. Yet, people labeled paranoid are readily committable, while drunken drivers are not.

Some types of dangerous behavior are even rewarded. Race-car drivers, trapeze artists, and astronauts receive admiration and applause. In contrast, the polysurgical addict and the would-be suicide receive nothing but contempt and aggression. Indeed, the latter type of dangerousness is considered good cause for commitment. Thus, it is not dangerousness in general that is at issue here, but rather the manner or style in which one is dangerous.

● ● ●

Let us now analyze commitment from a sociopsychological standpoint. In general, that conduct tends to lead to commitment which appears abnormal to the layman. Such crudely offensive social behavior cannot, however, be readily correlated with psychiatric diagnoses. Nevertheless, psychiatrists tend to label this sort of behavior psychotic. Thus, the expressions "psychosis" and "behavior justifying commitment" overlap, and in effect often mean the same thing. Indeed, persons whom psychiatrists may consider psychotic are usually left undisturbed so long as they do not annoy others. Ezra Pound, for example, was released from psychiatric confinement with the explanation that although he was still seriously ill mentally, he was no longer dangerous.

A crucial consideration is the issue of social disturbance. If a person is old and cannot care for himself, he creates a social disturbance and may be committed. If a person threatens to kill himself—but does not do so—he too creates a social disturbance and, in a way, asks to be committed. If a person lays claim to ideas or beliefs or sensations that threaten society—for example, beliefs of being persecuted (called "delusions"), or sensations of seeing or hearing (called "hallucinations")—he too creates a social disturbance and may be committed. Finally, if a person commits acts which violate social rules—for example, by engaging in forbidden modes of sexual gratification—he too creates a social disturbance and may be committed.

The similarities between committable mental illness and crime thus emerge. In both, the person "offends" society, and is therefore restrained. The motives for restraining the mentally ill person are ostensibly therapeutic, whereas for the criminal they are allegedly punitive. This distinction, however, cannot be defended satisfactorily. State hospitals have been notorious for their neglect, and indeed, abuse, of the mental patient. There is evidence that incarceration in a mental hospital may be more harmful for the personality than incarceration in a prison.

If so, irrespective of the motives that animate those who commit, the actual effect of mental hospitalization may still be punishment.

Another crucial factor in commitment is social role. Our problem may now be formulated by asking: Who annoys whom? It is a fact that the vast majority of committed patients are members of the lower classes. Upper-class persons are virtually immune from this sort of social restraint. This point deserves emphasis.

Before the law, all men are equal. This at least is the intention of the law. We know, however, that when in legal jeopardy, the wealthy and well-educated often fare better than the poor and uneducated. Nevertheless, the whole tradition of Anglo-American law has been to support efforts to make the judicial process "fair." No such considerations of fair play enter into the game of commitment. Indeed, commitment is, in part, a symptom of class struggle—not exactly in Marxist terms, but a class struggle nonetheless. Let me illustrate what I mean. In the military service, an office may send an enlisted man to the hospital for psychiatric observation. This may appear to be a request for a medical study, but it is not. Rather, it is a charge of probable mental illness, similar to an accusation of wrongdoing. In effect, the person requesting the examination says: "This man is probably crazy. See if it is so." The roles in this situation cannot be inverted. The enlisted man cannot request a psychiatric examination of his officer.

The assumption that members of one group can do wrong but members of another cannot, can frequently be detected when the issue of a person's mental condition is raised. In the school, administrators and teachers may regard students as posing psychiatric problems, but not vice versa. Similarly, in psychoanalytic education, training and supervising analysts may decide that candidates need further analysis. Here too, the student is powerless to do anything about the training analyst's "mental health," even when the latter is obviously disabled, for example by senility. In courts of law, the same rule prevails: only the sanity of the defendant can be questioned, not that of the prosecutor or the judge.[5]

Involuntary civil commitment should be abolished.

All provisions for involuntary mental hospitalization should be abolished. Like the institution of slavery, the institution of hospital psychiatry, as we know it, must go.

Legal provisions for so-called psychiatric emergencies are, of course, necessary. I believe that the existing provisions for dealing with medical emergencies and with crimes are adequate. Psychiatric emergencies fall into one of two categories. The passive, stuporous, uncommunicative patient is one type. Legally, he should be treated like the unconscious medical patient. The other is the aggressive, paranoid person, who threatens violence. Legally, he should be treated like a person charged with an offense; psychiatrically, it would be desirable, of course, if he were not incarcerated in an ordinary jail, but in a prison-hospital, where he could receive both medical and psychiatric attention.

True psychiatric emergencies are rare. They constitute only a small proportion of cases of involuntary hospitalization. Moreover, in this group, the patient often suffers from bodily illness or intoxication—for example, brain tumor or diabetic hypoglycemia. Such patients should therefore be hospitalized in medical, not mental hospitals. Like hospitalization for medical emergencies, this type of confinement should last only until the patient regains his powers.

In the scheme I am proposing, two classes of people could no longer be forced to submit to psychiatric hospitalization. The first is composed of persons threatening to commit suicide; the second, of those considered mentally ill by others, who refuse to submit to psychiatric treatment. . . .

Mental hospitals, both private and public, should be restricted to the care of consenting, voluntary, adult patients. Both the hospital and the patient should be treated as independent, contracting parties. Patients should be free to enter or leave the hospital at will. Similarly, psychiatrists and psychiatric hosptials should be free to refuse to accept patients they do not want. In brief, the power of both patients and psychiatrists should be curtailed. Thus, patients should be deprived of the power to coerce psychiatrists, for example, by a threat of suicide; psychiatrists should be deprived of the authority to coerce patients, for example, by a threat of commitment. The power of both parties should be limited by law to persuasion. If persuasion fails, each should be allowed to act autonomously, in its own best interests.

The therapeutic tasks of such voluntary psychiatric institutions might range from social rehabilitation to intensive individual psychotherapy. However, protection of the public from harm by so-called mental patients would *not* be one of them. There would be no need—indeed, it would be absurd—to copy the penal model. Psychiatric hospitals, like school dormitories, medical hospitals, museums, or personal homes, would be at once "open" and "closed." Like the inhabitants of these places, those in mental hospitals would be fully responsible for their acts. Mental hospital personnel should have no more concern about the antisocial conduct of their patients than should, say, a medical school faculty have of its students.

The mental hospital should be a new kind of institution, resembling neither prison nor medical hospital. Its purpose would be to provide the kind of help rendered today by many psychiatrists, psychologists, and social workers. These services are more comparable to those obtainable in certain schools, hotels, vacation resorts, and aboard ocean liners, than to those furnished by ordinary hospitals. Accordingly, in mental institutions (the term "hospital" would only be distracting) few physicians would be needed, and they would care only for bodily diseases. Until new standards are developed, personnel for this sort of organization should be recruited from those who demonstrate interest and skill in this type of work, not from those who meet the existing, but irrelevant, institutional qualifications.

This type of institution would be unsuitable for many persons who are now confined in mental hospitals. Those who break the law, but are now classified as mental patients, should be held in what I call "prison hospitals." Children regarded as mentally ill would also require another kind of facility. Minors do not have the legal rights of adults. Hence, a "therapeutic" program designed especially to safeguard the legal rights of adults would be inappropriate for them. Finally, the mentally retarded, whether child or adult, would also need a different type of institution.[6]

Involuntary civil commitment remains a reality to be dealt with; however, because psychiatrists and mental patients are natural adversaries, special attention should be paid to patient rights and the risks of mental hospitalization.

The Antagonistic Character of the Relationship Between the Involuntary Mental Patient and the Psychiatrist Should Be Frankly Recognized and Publicly Acknowledged. We must begin by candidly acknowledging the role of the hospital psychiatrists, vis-à-vis his patient. Such a psychiatrist, especially if he works in a state hospital, is not the patient's agent. The law, the mental patient, and the public must cease to look on hospital psychiatrists—and perhaps even on current psychiatry as a profession—as the patient's helpers and friends. To be sure, sometimes they *try* to be. But more often they are the patient's adversaries. Perhaps this is a shocking statement. I shall try to explain it.

The relationship between hospital psychiatrist and mental patient is one of oppression disguised as benefaction. The institutional psychiatrist, though not necessarily the patient's enemy, is neither his friend nor his therapist. I believe that there is a conflict between them.

Let us compare this with the struggle between industry and labor at the turn of the century. To solve that problem, American legislation embraced the principle that workers have a right to organize and strike. I believe that mental patients should have a similar opportunity to protect themselves against the psychiatrists who coerce them. . . .

The problem of "liberating" the hospitalized mental patient from his psychosocial, religious, and legal shackles is exceedingly complex and difficult. It calls to mind the socioeconomic problems of so-called underdeveloped nations. Because of a low level of education and industrialization, it is extremely difficult for such nations to get going in a cycle of increasing education, increasing industrialization, and increasing democratization. Similarly, it is often a lack of social feeling or interest that causes a person to become a mental patient. This deficiency prevents him from engaging in organized social activity with his peer group. Hence, he remains isolated, and the benign circle of organizing, learning, acquiring new skills, approaching equality with his superiors, never begins. Like underdeveloped nations, mental patients need "foreign aid." But such "aid" can easily be destructive. The mental hospital patient needs help, but not in the form of housing, food, and tranquilizers. Such aid only perpetuates the infantile, disabled role for the patient.

In my opinion, what the mental hospital patient needs is to acquire the spirit of liberty and, indeed, of revolt. I propose that we supply him with an agency to foster this.

A Watchdog Agency Should Be Created to Protect the Rights of the Mental Patient. The mental patient needs an agency to counteract the power of the hospital psychiatrists. It should consist of a corps of lawyers, psychiatrists, social workers, and perhaps others, and be independent of the department which operates the state mental hospitals.

This agency would assist persons threatened with commitment and those already hospitalized. For instance, when a wife files a petition to commit her husband, it would be the duty of this agency to provide capable persons to investigate the possible alternatives to commitment. They could help the husband obtain a separation or divorce from his wife, or help him rebut her accusations of mental illness.

This agency would thus be entrusted with the task of promoting the "mental patient's" interests as he defines them. The hospitalized mental patient could call on the resources of this facility if he should wish to leave the hospital, obtain a driver's license, or secure any other lost rights or privileges which he is ill-equipped to regain.

Lack of commitment to this enterprise, or inadequate financial support for it, could lead only to failure. However, if properly implemented

I am confident that such an agency could foster a significant improvement in the conditions of the mentally ill in America.

Mental Hospitals Should Cease to Be "What Else" Institutions. When people do not know "what else" to do with, say, a lethargic, withdrawn adolescent, a petty criminal, an exhibitionist, or a difficult grandparent—our society tells them, in effect, to put the "offender" in a mental hospital.

To overcome this, we shall have to create an increasing number of humane and rational alternatives to involuntary mental hospitalization. Old-age homes, workshops, temporary homes for indigent persons whose family ties have disintegrated, progressive prison communities— these and many other facilities will be needed to assume the tasks now entrusted to mental hospitals. Some of the money and effort spent on mental hospitals should be devoted to such enterprises. As matters now stand, mental hospitals only waste our valuable human resources and funds. They also endanger our trusted political institutions and our personal liberties.

The Hospitalized Mental Patient Should Retain as Many of His Rights as Possible. At present, the involuntarily hospitalized mental patient is virtually without any rights. In theory, the committed mental patient is not incompetent. In fact, however, he may be treated as if he were. If the hospital psychiatrists decide to deprive the patient of a right, there is little he can do about it.

As an alternative, we could experiment with partial deprivation of liberty for the mental patient. In this connection, involuntary military service may serve as a model. A person conscripted for military service loses some of his freedom—for example, the freedom to pursue his occupation, to select his home or clothes, to move about freely, and so forth. He retains, however, the right to marry and divorce, to enter into valid contracts, to vote, and many others. The point is that the conscripted solder surrenders *only* those rights which are required by the duties of soldiering. The deprivation of rights cannot be justified on this ground—for example, censoring the serviceman's mail or reading materials—offends our sensibilities. It would also be unconstitutional.

The same principles should apply to the loss of freedom incurred by the involuntarily hospitalized mental patient. Let us suspend only those freedoms which are necessary for settling the dispute that caused him to be defined as mentally ill. For example, instead of committing the alcoholic husband who abuses his wife, the court could order him to cease annoying her. Subsequent violations of such orders could be treated by judicial, not psychiatric, penalties. The court would thus regulate only the patient's relationship with his wife. His liberty would remain otherwise unimpaired. Accordingly, the husband would not be forced to submit to psychiatric treatment he does not want; nor would he be prevented from working, making telephone calls, writing letters, and so forth. Current commitment laws deprive such a person of all these freedoms. In sum, the committed patient's loss of rights should be partial rather than almost total.

Involuntary Mental Hospitalization Should Be Discouraged. Frequently, when people do not know what to do about a human problem, they may try to resolve it by committing one of the parties to the conflict to a mental hospital. Thus, husbands may prefer committing their wives to legally separating from them or divorcing them. Physicians may prefer committing a difficult patient to withdrawing from the case. Policemen and district attorneys may prefer committing certain offenders to prosecuting them. And so forth.

In each of these instances, commitment offers—at least temporarily—an easy solution to a difficult situation. If, however, we consider involuntary mental hospitalization a serious evil, we should search for more effective means of coping with these problems. Moreover, if we do not discourage easy commitment, there will never develop the social tension which may be necessary for creating adequate facilities for, say, indigent old people.

The present practice of admitting to the state mental hospitals people of all sorts, whether "mentally ill" or not, represents the persistence of an old habit: this was the function of the insane asylum in the eighteenth century. This practice cannot be justified any longer. Under the same roof, how can psychiatrists provide for the needs of such diverse persons as juvenile schizophrenics and indigent old people dying of cancer, drug addicts and depressed housewives, petty criminals and religious paranoiacs? They cannot—but often justify what they do by humanitarian motives and the pressure of social needs. In the long run, however, inadequate or misdirected stopgap measures of this kind serve only the self-seeking interests of psychiatrists, for whose services such tactics generate an ever increasing demand. At the same time, the welfare of the sufferers is sacrificed.

People Should Be Educated About the Dangers of Mental Hospitalization. My final proposal, if adopted, would reverse many current practices in mental health education. Instead of comparing mental health to physical health, and exhorting people to use psychiatric services as much as possible, I suggest clarifying and emphasizing the differences between them. These I consider the more significant. Likewise I suggest stressing the similarities between the roles of prisoner and mental hospital patient. If we expect people to conduct themselves responsibly, we must tell them not what is "good" for them, but what is true.

I believe, further, that so long as our mental health facilities are inadequate, we should not urge people to use psychiatric help as much as possible. Instead, we should emphasize the risks. Curiously, [especially in the past] psychiatrists seem to be quite immune to the hazards that threaten nonpsychiatric physicians and various medical facilities (such as hospitals and pharmaceutical companies). Radiologists and surgeons, for example, who do not inform a patient of the dangers of a procedure, fail to secure "informed consent." This renders them liable for damages, if the patient is harmed as a result of their actions. In other words, the physician will be liable for damages even if his performance was faultless, and the patient suffered merely as a result of risks inherent in the procedure.

This principle was the basis for awarding compensation to the persons who contracted poliomyelitis from injections of Salk vaccine manufactured by the Cutter Laboratories. As stated in *Modern Medicine,* "In the Cutter suit, no judge or jury has found the laboratory negligent in its manufacture of the vaccine, but damages were awarded on the grounds that *Cutter had breached an implied warranty since the vaccine caused the disease it was intended to prevent.*" Because the public was not warned of the risk of contracting polio from the vaccine, the court held the manufacturer responsible for an "implied warranty."

The Cutter affair, tragic though it was, is a relatively minor instance of injuries incurred by patients as a result of their having been misinformed. The faulty polio vaccine affected less than fifty persons, some only slightly. Compared to the thousands, perhaps hundreds of thousands, who have been injured by mental hospitalization—without having been fully apprised of the risks inherent in this form of "treatment"—the Cutter affair will seem like a raindrop in the ocean. Approximately a quarter-million people are hospitalized in mental institutions every year. A significant proportion is injured as a result. Nevertheless, contemporary mental health propaganda (it cannot very well be called "education") is silent about the hazards to which a person exposes himself when he enters a mental hospital, or to which he exposes those whom he causes to be hospitalized. It may be argued that there are certain unavoidable risks inherent in mental hospitalization. Indeed, there are. But this only emphasizes that all those responsible for recommending or providing this type of care ought to be duty-bound to inform the patients, and the public, of the exact dimensions of this risk. If, instead of providing accurate information, they indulge in spreading propaganda—then, I submit, they should be held legally responsible for the damages that may result, from mental hospitalization.

•   •   •

Pinel may have struck the chains of iron from the hospitalized mental patient but the chains of the law are still fastened on him. Who shall sever these legal restraints? Perhaps it will be attorneys. They have already helped the medical patient in his struggle against coercive practices by (nonpsychiatric) physicians. Although unpleasant for doctors, malpractice suits fulfill two important functions. First, they secure money damages for patients injured as a result of certain medical procedures. Second, they underscore the fact that a person's body belongs to himself, not to his physician. The latter assumes paternalistic control over it at his own peril.

In psychiatry, and especially in the hospital practice of it, physicians frequently exert paternalistic control over their patients. Perhaps through litigation, attorneys could dislodge this oppressive relationship. An individual's personality, no less than his body, should belong to him, not to his self-appointed psychiatric guardians. Anything that would move us toward this goal would contribute immensely to the furtherance of human liberties, and hence, in my view, to better "mental health" as well.[7]

7

Three Questions and Answers on Contentions

Question 1: Cannot therapists help people to deal with problems even if these people are not mentally ill?

Answer: Autonomous psychotherapy, although not literally therapy, can with integrity help clients by preserving their autonomy and maintaining the economic and contractual basis of their relationship.

The traditional analyst lays down certain rules for the patient and justifies them by appealing to the interests of "therapy." This is a deceptive argument, easily misused; we should be wary of it. In actuality, there is no such thing as "therapy"; there is only a particular therapist, a particular patient, and their communications, especially their promises, to each other. In principle, the "needs of analysis" require and justify the idea that the therapist and the patient follow certain rules. In practice, however, "the therapy" has no needs; only the therapist and the patient do.

It is therefore not enough for the analyst to mouth his commitment to the ethic of autonomy; he must live it. If the ethic of autonomy is fundamental to psychoanalysis, its practice must begin at home, in the analytic situation. This is the most important reason for the analyst not to impose various kinds of rules on the patient, other than the minimal and agreed-upon rules necessary for autonomous psychotherapy.

These considerations converge on a single proposition: to preserve the patient's autonomy in the therapeutic situation, the analyst must avoid all unnecessary coercion. Since the only thing the analyst really needs (or ought to need) is money, the only legitimate demand on the patient is money. Indeed, what other demands can the analyst, as an autonomous therapist, have? Surely he cannot require the patient to lie on the couch or free-associate, to refrain from sexual misbehavior or law-breaking, or any of the myriad things that therapists demand from their patients.

Like everyone else, the analyst is a real person; he has real needs. But in analysis he can expect the patient to satisfy *only one* of his needs, namely, his need for money. Practicing analysis is a profession; it is the way the analyst makes a living. This is why it is "realistic," psychologically and socially, for the patient to pay the analyst.

If the analyst expects the patient to satisfy other needs, he vitiates the analysis. For example, the therapist may have a need to be a good parent, to be loved, and admired, to be forgiving, to succor the weak to make secret alliances with patients against the outside world, to play doctor, to remake personalities, and so on. But why expect the analysand to satisfy them? In my opinion, the patient should no more satisfy any of these (or other) needs than he ought to satisfy, for example, the analyst's craving for sexual pleasure. The therapist must fulfill his aspirations and needs through objects other than the patient. I repeat, the analysand owes *only* money to the analyst. Needless to say, the patient's self-transformation will cost him more than just money; but the extra cost is not payable to the analyst.

The stipulation that the analysand be deprived of certain opportunities to satisfy the needs of the analyst may also be the source of difficulties; it is necessary to understand these and guard against them. For example, the analyst may come to believe that he "gives" too much to the patient and "receives" nothing from him in return; this will make the therapist feel bountiful and magnanimous and, reactively, perhaps demanding as well. The situation is comparable to certain relations between child and parent or between husband and wife where each feels either exploited by his partner or guilty toward him. How can we avoid this?

The best safeguard is the economic basis of the analytic relationship. The analyst usually needs the money that the patient pays him. For the therapist, the fee is tangible evidence that he "receives" something from the patient; he will therefore be less likely to feel exploited (especially if he considers the fee high enough). However, for the money transaction to have the significance I am here attributing to it, the analyst must feel comfortable about it. If he denies or minimizes what money means to him, he will deprive the patient of paying him with money *only* and will burden the patient with expectations of other kinds of "payment." If, on the other hand, the analyst overvalues money, he will make other mistakes. Fearful of losing the patient, he will set his fee too low and resent it. Greedy to make as much as possible, he will set his fee too high, and his patient will resent it. Or the analyst will abandon analysis altogether and sell the patient whatever he seems to want to buy.

If the analytic contract is properly negotiated, the fee should satisfy both parties. The analyst ought to feel that he is well paid for his services, and the analysand, that he owes the analyst only money and only as much as he can afford. Again, this has certain practical implications. The contract for the fee—or, more generally, for the amount the patient owes the analyst—is often broken in two ways. First, the analysand may refuse to pay or be delinquent in paying; if the analyst does not stop the treatment but reduces the fee or lets the patient accumulate a debt, he will have ended the analytic relationship and created instead a psychotherapeutic situation that is neither analytic nor autonomous. Second, in response to the analyst's expectations or from his own motives, the analysand may wish to do more for the analyst than pay his fee (e.g., finance his research, give him valuable gifts, and so forth); if the analyst lets the patient overfulfill his contract, he will have succeeded in destroying the analytic relationship.

The conditions that I have outlined are those of successful analysis; they create an atmosphere in which the patient realizes that the therapy, is his, not someone else's. On the other hand, if the therapist lays down various rules—such as requiring the patient to lie on the couch, to free-associate, to report his dreams—he inevitably creates a situation in which the patient can cooperate or refuse to cooperate, can be a good patient or bad patient, and so forth.

All these possibilities and the complications that result from them are avoided if the analyst renounces the traditional role of doctor or therapist who tries to do a job *on* the patient or *on* his sickness. Instead, by adopting the role of expert who sells his services and becomes contractually obligated to his client, the therapist retains just enough power to discharge his duty, that is, to play the role of analyst. The therapist needs no power beyond this, for it is not necessary for him to judge whether the client is a good or bad patient or to participate as an authority in the client's extra-analytic life; indeed, the possession of such power interferes with the performance of the analytic task.

The rules of the analytic game serve a single, basic aim: to preserve the integrity of the analytic relationship. It is impossible to play contract bridge if one of the players is allowed to cheat because he complains of a headache. In proportion as a contract can be broken, it is not a contract. This and this alone is why the analyst must eschew the roles of doctor and psychiatrist. These are status roles, not contract roles; they give their bearers the right and indeed the responsibility to take matters into their own hands, and, if necessary, "save the patient from himself." But, if the analyst wants to save a patient from himself, he cannot analyze that patient. Otherwise it is a mockery to speak of the patient as an autonomous agent. A a great many people *are* able and willing to conduct themselves as self-responsible analytic patients, but the therapist can never discover who they are unless he himself acts autonomously, that is, contractually.

The therapist who is comfortable in the role I have indicated will find many patients who not only accept this arrangement but like it. This need not surprise us. Patients who consult analysts often want analysis, not something else. Accordingly, they are pleased to find an analyst who sells analysis, not something else. Many patients do not want the psychotherapist to do things other than psychotherapy. However, they become confused when the therapist seems willing, indeed, eager to perform other activities as well. Thus, complications in psychotherapy arise not so much from the patient's demands for non-psychological interventions as from the therapist's eagerness to play doctor.

To be sure, some patients may not wish to buy a purely psycho-therapeutic or analytic product. The therapist's obligation is to make clear what he sells. If the patient wishes some other type of therapeutic commodity, he will soon stop seeing the analyst and perhaps seek another therapist. If, however, the arrangement seems satisfactory to him, it will be so without the therapist having made any false representations.

The autonomous therapist offers to sell *only* his skills as an ana-lyst. If the patient is sick, he must consult a physician; if he wishes to obtain drugs, he must do so from someone other than the analyst; and so forth. Some analysts do indeed conduct themselves in this way. Many others, however, do not; they prescribe drugs and even use con-vulsive therapy while "analyzing" the patient. They justify this dilution of the analytic role by claiming that the patient "needs" such adjuvant therapies and by asserting that they are, after all, physicians and should therefore offer the patient all their medical skills. This is nonsense.

To be sure, the therapist has every right to practice in this way. If his patients benefit, the therapist's reward will be a lucrative practice. Nevertheless, the foregoing argument is nonsensical or worse because it undermines the analytic contract and thus destroys psychoanalysis as autonomous psychotherapy. We may grant the claim that the patient in analysis may need drugs and many other things as well. My point is this: if the therapist is to do his job as analyst correctly, and well, he cannot provide other services. Nor does he need to; the patient is free to secure them from others.

The additional argument that the analyst is a physician and hence owes the patient the full range of his knowledge and skills is absurd.

The therapist owes the patient no more and certainly no less than what he contracts for; if he promises the patient only psychotherapy, he owes him only psychotherapy. Furthermore, the fact that the therapist is a physician is largely a historical accident; his medical training and credentials help him little, if at all, with his task as psychotherapist.

It is also possible that the therapist possesses skills additional and quite unrelated to those of analyst and physician. For example, the therapist may be an expert bridge-player, accomplished musician, or experienced investor in the stock market. Suppose the analysand wishes to take advantage of one of these skills? Will the analyst teach the patient how to play bridge, play the piano, or make money in the stock market? If he lends the patient his medical skills, why not lend him his other skills? I mention this line of reasoning, not only to clarify this issue, but also to suggest an explanation that may help some patients to understand why the analyst refuses to help in any way except by analyzing. The limitation of the analyst's role may disappoint the patient. But it is only the disappointment not dispelled by such realistic explanations that can be subjected to fruitful analytic scrutiny.[1]

Answer: Although the relationship is nonmedical, pseudo-therapeutic, and often fraudulent, sex "therapy" may for various reasons lead to alleviation of some sexual problems.

Instead of regarding sexual dysfunctions as diseases, we could more profitably regard them as the solutions of certain life tasks—that is, as the expressions of the individual's life-style. Consider, for example, the man who completes the sex act very quickly (which Kinsey regarded as normal, but which is now conventionally called premature ejaculation). The man himself may be dissatisfied with his performance, or he may not be. We might look upon him as we do a man whose idea of eating a meal is to gulp down a hamburger and french fries in three minutes flat. Such a person is assuredly no gourmet: he does not know how to eat like a gourmet—that is, how to stretch a seven-course meal with drinks over three hours and enjoy every minute of it. Similarly, the quick sexual performer is not a sexual gourmet: he does not know— for whatever reason—how to have leisurely sex. If he wants to change this, he must learn new patterns of sexual performance. This task can be achieved in many ways—ranging from self-help through reading, practice, and the assistance of experienced and sympathetic sexual partners to a variety of systems of counseling, psychotherapy, or so-called sex therapy. Although I am generally critical of, and skeptical toward, professional approaches to sexual problems, nothing I say is intended to imply that all medical, psychological, or psychiatric help for persons who seek such assistance for their sexual difficulties is worthless.

We must remember that, in its day, exorcism "worked" too. That it worked is a fact—but that fact does not prove that the persons so helped were possessed by demons. Certain new (as well as old) sex therapies work—in the sense that they may enable some persons to engage in sexual activities more freely, competently, or pleasurably than they could previously. It does not follow, however, that this proves the validity of the sex therapists' claims about their ideas or interventions. The mode of action of the new sex therapies is easily explained along simple, common-sense lines. Clients seeking sex therapy accept their therapists as authorities—as expert healers, physicians, scientists. This enables the experts to grant patients absolution for sexual ignorance or ineptness, and permission to engage in sexual acts that they formerly feared or considered forbidden. . . .[2]

Question 2: Is our system of "treating" deviant behavior the most abusive?

Answer: The actual use of psychiatric diagnoses to control dissidents in the Soviet Union is greater than in the West and the range of behaviors deemed to be "illnesses" justifying deprivations of freedom is much wider.

The proposition that the real meaning of schizophrenia has always been, and continues to be, "crazy" and therefore "commitable," is supported by the widespread use of this "diagnosis" in Soviet Russia. If the Russian authorities had only wanted to demean and insult their dissidents, they and their psychiatric lackeys could have pinned any derogatory psychiatric diagnosis on them. They could have called them manics or obsessionals or homosexuals. Why, then, did they choose to call them schizophrenics? Because, more than any other psychiatric diagnostic term, *schizophrenia* carries with it the implication that the person so "diagnosed" is crazy, does not know what he is doing, is not responsible for his behavior, and should be so "treated." This explains why *schizophrenia* has justified, and continues to justify, the imposition of involuntary psychiatric interventions on the "patient" so diagnosed.

While an adequate presentation and discussion of Soviet barbarities justified by appeals to "schizophrenia" would require a book, I want to offer a few remarks to illustrate the actual, as against the abstract, meaning and use of this term. The following quotations are from an interview with a Russian psychiatrist, Dr. Marina Woikhanskaya, who identified herself as follows:

I left the Soviet Union on the 11th April, 1975, and in the Soviet Union I have been working as a psychiatrist for the last 12 years. I worked in one of the largest city hospitals. I was very fond of my patients and very proud of my work for it was one of the most humane types of work that could exist.

In 1974 she at last realizes that the situation is not quite so idyllic. But of course she still loves the system: "I learned that in various hospitals in the Soviet Union there are quite a number of so-called dissidents." Schizophrenics, however, are never "so-called" to Woikhanskaya. They are "real." She believes in schizophrenia as firmly as she believes in Marxism. "This problem [i.e., the "abuse" of psychiatry] worries me greatly," she says, "and it worries honest Soviet psychiatrists greatly." What "honest psychiatrists" actually do in the Soviet Union we soon learn, all too clearly, from her answers to the interviewer's pointed questions:

> *Question.* How frequently in general psychiatric cases, that's apart from the dissidents, is compulsory treatment undertaken in the Soviet Union?
> *Woikhanskaya.* A mentally ill person has no rights in the Soviet Union and it is entirely the decision of the doctors to send this person to hospital or not, and if the doctor thinks that there is any danger of this person behaving in an unpermissible way, to hospital this person goes.
> *Question.* And that applies to all psychiatric cases?
> *Woikhanskaya.* Yes.

Then we learn about schizophrenia in Russia, and realize, if only we are willing to face it, how little this "disease" has changed from Bleuler's Zürich to [present day] Moscow:

> *Question.* If the dissidents are admitted officially, there must be some official diagnostic category which they come under and there must be criteria which they have to fit in order to be admitted in this way?
> *Woikhanskaya.* The diagnosis is of a boring and consistent type. Slow Schizophrenia, Reforming Syndrome, Chronic Schizophrenia, Creeping or Smouldering Schizophrenia, and Syndrome of Reform Seeking Schizophrenic types. . . . They are given insulin treatment, they are given E.C.T. treatment. They are not ill, but the treatment, yes, is the standard one for ill people.

Here it is, all of it, in pure.culture: "Seeking reform" as "schizophrenia"; the psychiatric incarceration of the "patient"; and his involuntary "treatment." If linguistic philosophers and semanticists are right in insisting that what a word means must be inferred from the way it is used, then this is what *schizophrenia* means—not just in Communist Russia but everywhere.

A brief case history of the "diagnosis" and "treatment" of a "dissident" was published in a recent issue of the *New Statesman.* It complements and amplifies Dr. Woikhanskaya's account.

A young man, Jan Krilsky, a Jew and a Zionist, is arrested in the USSR for entering a factory illegally, with a friend's pass. The police ask: Who would he fight for in the event of war between Israel and Russia? Israel, he answers. Here is what happened next:

> His father, called by the KGB, agreed to his son's committal to Jaroslavl [a city near Moscow] mental hospital for treatment for schizophrenia, but only, he claims, in desparation to avoid a long prison sentence. (Jan was now 18.) The treatment was of course injections of sulphazine, purified sulphur in peach kernal oil, which sent his temperature soaring to 41C (105.8 F). There is no modern use for the drug, according to Dr. Harold Merskey, a London psychiatrist and chairman of the Medical and Scientific Committee for Soviet Jewry. . . . The boy was moved to Yakovenko closed mental hospital in Moscow and six months later released as "well" by a commission of doctors. . . . [Later], while he was under arrest, the KGB drafted a letter to Foreign Minister Gromyko about his desire to go to Israel, and Jan signed angrily. This was tantamount to a confession of madness. In the space of a few weeks, he was shunted from one hospital to another.

Receiving these free benefits of the Russian health care system was evidently enough to make even Jan's father, who had been a loyal Communist Party member for fifty-two years, see the light:

> By now, Julius, the father, had had enough. He submitted an official request for the family to be allowed to emigrate to Israel. . . . [Whereupon an old criminal charge against him was reopened, and the court] committed Jan to a mental hospital "until he recovers from militant Zionism."

However glaring these "psychiatric abuses" may seem, the concepts and methods of the Russian psychiatric gangsters who perpetrate them are legitimized and supported by their colleagues in the West. Even Kendell, now the acknowledged dean of British psychodiagnosticians, shies away from criticizing them! In his comprehensive book, *The Role of Diagnosis in Psychiatry,* where he never mentions the psychiatric repression of deviants in Russia or elsewhere, he states:

> The Russian concept of this illness [schizophrenia] embraces three subtypes, periodic, sluggish, and shift-like schizophrenia, which are not recognized elsewhere. In general, Russian psychiatrists appear to be influenced more by the course of the illness and less by its actual symptomatology than other European psychiatrists, a fact which has some bearing on recent political controversies.

The Russian psychiatrists who make and support such diagnoses of schizophrenia on "dissidents" are, of course, members of the same international psychiatric organizations as are Western psychiatrists— and as are the American psychiatrists who make and support the diagnoses of schizophrenia on "madmen" like Ezra Pound and James Forrestal. "Patients" like these form the "clinical" base on which "researchers" rest their recommendations for its proper treatment.[3]

● ● ●

. . . In the Soviet Union patients, especially mental patients, are more like prisoners on parole than free citizens contracting for medical services, and physicians, especially psychiatrists, are more like parole officers than physicians providing medical services. The result is that personal and social problems of all kinds, and especially political deviance, are defined and treated as psychiatric diseases even more readily in the USSR than in the US or UK.

J. K. Wing, a British psychiatrist who had visited the Soviet Union on four occasions, accounts for some of the differences between Russian and British psychiatry in this way:

> The diagnostic system used by many Soviet psychiatrists is different from that incorporated in the International Classification of Diseases. In particular, the term "schizophrenia" is used to describe conditions which British psychiatrists would label in other ways. This clinical difference partly explains the different concept of "criminal responsibility," but another large component of the difference is political rather than medical.

No physician anywhere would acknowledge that there are political reasons for diagnosing lobar pneumonia or myocardial infarction differently in capitalist and communist countries. Although American and British psychiatrists are now beginning to acknowledge that there are political reasons for diagnosing schizophrenia differently in their countries and in Russia, they continue to insist that schizophrenia is, nevertheless, a disease, just like lobar pneumonia and myocardial infarction. Because some Russian psychiatrists "misuse" the names of certain psychiatric diseases, so these Western psychiatrists argue, is no reason for doubting the validity of the diagnosis when "correctly" applied, or the "reality of the disease it names." Wing actually describes the way the term *schizophrenia* is used in Russia to justify controlling deviants, but this seems not to affect his acceptance of the label as the name of a bona fide medical disease:

> As we have already seen, the concept of mental illness, particularly schizophrenia, is a good deal wider [in USSR] than in the UK, including quite a

lot of what we would call personality disorder. None of the people whose case histories I have heard were suffering from schizophrenia in the same sense of the florid central syndrome recognized by psychiatrists everywhere. There are two main groups: one composed of people who had been admitted [*sic*] to mental hospitals long before they had become political dissenters (though not for what I would call "schizophrenia"); the other comprising people who have developed complex economic and social theories which they put forward as alternatives to currently orthodox Marxism. . . . Most British psychiatrists would probably not make a diagnosis of schizophrenia (or any kind of mental illness) in such cases.

Obviously, the distinction between voluntary and involuntary mental hospitalization is quite meaningless in Russia. All mental patients are actually like prisoners or paroled prisoners: none is, or feels, free to decide whether he should be treated in the hospital, clinic, or not at all. Although Wing seems rather insensitive about the issue of human rights in psychiatry, he notes that while on paper there is a difference between committed and voluntary mental patients, it is a difference not demonstrable in practice:

> I tried to discover whether a patient not under certificate is free to leave the hospital "against advice," but it seemed very difficult for my informants to envisage such a case. After a great deal of questioning they did finally say that it would be possible but they could not recall it happening.

It does not seem to occur to Wing that in a country where people cannot even move from one city to another without the permission of authorities, it would not occur to them to try to leave mental hospitals "against advice." And it does not seem to occur to psychiatrists—or to the biologists, chemists, and geneticists who base their work on psychiatric diagnoses—that "schizophrenia" has more to do with freedom and slavery than with health and disease, more with semiology than biology, more in short, with politics than with genetics.[4]

Question 3: What are the differences between Szasz and other critics of psychiatry?

Answer: While Szasz is joined by others such as R. D. Laing in criticizing psychiatry, Szasz's arguments and politics differ substantially from Laing's. Where Laing appears to glorify the oppressed schizophrenic as morally superior, Szasz denies the superiority of *both* the schizophrenic and the psychiatrist who oppresses him.

One of the developments since the first publication of *The Myth of Mental Illness* and attributable in no small part to its influence, is the so-called anti-psychiatry movement. This movement, like the movement of traditional psychiatry which it seeks to supplant, is also centered on the concept of schizophrenia and on helping so-called schizophrenics. Because both the anti-psychiatrists and I oppose certain aspects of psychiatry, our views are often combined and confused, and we are often identified as the common enemies of all of psychiatry.

It is true, of course, that in traditional, coercive psychiatry, the anti-psychiatrists and I face the same enemy. So did, in another context, Stalin and Churchill. The old Arab proverb that "the enemy of my enemy is my friend" makes good sense indeed in politics and war. But it makes no sense at all in intellectual and moral discourse.

I reject the term *anti-psychiatry* because it is imprecise, misleading, and cheaply self-aggrandizing. Chemists do not characterize themselves as *anti-alchemists,* nor do astronomers call themselves *anti-astrologers.* If one defines psychiatry conventionally, as the medical specialty concerned with the diagnosis and treatment of mental diseases, then one is, indeed, committed to "opposing" psychiatry as a specialty—not of medicine but of mythology. However, since I believe that people are entitled to their mythologies, this opposition must be clearly limited to the use of force or fraud by the mythologizers in the pursuit of their ersatz religion. This is why I have always insisted that I am against involuntary psychiatry, or the psychiatric rape of the patient by the psychiatrist—but I am not against voluntary psychiatry, or psychiatric relations between consenting adults.

On the other hand, if one defines psychiatry operationally, as consisting of whatever psychiatrists do, then it is necessary to identify and articulate one's attitude toward each of the numerous practices in which psychiatrists engage. I have tried to do this in several of my publications, always indicating what I oppose, what I support and why. As against this analytical approach, the very term *anti-psychiatry* implicitly commits one to opposing everything that psychiatrists do— which is patently absurd. In any case, anti-psychiatrists do not clearly state whether they object only to involuntary psychiatric interventions, or also to those that are voluntary; to all involuntary psychiatric interventions, or only those practiced by their political adversaries. They do not frankly acknowledge whether they support real tolerance for contractual psychiatric interventions, or only "repressive tolerance" for (against) them—because such practices occur in an "exploitative-capitalist" context of free market and free enterprise.

Actually, as we shall see, the anti-psychiatrists are all self-declared socialists, communists, or at least anti-capitalists and collectivists. As the communists seek to raise the poor above the rich, so the anti-psychiatrists seek to raise the "insane" above the "sane"; as the communists justify their aims and methods by claiming that the poor are virtuous, while the rich are wicked, so the anti-psychiatrists justify theirs by claiming that the "insane" are authentic, while the "sane" are inauthentic.

Ronald Laing, who with David Cooper originated the so-called anti-psychiatry movement, began his work with the study of schizophrenic persons. His first book, published in 1960, is titled *The Divided Self*—an almost literal translation of the Bleulerian Greek term *schizophrenia,* and a virtual repetition of the classic psychiatric view of the schizophrenic as a "split personality." Four years later, with Aaron Esterson, Laing published *Sanity, Madness and the Family.* Subtitled *Families of Schizophrenics,* it is a report on the study of eleven hospitalized schizophrenic patients and their families. Nowhere in this book do the authors identify the legal status of any of the "schizophrenics"—that is, whether they are voluntary or involuntary patients. There is also no mention of what, if any, roles Laing and Esterson played in depriving these persons of their liberty, or, if they were deprived of their liberty by others, what, if any, roles the two authors played in trying to help them to regain it.

Subsequently, Laing has, on some occasions, rejected the idea that schizophrenia is a disease, but he has continued to "treat" it. The fame of Kingsley Hall—Laing's "asylum" for managing madness—rests almost entirely on the claim that it offers a method of helping "schizophrenic patients" superior to those offered by other psychiatric institutions or practitioners.

I have long maintained, and continue to insist, that if there is no disease, there is *nothing* to treat; if there is no patient, there is *no one* to treat. Insofar as others make the same claim—that is, that schizophrenia (and mental illness generally) is not a disease—they are compelled, by the logic of language alone, to conclude also that there is no "treatment" for it. However, inasmuch as many persons whom psychiatrists diagnose as schizophrenic seek help—especially if "help" is not forced on them and if they don't have to pay for it—we are confronted with the social reality of "psychotics," supposedly lacking "insight" into their "illness," clamoring for its "treatment."

Laing accepts such persons as "residents" in his "communities" and legitimizes them as "sufferers" who, because of their very "victimization," are more worthy than others. There is thus built into his system of asylum care a moral-economic premise which is inexplicit but is all the more important for being so. It is, moreover, the same premise that animates large numbers of men and women today throughout the civilized world. Briefly put, it is the premise that it is wicked for people to purchase, for money, medical or psychiatric (or anti-psychiatric) help, but it is virtuous to "purchase" it for suffering. I shall say more about this moral dimension of the therapeutic nexus presently. Here it should suffice to note that in espousing this position, Laing is hardly unconventional. On the contrary, he places himself squarely midstream of the main current of contemporary thought and sentiment about "health care." This current, in both communist and capitalist countries, is now fully Marxist—adopting, for "suffering situations," the famous formula: "From each according to his abilities, to each according to his needs."

Economically, Laing has thus replaced the coercion of the mental patient by the psychiatrist on behalf of the citizen, with the coercion of the taxpayer by the government on behalf of the mental patient. Formerly, sane citizens could *detain* those whom they considered to be mad; now they must *maintain* those who undertake to "journey" through madness.

I say this because even if a person is, in his current situation, unmolested by his family and employer, by the police and psychiatry—in other words, even if he is not actually harrassed or persecuted in any way whatever—Laing still accepts him as a resident at Kingsley Hall and legitimizes him as a bona fide sufferer. I am not contending that such persons may not, in fact, suffer—at least in the sense which most persons often suffer from the slings and arrows of outrageous fortune. I am contending only that it does not follow logically or morally that such persons are entitled to services extracted by force or fraud from others—whether those "others" be indentured torturers in old-fashioned state hospitals or indentured taxpayers in new-fashioned welfare states. I am trying to make explicit here something which, so far as I know, is never made explicit either by Laing and his followers, or by their critics—namely, that the cost of the care of the "residents" in the Laingian asylums is mainly borne by the British taxpayer; and that the British taxpayer has no more of a direct vote on whether or not he wants his hard-earned money spent that way than did the American taxpayer on paying for the war in Vietnam. Ironically, while Laing's tongue lashes society for driving people mad, his hands are picking the taxpayers' pockets.

Furthermore, anti-psychiatrists resemble psychiatrists and psychoanalysts in their insistent inattention to whether the so-called mental patient assumes his role voluntarily or is assigned to it against his will. Psychoanalysts, psychiatrists and anti-psychiatrists all theorize about neurosis and psychosis, hysteria and schizophrenia, without acknowledging whether persons so identified seek or avoid psychiatric help; whether they accept or reject being diagnosed; whether they claim to be suffering or others impute suffering to them. Thus all of these seemingly different, and sometimes even antagonistic, approaches to so-called psychiatric problems display this crucial similarity: each regards the "patient" as a "case"—indeed, as a "victim." To the psychiatrist, the "schizophrenic" is a victim of an elusive disease of the brain, like neurosyphilis; to the psychoanalyst he is a victim of a weak ego, a powerful id, or a combination of both; and to the anti-psychiatrist, he is a victim of an intrusive family and an insane society. Each of these creeds and cults diminishes and distorts the "patient" as the person he really is; each denies his self-explanatory act of self-definition. Thus, the psychiatrist denies the "schizophrenic's" right to reject confinement, and attributes his desire for freedom to lack of insight into his illness and his need for treatment of it; the psychoanalyst denies his right to resist analytic interpretation, and attributes his noncooperation with the analyst to an "illness" that renders him "inaccessible" to analysis; and the anti-psychiatrist denies his obligation to care for himself and to obey the law, and views his penchant for social rule violation as proof of his superior moral virtue.

The result is a lumping together—in psychoanalysis, psychiatry, and anti-psychiatry—of the most dissimilar kinds of persons. For example, persons able but unwilling to take care of themselves are placed in the same class with those willing but unable to do so; persons who are guilty but claim to be innocent are placed in the same class with those who are innocent but claim to be guilty; and persons charged with and convicted of lawbreaking are placed in the same class with those who are neither charged with nor convicted of any offense. In psychiatry and psychoanalysis, each of these types of persons may be categorized as "schizophrenic"; in anti-psychiatry, such categorization of persons as "schizophrenics" is, on the one hand, criticized as erroneous, and on the other hand, embraced as identifying a specific group of individuals distinctively victimized by others and especially suitable for Laingian methods of mental treatment. In all of these ways, the similarities among psychiatry, psychoanalysis, and anti-psychiatry in their approach to "schizophrenia" seem to me to far outweigh the differences among them.[5]

•   •   •

My suggestion that we regard the sane and the insane on the one hand, and psychiatrists and anti-psychiatrists on the other, as adversaries, each claiming superiority for himself and inferiority for his opponent, invites putting these images in the broader perspective of other superior-inferior relationships and their characteristic mythologies. I have remarked on this theme elsewhere, in connection with my analysis of the relationship between institutional psychiatrist and institutionalized mental patient and its similarities with the relationship between inquisitor and heretic. Here I want to extend this sort of analysis to the relationship between psychiatrist and anti-psychiatrist, with particular emphasis on the moral character of their respective claims.

In one of his brilliant, early essays Bertrand Russell has furnished a framework into which this controversy fits perfectly: "One of the persistent delusions of mankind," Russell suggests, "is that some sections of the human race are morally better or worse than others. This belief has many different forms, none of which has any rational basis." After remarking on how this human predilection finds its most obvious outlets in the chauvinism of sex, nationality, and class, Russell notes that some people prefer to admire and aggrandize groups to which they do not belong—from which, indeed, they are excluded:

> A rather curious form of this admiration for groups to which the admirer does not belong is the belief in the superior virtue of the oppressed: subjected nations, the poor, women and children. The eighteenth century, while conquering America from the Indians, reducing the peasantry to the condition of pauper laborers, and introducing the cruelties of early industrialism, loved to sentimentalize about the "noble savage" and the "simple annals of the poor." . . . Liberals still continue to idealize the rural poor, while intellectual Socialists and Communists did the same for the urban proletariat.

Russell suggests that there is something in the nature of the power relations between those who dominate and those who are dominated, and in the nature of human nature, which, together, generate these compensatory images of the superiority of the inferior. One of the most typical of these was, and remains, the mythology of feminine superiority about whose Victorian form Russell offers this observation: "The belief in their [women's] 'spiritual' superiority was part and parcel of the determination to keep them inferior economically and politically."

Insofar as the anti-psychiatrists maintain that the insane are superior to the sane—which is one of their most important doctrinal tenets—they seem to me to begin where the female superiorists have left off. They merely substitute for the "superior virtue" of oppressed women the "superior sanity" of oppressed schizophrenics. This particular game of the anti-psychiatrists seems to me to be both crude and contemptible, for the result of the idealization of the "authenticity" of insanity, of the romanticization of the "breakthrough" of psychosis, can be only one of two things, both of which I oppose.

On the one hand, the mythology of the superiority of the psychotic, like that of the superiority of women, may be part of the psychiatrist's determination to dominate him, not crassly as a lunatic, but covertly as a lost tourist. Or it may be a genuine effort to replace the special powers and privileges of the psychiatrist with those of the psychotic, in the tradition of the Christian program of replacing "the first" with "the last" or the communist program of replacing the rule of the capitalists with the "dictatorship of the proletariat."

Looking at the countless pairings of oppressors and oppressed, one must ask oneself: Why would anyone believe in the myths of the superiority of either? It is possible to answer this question with some useful generalizations. In the main, people will believe in the superiority of the oppressor when the oppressor occupies a favored position— for example, as a man or psychiatrist; or when they seek the oppressor's protection—for example, as a child or hospitalized mental patient; or when they wish to play a complementary role—for example, as wife or psychotic. On the other hand, people will believe in the superiority of the oppressed—for example, women and psychotics mainly when they feel guilty toward them. Support for the countermythology is thus much less secure than for the mythology; this difference accounts for the much greater stability of the former as compared to the latter. Russell's remarks in this connection, are perhaps more relevant today to the situation in psychiatry and anti-psychiatry than to any other aspect of the power politics of the human tragicomedy:

> As it appears from the various instances that we have considered, the stage in which superior virtue is attributed to the oppressed is transient and unstable. It begins only when the oppressors come to have a bad conscience, and this only happens when their power is no longer secure. The idealizing of the victim is useful for a time: if virtue is the greatest of goods, and if subjection makes people virtuous, it is kind to refuse them power, since it would destroy their virtue. . . . It was a fine self-sacrifice on the part of men to relieve women of the dirty work of politics. . . . But sooner or later the oppressed class will argue that its superior virtue is a reason in favor of its having power, and the oppressors will find their own weapons turned against them. When at last power has been equalized, it becomes apparent to everybody that all the talk about superior virtue was nonsense, and that it was quite unnecessary as a basis for the claim to equality.

It is precisely this sort of commonsense, middle of the road position to which I have tried to cleave in my approach to that still relatively unexplored dimension of domination and subjection—the relations between mad-doctors and madmen, psychiatrists and psychotics, schizophrenia experts and schizophrenics. Thus, I have tried to destroy the mythology of the medical superiority of psychiatry and psychoanalysis over legal and religious principles and practices of social control, and of the moral superiority of psychiatrists and psychoanalysts over people generally and so-called mentally ill persons in particular. At the same time, I have tried to avoid idealizing insanity as supersanity, and mythologizing the madman as a person of superior artistic, moral, or psychological gifts, virtues, or powers.[6]

PART THREE

MAJOR CRITICISMS AND DEFENSES

Introduction

Chapters 8 and 9 present key critics and criticisms of Thomas Szasz's value applications and contentions. Our previously published responses to these critics are also included. In addition, we present a transcript of a radio debate originally broadcast on WBAL radio in Baltimore, Maryland.

Psychiatrist Ronald Pies along with attorneys Michael Moore and C. G. Schoenfeld attack both the philosophical bases of Szasz's contentions regarding the myth of mental illness as well as the contentions themselves. Pies focuses on the competing concepts of disease which he claims invalidate Szasz's assertion that "mental illness" is mythical. Moore echoes many of the points made by Pies and comes to the following conclusions: what we call "mental illness" is quite appropriately considered "disease" and the absence of rationality is with equal appropriateness considered a symptom of that disease. Schoenfeld's arguments represent a typical broadbased attack on Szasz's contentions and the rationales underlying them.

To these criticisms we offer responses that we believe to be consistent with Szasz's writings. In many cases we argue that his critics have simply failed to interpret correctly what Szasz has said and, consequently, are responding to misrepresented claims. In other cases, we try to demonstrate that certain criticisms simply reflect competing philosophical starting points or faith assumptions that are irresolvable.

In the final section we provide the reader with a discussion of Szasz's values and contentions between the author and nationally prominent forensic psychiatrist, Dr. Jonas Rappeport. This discussion provides give and take respecting a wide range of practical issues and circumstances involving institutional and forensic psychiatry as well as integrating theoretical concerns. We believe that the discussion format illustrates the stimulating challenges for policy-making generated by Szasz's provocative analysis.

179

8

The Critics

Michael S. Moore

Some Myths About "Mental Illness"

Often mental illness is said to be a myth, not just in the sense that it does not exist, but also in the sense that no one is in fact mentally ill. The claim, in other words, denies not just that "mental illness" is a name of some thing, but that "mentally ill" is ever truly predicable of a person. The claim is that no one is really mentally ill.

This claim that mental illness is a myth is put forward as an empirical discovery—all of those people that have been thought to be mentally ill (i.e., irrational) are in fact just as rational as you and I. Szasz makes this claim when he argues that "insane behavior, no less than sane, is goal-directed and motivated . . ." and concludes from this that we should regard "the behavior of the madman as perfectly rational from the point of view of the actor. . . ." Braginsky and co-workers purport to have made the same "discovery" regarding schizophrenics:

> The residents who remain in 'mental hospitals' are behaving in a perfectly rational manner to achieve a personally satisfying way of life—often the most satisfying of which they are capable . . . in a certain sense an individual *chooses* his career as a mental patient; it is not thrust upon him as a consequence of his somehow becoming 'mentally ill.' But in just what sense does the individual 'choose' his career? In our view, having and maintaining the status of mental patient is the outcome of *purposive* behavior. Furthermore, given the life circumstances of most of the persons who become and remain residents of mental hospitals, their doing so evinces a realistic appraisal of their available alternatives; it is, in short, a *rational choice.*

From *Archives of General Psychiatry* 32 (1975): 1485–1490.

181

The central thrust of this form of the argument is not to claim that "mental illness" or "mentally ill" are meaningless — their meaning is assumed to be closely connected with that of "irrational" — but to dispute as a factual matter that there are persons who fit the agreed-upon definition of mental illness (irrationality). In fact, however, what has been done here is not to present a discovery of new facts, overlooked by orthodox psychiatrists because of their own self-interest or whatever, but rather to stretch our concepts of "rationality" and "purposive behavior" to accommodate within their criteria facts well-known to orthodox, as well as radical, psychiatrists. The facts — the behavior of patients — are often undisputed. What is disputed is the precise nature of the criterion to be applied in judging the behavior as rational or not.

As the above quotations from Szasz and Braginsky et al. make clear, the notion of rationality relevant here is linked to the actor having reasons (purposes, motives) for his actions. A more precise account of the relationship between an agent being thought to be rational and his acting for reasons may perhaps best be brought out by the following schema of reason-giving explanations. When we explain an action by giving the actor's motive, the following premises are involved:

1. Agent X wants result R to obtain.
2. X believes that in situation S, action A will cause R to obtain.
3. X believes that he is in situation S.
4. If X believes that he is in situation S and believes that in S action A will cause R to obtain, and if X wants R to obtain, then, ceteris paribus, X will do A.
5. Ceteris paribus.

With these premises, it follows that X will do A.

In ordinary English, in order to make out a motivational explanation we need to know what the agent wanted and what he believed about the situation and his abilities to achieve through action what he wanted. In addition, we need to know that he is a rational creature in the fundamental sense of "rational" defined by the fourth premise, that is, one who, other things being equal, will act so as to further his desires in light of his beliefs; and we need to know that other things are in fact equal, namely, that the agent does not have desires and beliefs that conflict with the desires and beliefs on which he is about to act.

The actions of the mentally ill may be nonrational or irrational in any of the five following corresponding senses: (1) R may be an unintelligible thing to want, such as soaking one's elbow in the mud for its own sake; (2) the belief that A will lead to R may be an irrational belief (e.g., a belief that saying "storks" instead of "stocks" will make one a mother); (3) the belief that one is in situation S may also be irrational (e.g., a belief that one is being persecuted by spirits); (4) there may be no set of beliefs and desires, no matter how bizarre, by virtue of which one can make out the action as the rational thing to do; or (5) the beliefs and desires of the particular practical syllogism may be inconsistent with other standing beliefs and desires.

The rationality of an *agent* is a function of the rationality of his actions over time. The more irrational behavior we observe of an individual in any of these five senses, the less rational we will judge him as an agent to be.

By and large, the empirical version of the myth argument is only intended to show that the behavior of the mentally ill is rational in the fundamental sense defined by the fourth premise above, i.e., there is *some* set of beliefs and desires (no matter how bizarre) furthered by the act in question. The crunch for even this limited attempt at making out the behavior of the mentally ill as rational comes in making more precise the nature of the beliefs and desires of mental patients in terms of which their actions are to be so adjudged. More specifically, the fudge occurs with the use of *unconscious* beliefs and desires to fill in where we all know that mental patients did not consciously guide their actions to achieve such goals in light of such beliefs. Braginsky and colleagues are explicit about this: "It is obvious that rational goal-directed behavior does not guarantee that the individual appreciates what he is up to." Szasz is particularly transparent in his glossing over of this distinction:

> In describing this contrast between lying and erring, I have deliberately avoided the concept of consciousness. It seems to me that when the adjectives "consciously" and "unconsciously" are used as explanations, they complicate and obscure the problem. The traditional psychoanalytic idea that so-called conscious imitation of illness is "malingering" and hence "not illness," whereas its allegedly unconscious simulation is itself "illness" ("hysteria"), creates more problems than it solves. It would seem more useful to *distinguish between goal-directed and rule-following behavior on the one hand, and indifferent mistakes on the other.* . . . In brief, *it is more accurate to regard hysteria as a lie than as a mistake.* People caught in a lie usually maintain that they were merely mistaken. The difference between mistakes and lies, when discovered, is chiefly pragmatic. From a purely cognitive point of view, both are simply falsehoods.

The fudge occurs in the shift from our judgments of rationality being based on the agent's conscious beliefs and objectives to a notion of rationality by virtue of which we adjudge an action at least minimally rational if we can posit any set of beliefs or objectives with which we can explain the action. The problem is that it is notoriously easy to posit beliefs and desires to explain any finite sequence of the behavior of anything. Simply pick a consequence of the behavior and label it the objective, pick a set of beliefs by virtue of which it would appear likely that such a consequence would indeed ensue as a result of the behavior, and one is then in a position to adjudge the behavior as rational, relative to that objective and that set of beliefs. The shedding of leaves by a tree, the falling of stones, the pumping of blood by the heart, and the most chaotic word-salad of a schizophrenic are all "rational" activities judged by such a standard. The "action" of a tree in shedding its leaves is rational, if we suppose that it desires to survive the coming winter, and believes that the only way to do this is to lower its sap level, thereby killing off its leaves. The same analysis can be applied to stones, hearts, and schizophrenics.

The reason such explanations are so easy to manufacture is because without the requirement that an agent be conscious of the beliefs and the desires by which we (and he) judge his action as rational, there is no means of fixing the nature of such beliefs or wants independently of the behavior to be explained and adjudged. Behavior is by itself inherently ambiguous as a criterion for such matters. If we know by some independent means that an agent believes that action A will lead to result R, and he does A, we have good grounds for attributing to him a desire for R; if we know that he desires R, and does A, we have equally good grounds for supposing that he believes that A will lead to R. However, if we know neither his beliefs or his desires, but only that he does A and that A does result in R being the case, we have no means of singling out R as his motive, for any other consequence of A would do as well. "There is nothing in a pure behaviorist theory to prevent us from regarding each piece of behavior as a desire for whatever happens next."

Szasz can thus ignore the conscious/unconscious distinction only at the price of significance. What he fails to realize is that any behavior can be seen as rational (or as in accordance with rules of a game, or as furthering certain goals—Szasz's substitute criteria for consciousness); if one allows oneself the freedom to *invent* the beliefs and desires in terms of which the behavior is to be so viewed.

It may be objected that good sense at least seems to be made in the use of unconscious beliefs and unconscious desires in explaining human action, even in orthodox psychoanalysis, and thus that the foregoing must be an inadequate account of motivated action and, hence, of rational action. As Stuart Hampshire and Dilman have pointed out, unconscious beliefs and unconscious desires can make good sense, so long as they are used in a way that ties them to consciousness. One may have the same independent grounds for ascribing beliefs and desires to an agent if his first person statements of his *memory* of them are accorded the same authority as are his normal, first person, present tense reports of them. When in successful psychoanalytic therapy the patient comes to know his motives or beliefs, he comes to know them in the same noninferential, nonobservational way as we all normally know our own motives, and in such cases it makes sense to grant the usual authority to his sincere avowals of what they are. As long as the nature of such beliefs or desires is dependent on authoritative statements of the agent who himself remembers them (as opposed to inferring them from observing his own behavior or acceding to the authority of his analyst), significant explanations of his behavior can be formed using such unconscious motives.

So restricted, how much of the behavior of the mentally ill can even be said to be unconsciously motivated? Are there sets of beliefs and desires, conscious or unconscious, that explain the peculiar string of words and sounds sometimes uttered as a kind of word-salad by the mentally ill? Can one give such an explanation of the actions-by-omission of the vegetating catatonic, or of the violent actions against self-interest such as beating one's head against the wall? Note that the question is not whether one can or cannot come up with legitimate *causal* hypotheses about why the patient is in the state he is in. Nor is the question whether or not one can *invent* some set of beliefs and desires which, *if* the patient had them, would render his action rational. Rather, the question is whether such patients are performing an action for reasons which they either recognize, or if sufficient effort were made, could come to recognize, or if sufficient effort were made, could come to recognize as an action *they* were doing for reasons *they* found sufficient. Put this way, much of the behavior by which the more extreme forms of mental illness are diagnosed remains unmotivated and hence nonrational.

In any case, such behavior of the mentally ill as can be legitimately explained by reference to unconscious beliefs or unconscious desires is not fully rational. By hypothesis, such behavior is minimally rational because motivated. It is typically *irrational* however, in each of the several other senses of "rationality" mentioned earlier—the desires may be unintelligible, the beliefs about means irrational (or at least the means/end calculation grossly inefficient), the beliefs about the situation in which the actor finds himself irrational, or the beliefs and desires inconsistent with standing beliefs and desires. . . .

It is sometimes believed that the rationality of beliefs is not a matter that can be objectively judged and that calling them irrational is simply a pejorative way of saying that they are false. While the topic of rational belief is a difficult one, prima facia the most obvious way to differentiate beliefs that are irrational from those that are merely false is by looking at the influence relevant evidence would have on the holder of the belief. It is characteristic of irrational beliefs that their holder maintains them despite countervailing evidence or despite inconsistencies with other beliefs he has. There is a fixed or frozen nature about such beliefs, in the sense that they are not correctable by relevant evidence. Irrational beliefs are held with a strength (relative to other beliefs the actor has) disproportionate to the evidence known to the actor. Thus the man "who believes very strongly that his brother is trying to poison him (in spite of appearances) and who believes, rather weakly by comparison, that Boston is north of New York is likely to be flying in the face of evidence and the claims that the evidence renders likely"—he is likely, in other words, to be irrational in his belief of his imminent poisoning.

The empirical version of the myth argument fails because it is empirically false. By our shared concept of what it is to be rational, the mentally ill are not as rational as the rest of the population. Only by muddling the concept of rationality have the radical psychiatrists appeared to call into question this obvious truth. Only by attributing unconscious beliefs and desires to the mentally ill for which there is no evidence, or only by referring to beliefs that are themselves irrational can motives be found for the peculiar behavior symptomatic of mental illness. Neither of these moves satisfies what we usually mean by "rational" as applied to actions and agents. One may, of course, like Humpty Dumpty, choose to make a word like "rationality" mean what he pleases, but surely it is unhelpful when one does so to then present the manufactured match between the facts and the new criteria for the word, as a discovery of new facts, previously overlooked because of the willful blindness of self-interested psychiatrists or whatever. To do so is to create one's own myths.

In *The Concept of Mind,* Ryle made popular the notion of a category mistake. His motive for using this notion was to avoid having to take a position on the ontological status of mental entities. The dualism attributed to Descartes, i.e., the two-worlds view that there are minds and there are bodies, each in their own species of existence, is untenable for all of the reasons Ryle recounts throughout the whole of the book. Yet neither form a monism—that there are only minds (idealism) or there are only bodies (physicalism)—seems to do justice to the way we speak of ourselves as human beings. We do use mental terms such as "belief," "desire," "pain," etc., in apparently significant discourse, and yet when one attempts to say something about the entities to which such terms ostensibly refer, one is baffled. How does one describe a belief? What properties can one give it? Does it have physical extension? And if it has no such properties, what sort of a thing is it anyway?

Ryle wants to avoid answering these questions about the ontological status of mental entities. One kind of question we do not have to answer is a question that is not meaningful. Ryle wants to say that the question "Are there bodies and minds?" is not meaningful, because a category mistake has been made in conjoining a term in one category ("bodies") with a term in another ("minds"). It is like conjoining hopes, the tide, and the average age of death to say (in the same logical tone of voice) that all three are *rising*. Ryle explicitly avoids the snare of saying that there are two species of existence (dualism); he is operating on the level of language only, claiming that we use the word "exists" in two different senses when we speak of bodies and when we speak of minds. Hence, a difference of linguistic categories for Ryle does not imply a difference in ontological status (nor does it exclude it).

One of the particular category mistakes that Ryle is at pains to correct throughout his book is the assumption that "there are mechanical causes of corporeal movements and mental causes of corporeal movements." For Ryle, this statement contains a category mistake because it is a conjunction of words in different categories—specifically, the names of the candidates for mental causes, such as "belief," "desire," "volition," and the like, are in a different category from the kinds of words we use to label mechanical causes. Ryle later brings out this difference: he likens mental words, such as "desire" or "motive," to dispositions and contrasts them with mechanical causes. His well-known example is the broken window; one sense of explaining the shattering of a window is because a rock hit it; another sense of explaining this breaking is because the glass was brittle, i.e., because it had a tendency to break when hit by a hard object. The first form of explanation is to refer to a mechanical cause and the second to a dispositional property. Ryle construes motive words such as "vanity" or "greed" similarly to words such as "brittle" or "soluble"; such words do not cite a cause, but a tendency of persons or objects to behave in certain sorts of ways.

By his examples, vocabulary, and explicit citation, Szasz makes it clear that he has read Ryle with approval. He begins, for example, Part 1 of *Law, Liberty, and Psychiatry* with a quote from Ryle on the nature of myths:

> A myth is, of course, not a fairy story. It is the presentation of facts belonging in one category in the idioms belonging to another. To explode a myth is accordingly not to deny the facts but to re-allocate them.

"Mental illness" is a myth, then, in the same way that other mental terms are myths—it is as improper to place mental illness in the same category with real illnesses (read as physically caused illnesses) as it is to treat "belief," "desires," "perception," etc., as the names of mechanical or paramechanical causes.

There are, in fact, a number of distinguishable uses of the doctrine of categorical differences made by Szasz in his attack on mental illness as a myth, which include the following: (1) his primary use is to focus on "mental" in the phrase "mental illness" and to argue that mental illness is a myth (and hence a sick mind is a myth). (2) He also focuses on "illness," to argue that the latter term necessarily refers to physicochemical goings-on in the body; thus, saying that a mind could be ill is absurd because only physical bodies can be ill (in the ordinary meaning of "ill"). (3) Szasz also utilizes the doctrine of category differences to inveigh against any use of the names of particular mental illnesses, such as "schizophrenia," "hysteria," etc.; the argument here is that the names of particular illnesses illicitly conjoin words referring to behavioral tendencies with words referring to physiological happenings in the brain, as well as with words whose only reference is to mental experience—a clear example, for Szasz, of a category mistake. (4) Fourthly, and finally, because of the categorical differences between mind words and brain words,

Szasz appears to believe that it is logically impossible to establish correlations between the mental and behavioral-based syndromes we call mental illnesses, and the brain events that may cause them; hence, the scientific aspirations of psychiatry, and the medical treatment of mental illness, are forever condemned to frustration because the aspirations themselves are logically absurd.

It should be noted that the first two of these arguments deal with "mental illness" in general and the second two deal with the names of particular illnesses. For clarity, it helps to keep these two discussions separated, even though they are obviously related. Thus, I shall proceed to discuss Szasz's use of the doctrine of categorical differences in the four-part order set forth above. The ultimate conclusion of all of them, it is worth emphasizing, is that mental illness, and mental illnesses, are myths.

1. What is a sick mind? Surely a large part of the appeal of the myth argument stems from the difficulty one has in answering this question. One may indeed be tempted by the radical psychiatrists' reply that only bodies can be sick and that minds are not the sorts of things that can be either healthy or ill. Yet a good deal of the attraction of this argument should be eliminated once it is realized that the difficulty we have in saying anything very intelligible about what a sick mind is stems directly from the difficulty we have in saying anything intelligent about what a mind is. For, unless one is prepared to jettison our talk about minds in toto (as Szasz plainly is not), merely pointing out that "mental illness" has no clearer reference than does "mind" itself is hardly a sufficient basis for labelling it a myth.

Fixing the reference of "mind" and mental words generally is notoriously difficult, yet, in fact, we can leave the question of reference open, and still see that in no pejorative sense is a sick mind a myth. One may adopt any nondualistic position on the ontological status of mental entities (the popular ones presently being logical behaviorism, which asserts that minds are hypothetical constructs from behavior; materialism, which asserts that minds are (identical with) an as yet unknown set of physiological phenomena; functionalism, which contends that minds are functional states of physical systems; or Ryle's own position, that one may avoid the question because it cannot be meaningfully framed.) Perhaps "mind" and other mental terms are not even referential in character, as has also been suggested, so that we need not worry about what sorts of things minds are. Whichever of these positions one adopts about what minds are, he is immune to the kind of criticism Ryle directed against Cartesian dualism (criticisms that Szasz and others would redirect against the supposedly dualistic assumptions inherent in "mental illness"); in none of them does one presuppose the existence of some funny, nonmaterial mind substance. In none of them need one who speaks of mental illness be committed to "paramechanical myths" about ghostly mind-things being "injured" in some nonspatial way. "Mental illness" can make perfectly good sense—as much so as 'mind' and mind words generally – no matter which of these general positions one takes as to the reference of mental terms, even if the position adopted should be that none of them refer to anything.

The question, "What is a sick mind?" can be left aside in favor of a more useful question – "Does 'mental illness' have as significant a descriptive/explanatory use as other mental expressions?" If it does not, then "myth" is as good a perjorative label as any; but if the phrase does have a significant use, then no amount of Rylean exorcism as to the phrase's supposedly ghostly referents can be a sufficient reason to eliminate it from our vocabulary.

Our mentalistic vocabulary may conveniently be divided between experiential terms and those terms that we use to describe and explain human actions. Thus, when we predicate "is in pain," "is feeling tired," or "is seeing an orange afterimage" of another, we are ascribing mental experiences to him; when we predicate "is murdering," "is hiding," "is intending to hide," or "is desiring a yacht" of another, we describe his doings as actions and explain such actions by his (mental) intentions, desires, beliefs, motives, etc. Since the concept of mind is intimately connected with our concept of what it is to be a person, predicating mental experiences, actions, and intentions to another being is not only necessary before we will say that he has a mind, but also before we will think of that being as a person.

"Mental illness" is used to deny that all of the mind words can be properly predicated of another. Specifically, it is used to deny that the action/intention predicates are as regularly or as properly applicable to the mentally ill as they are to more normal persons. This is merely a corollary of saying that the mentally ill are not as rational as the rest of us, in these senses of "rational" discussed earlier. For those senses of rationality are all linked to our usage of the action/intention predicates. If an individual is irrational in the sense that his desires are unintelligible, or that his beliefs are irrational, or that the set of his beliefs or desires are inconsistent, then the action/intention mode of explanation begins to break down. If the individual is so far gone that for some of his actions we are unable to make out any set of beliefs or desires, no matter how bizarre, or inconsistent, then this mode of explanation breaks down entirely. Although no one would deny that the mentally ill have mental experiences (indeed, they typically have something of a surplus), the diminished rationality of the mentally ill does entail a diminished applicability of the other part of our mentalistic vocabulary, the action/intention predicates.

If we observe enough behavior of the same individual for which we are unable to apply the action/intention predicates, we will come to regard that individual differently than most of our fellows, differently, because we lack *the* form of description/explanation of his behavior by virtue of which we understand ourselves and others in daily life. To make out another being as a person fully like us, we need rather regularly to be able to see his actions as promoting desires we find intelligible in light of beliefs we find rational.

A "sick mind" is thus properly predicated of an individual when we are unable to presuppose his rationality to the same extent as we do for others. A sick mind is an incapacity to act rationally, which, in the senses of "rational" here used, means an incapacity to act so as to further intelligible desires in light of rational beliefs.

In so using "mental illness," one is thus committed to no funny, non-material substances that are in some nonspatial way injured or impaired. "Mind" and other mind-terms may not refer to such paramechanistic myths, but then, "mental illness" doesn't either. To say that someone's mind is ill is only to say that his capacity for rational action is diminished, that the subject himself is irrational. Since "mind" in Ryle's own analysis is the name of all such capacities for intelligent performances, a lack of some of them may as properly invoke mind words as may the possession of them. To the extent that one is willing to say of another, "he has a mind" (or, "he is a person"), then to the same extent should one be willing to say, "his mind is defective" (or, "he is not wholly a person"), if he in fact lacks the relevant capacities.

2. Of course, if "illness" meant "deviation from an anatomical or physiological norm," as Szasz believes, then *mental* illness would still make no sense, for how can a mind (or capacities for intelligent performance) deviate from physical norms? Minds cannot be normal or abnormal vis-à-vis such physiological norms, and, Szasz argues, beliefs to the contrary are simply category mistakes.

Does "illness" properly predicated of a person mean that the person's bodily structure is abnormal in comparison with other people's bodily structure? The first thing one wants to say is that "illness" was a word in the English language long before anyone knew very much about anatomy or physiology, and thus, the meaning of the word cannot be a matter of statistical deviation from a physiological or anatomical norm (else the word would have had no use prior to knowing of such norms and such deviations). Still, one might think that our ancestors had a different concept of illness than we do. So, to press on to contemporary examples, consider the following two: first, imagine an individual possessed of a cubical stomach. This stomach, while abnormal in its physical structure, functions perfectly efficiently in digesting food, etc.; it thus allows its owner as long a life as people with normal stomachs. Suppose further, it causes him no discomfort and that it allows him to eat and drink the variety and quantity of foods and beverages available in his society. Despite the presence of an abnormal physical condition, no one would call this individual ill.

Next, imagine an individual who possesses a small gland common to all mankind. As with everyone else, this gland causes him pain, increases his chance of early death, and prevents him from eating a large number of foods. Despite the fact that this physiological condition (until corrected by surgery) is universal, no one would hesitate to label the state caused by it an illness, similar to tonsilitis or appendicitis.

What these examples show is that being ill, even physically ill, is not the same as being in a certain state, even if that state deviates widely from what is normal for human beings. Being ill is not a state in which one's bodily structure deviates from a statistical norm, as Szasz argues throughout his work. Such deviance from physiological norm is in itself neither a necessary nor sufficient condition to being ill. It is simply irrelevant.

While to say what "illness" does not mean is considerably easier than specifying what it does mean, being ill seems to involve something like being in a state of pain or discomfort, which, if not removed, may lead to premature death, and which, for its duration, incapacitates the patient from certain activities thought normal in our society. One might assume that such states are physically caused; but such assumptions are irrelevant to what we mean by "illness." There are presumably physical causes for us being in all kinds of states, such as being a thousand miles from Paris, or for being alert or angry, etc. *Whether* there are physical causes for such states, and if so, *whether* they are manifested by abnormal physical structures, is irrelevant to whether or not one is ill, alert, angry, or a thousand miles away from Paris. Merely discovering a physical deviation in no way tells us that the person whose body it is that deviates is ill. To properly predicate "illness" of another we instead need to know such things as whether he is in pain, is incapacitated, or is dying.

The reason this has been so well camouflaged by the radical psychiatrists is because the names of *particular* illness, such as "polio," "pneumonia," etc., do involve knowledge of physical causes. Whether one has polio or pneumonia is determined in part by knowledge of the virus involved. Yet whether one is ill (in general) is *not* determined by such causes; whether one is ill in general is determined by wholly different criteria, seemingly connected with pain, incapacitation, or a hastened death.

Once one appreciates this, then the propriety of terming hysterics (mentally) ill is also evident. The activities for which one is incapacitated by a paralyzed arm differ not a whit, no matter if the paralysis is anatomical or hysterical. In either case, one cannot, for example, play baseball or tend after one's father effectively, etc. The admittedly sincere reports of pain of an hysteric throat irritation are as good as evidence that the hysteric feels pain, as are such reports of one whose C fibers are really jingling with physiological pain signals due to a physically caused throat irritation. More generally, those whose capacity to act rationally is diminished because their memory, perception, reasoning abilities, or other mental faculties are impaired, are incapacitated from a normal life in our society no less, e.g., than is the chronic alcoholic whose short-term memory banks have been physically damaged by his long-term drinking habits (Korsakoff syndrome).

Being in a state properly called "ill," then, does not depend on one's knowing or even in the first instance of there being, any particular physiological condition. It depends on one's being in a state characterized (roughly) by pain, incapacitation, and the prospect of a hastened death. There is nothing mythical about such states, whether they be due to a broken leg or a broken home. . . .

Ronald Pies

On Myths and Countermyths

To place Szasz's view of disease in historical perspective, some of its salient features should be noted. First, it holds that the "original" meaning of disease entailed the presence of some kind of lesion, and furthermore, that Virchow established this notion, whereas Bleuler subverted it. Second, Szasz maintains that there is now "no such thing" as schizophrenia, but that if physicochemical lesions can be correlated with schizophrenia, then it, too, will be a disease. Let me defer criticism of these claims and examine the notion of disease in historical perspective.

Szasz maintains that "until the middle of the nineteenth century," illness entailed some visible deformity or bodily lesion. In fact, however, this pathoanatomic view has been merely one of many competing notions of disease, most of which date from antiquity. Indeed, a crucial dichotomy in the philosophy of medicine may be traced to the rival medical academies of Knidos and Kos, in ancient Greece. Knidos, the school of Aesculapius, recognized only the "disease"—the "separate morbid entity subservient to general rules of pathology." The more empirical school of Kos, associated with Hippocrates, emphasized that there existed only "the sick individual with his particular kind of misery." In effect, these two schools saw disease either as a specific *lesion,* or as a *phenomenon* whose character was deter-mined by the patient's manner of presentation. It should be clear, then, that the former view did not originate with Virchow, and that the latter did not arise from a "concerted effort" by Bleuler and his cohorts to "change the

From *Archives of General Psychiatry* 36 (1979): 140–142

criteria" of disease. The criteria of disease have *always* been in dispute, though theories have waxed and waned in popularity.

But what, precisely, did Virchow say about disease? There is no question that he assumed cellular derangements to be the *basis* of disease; it is far less clear that Virchow *identified* disease with such pathologic processes. Indeed, L. J. Rather notes that Virchow "violently rejected Rokitansky's claim that diseases were at all times open to morphologic investigation." Virchow himself wrote as follows:

> One can have the greatest respect for anatomical, morphological, and histological studies. . . . But must one proclaim them, therefore, the ones of exclusive significance? Many important phenomena of the body are of a purely functional kind.

Szasz mistakenly attributes the criterion of "bodily function" to the influence of "modern psychiatry."

Virchow, of course, is best known for his maxim, *Es gibt keine Allgemein krankheiten, es gibt nur Local krankheiten.* There is no general, only local, disease. But Aschoff, Virchow's colleague, has argued that the latter wished merely to localize *lesions,* not diseases. (The distinction is between *Krankheiten* [disease] and *die Krankheit* [disease in general]). Virchow once commented that one could localize "diseases," but "not disease." If this interpretation is correct, the lesions to which Szasz constantly appeals would be the *basis* of disease, but not necessarily the sine qua non of disease. Here, an intriguing difference between Szasz and Virchow emerges. Szasz argues that: "Every 'ordinary' illness that persons have, cadavers also have. A cadaver may thus be said to 'have' cancer, pneumonia, or myocardial infarction." But Virchow writes that "Disease presupposes life. With the death of the cell, the disease also terminates."

This is a crucial point. For if, as Sir Clifford Allbutt concurs, "disease is a state of a living organism," it follows that when the organism dies, the disease terminates. Now, it is a rudimentary principle of pathology (as Szasz's view makes clear) that lesions persist after the death of the organism. But if lesions persist and disease terminates, disease cannot simply be the presence of lesions. (Note that Virchow claims not merely that we cannot "talk" of disease in a nonliving organism. His claim is not an *intentional* one, but an *ontological* one: disease terminates *as an entity* when the cell [or organism, as collection of cells] dies. The notion of the "intentional fallacy" will be elucidated later.)

Szasz, however, has referred to the additional criterion of "pathophysiology." This permits Szasz to escape the bind of a purely morphologic view of disease; such a view, as Kendall notes, "had been discredited beyond redemption" by 1960 — the year in which *The Myth of Mental Illness* was published.

But the notion of pathophysiology is not a simple one, depending, as it does, on "disordered function." As Kendell points out:

> There is no single set pattern of either structure of function. . . . Even in health, human beings and their constituent tissues and organs vary considerably in size, shape, chemical composition and functional efficiency.

Indeed, contrary to what Szasz seems to believe about his "basic and rigorous" definition of disease, the notion of pathophysiology proves to be not an *empirical* but a *statistical* term. One does not "observe" pathophysiology as one observes a rock; one merely observes physiochemical processes that may or may not be "pathological," depending on one's statistical norm. L.S. King has expressed his well:

> I recall a very precise young physician who asked me what our laboratory considered the normal hemoglobin value. . . . When I answered, "Twelve to sixteen grams, more or less," he was puzzled. . . . He wanted to know how, if my norm was so broad and vague, he could possibly tell whether a patient suffered from anemia, or [from] how much anemia. I agreed that he had quite a problem on his hands.

● ● ●

I will summarize this section as follows. First, there has never been a single set of criteria for the ascription of disease; the pathoanatomic view has coexisted with the patient-centered (phenomenologic) view since the time of Hippocrates. Virchow did not "establish" that pathoanatomic lesions are the sine qua non of disease; he seems to have regarded such lesions as the *basis* for any particular disease but regarded disease itself as something over and above mere lesions. For Virchow (contra Szasz), disease terminates when life terminates. Szasz's additional criterion of "pathophysiologic" change is not a well-defined empirical criterion but a broad statistical construct.

● ● ●

There is another point to be made, concerning the antithesis Szasz sets up between "having" and "being" or "doing." One can *have* a disease precisely because of the things one *is* or *is not, can* or *cannot do*. Indeed, we shall insist that both "organic" and "functional" diseases are often ascribed on this basis, *not* necessarily on the finding of a lesion.

Let us consider the things one "is" and "does" when one is said to "have" a migraine. The patient *is* in pain. He *goes* to the physician and *describes* this pain as left-sided cranial pain, preceded by flashing lights. When the pain comes on, the patient is apparently *unable* to *talk, walk or move.* It disappears after an hour or two. The physician diagnoses "migraine" and prescribes a mixture of ergotamine tartrate and caffeine (Cafergot).

The diagnosis is based on what the patient is and does or is not and cannot do—not on the finding of a lesion or even a pathophysiologic change. (The pathophysiology of migraine is poorly understood. Sacks roundly criticizes the evidence for the Latham-Wolff theory of vasoconstriction as "scanty, indirect and questionable." In any case, migraine is practically never *ascribed* on the basis of laboratory investigation or demonstration of a lesion; rather, it is ascribed on the basis of the patient's claims. For a more detailed description, consult *Migraine* by Sacks.) Later it will be seen that this is true of numerous "medical" diseases. Szasz falls into a form of *ignoratio elenchi* when he supposes he has proved that bodily illness is something one "has," by appealing to the presence of lesions: one does, indeed, "have" bodily illness, but not necessarily because one has a demonstrable lesion. Similarly, Szasz thinks he has demonstrated the essential difference between bodily mental illness by showing that the latter is ascribed on the basis of what one is and does; indeed, that is how mental illness is ascribed—the point is not at issue—but bodily illness is often ascribed in the same way.

●   ●   ●

Since Szasz rests his case against schizophrenia almost entirely on the premise that it is not a disease, we might well ask how clear this term is in modern medical usage. If it is less than clear, one might have serious doubts about labeling mental illness a "myth"—at least, as a *uniquely* mythologic term. And if current nosology should function with a definition of disease quite unrelated to that of Szasz's, one might again wonder whether Szasz's arguments wield much weight. I shall show that, indeed, the term disease is often ambiguous in current medical usage; and furthermore, that modern nosology does not depend on Szasz's pathoanatomic notion of disease.

L. S. King has spoken frankly of "the confusion surrounding the notion of disease," whereas Henschen has admitted that "to explain what is meant by disease in a few words is not so easy as one might think." Henschen makes the further point that, "One can have a strong sense of not feeling well although not even the most searching examination can detect any disturbance; it is not necessarily a case of an imaginary illness." But in light of Szasz's insistence on pathoanatomic and pathophysiologic criteria, one wants to know *why* this is not a case of an imaginary illness. Henschen is not making the trivial point that we are technologically incapable of "finding" such lesions. Rather, he construes disease as essentially "a failure of adaptability." This, of course, hearkens back to the Hippocratic concept of disease as centering around the uniquely "sick person." Scadding, arguing along similar lines, holds that diseased persons are those at a "biological disadvantage." This concept has been analyzed, by Kendell, in the following two components: reduced fertility and higher mortality. Kendall, in fact, has adduced evidence that schizophrenia fits these criteria.

Neither biological disadvantage nor failure in adaptability requires any reference to *lesions* or *altered chemistry*—though, in fact, these may underlie the problem. The term "pathology" arises from the root word "pathos"; originally, this referred to "passion" or "suffering." In his preoccupation with lesions, the physician would best be reminded that medical science began as a response to such suffering, what King aptly calls "the realm of pain, discomfort, and death." Indeed, ". . . it seems likely that the concept of disease originated as an explanation for the onset of suffering and incapacity *in the absence of obvious injury,*" [emphasis mine]. Maurice Natanson concurs:

> Prior to the problems of establishing the etiological basis of a disease entity, there is the problem of uncovering the phenomenal character of the disease in question . . . disease entities are human realities expressed in the life activities of fellow men. Disease [is originally recognized] not by experts, but by ordinary men.

If disease arose to explain suffering and incapacity *in the absence of obvious injury,* one has trouble with Szasz's contention that illness has traditionally meant a "visible deformity . . . or lesion" such as "a misshapen extremity, ulcerated skin, or a fracture or wound." But even if illness once meant what Szasz says it did, it no longer does. In the first place, our notion of disease is not value-independent; it often reflects very general ideas about "good" health, good looks, and good living. An example of a medical diagnosis that partakes of such evaluation is obesity. There is no uniform definition of this term nor are there consistent histopathologic or pathophysiologic changes in obese persons. (Compare what Craddock writes in *Obesity and Its Management.* "In the majority of patients, most metabolic differences between obese and normal people are ones of degree only, and are due to adaptation to an abnormal intake of food.")

Albrink admits that obesity "cannot be separated from nonobesity on a frequency distribution curve," and that it can be defined only as "adiposity in excess of that consistent with good health." But what is good health? Living to 60? To 70? Despite these problems of definition and the intrusion of societal values, one would certainly hesitate before deploring "the myth of obesity."

But Szasz might legitimately protest at this point. It is true, he might say, that some medical diagnoses are as fuzzy and value-centered as that of mental illness, but that does not touch the essential argument, namely, that one must demonstrate histopathologic or pathophysiologic change to have disease.

Well, in the end, such a definition becomes not a scientific statement but a rhetorical call to action. One may wish that disease were so defined, and one may advocate such a definition. But, as was said of J. M. Keynes' theory of probability, Szasz's definition of disease remains a "vestal virgin" in the harsh world of medical realities.

Consider the diagnoses of migraine, idiopathic epilepsy, Gilles de la Tourette syndrome, and dystonia musculorum deformans. None of these "diseases"—and they are regarded as such outside the psychiatric profession— is associated with consistent histopathologic or pathophysiologic changes. None meets Szasz's criteria for the ascription of disease. So where does that leave us? With the myth of migraine? Do we withhold phenytoin (Dilantin) from epileptics because they have no "disease"? (Although epilepsy can often be correlated with EEG changes, there is no consistent EEG pattern associated with epilepsy. Read J. Laidlaw and A. Richens', *A Textbook of Epilepsy*.) Szasz has held, as a general principle, that "there can be no treatment without illness." Yet he recognizes that "medical intervention" occurs in the absence of illness; e.g., in cases of abortion or vasectomy. What Szasz has not recognized is the need for *active treatment* of such "nondiseases" as epilepsy, migraine, and—I would suggest—schizophrenia. To advocate this is surely not to abandon the principles of informed consent and contractual therapy—two cornerstones of Szasz's ethos. It is merely to point out the utter impracticality of a strictly Virchowian notion of disease.

L. S. King, a clinical pathologist, correctly perceives that disease is ultimately "an arbitrary designation." It is not a matter of finding lesions but of making complex existential decisions: "We carve out whatever disease patterns we wish, in whatever way we desire." Nevertheless, there is an abiding process of selection that "filters out" some diseases and retains others: "A [disease] pattern has reasonable stability only when its criteria are sharp, its elements cohere, and its utility in clarifying experience remains high."

Schizophrenia, to be sure, needs refinement in all these respects. Yet it remains a useful term in describing a unique kind of "suffering and incapacity in the absence of obvious injury." To those who suffer with that elusive entity called mental illness, and who voluntarily seek treatment for it, we owe an open-minded and aggressive concern.

●   ●   ●

C. G. Schoenfeld

An Analysis of the Views of Thomas S. Szasz

My purpose here . . . is to examine in detail the basic thesis that Szasz has advanced in a series of articles and books during the past 15 years. This thesis is that: There is no such thing as mental illness (no such thing as neurosis, psychosis, insanity, "madness," and so on). To the extent that conditions now labeled mental illness may actually exist, they are really "problems in living" (ethical, social, legal, political and other problems). Hence, psychiatrists who diagnose and treat what they regard as mental illnesses are really persecutors, oppressors, and torturers, who sometimes even create the conditions they are supposed to cure; persons now labeled mentally ill should not be sent involuntarily to so-called mental institutions: if they commit crimes, they should be prosecuted and punished like everyone else.

There is no such thing as mental illness (no such thing as neurosis, psychosis, insanity, "madness," and so on).

To support his thesis that there is no such thing as mental illness—no such thing as neurosis or psychosis—Szasz fails to offer what one would suppose to be the "best evidence" of his viewpoint: clinical evidence. That is, he fails to offer his readers detailed descriptions, case histories, and the like of a representative cross section of persons whom psychiatrists usually judge to be neurotic or psychotic, but whom he has interviewed or examined as a psychiatrist, and whom he has demonstrated to be completely normal.

From *Journal of Psychiatry and Law* 4 (Summer, 1976): 245-263.

Persons who are terrified of heights, or of entering small enclosures, or of leaving their home; others who feel compelled, usually in the privacy of their bedroom or bathroom, to perform certain bizarre rituals; still others who steal things they neither need, use, sell, nor really want; so-called fetishists who literally worship certain articles of clothing or parts of the body; masochists who have an overwhelming need to be "disciplined" by being cursed, whipped, and even urinated and defecated upon; exhibitionists who cannot resist exposing their genitals in public, and particularly in front of small children. It is clinical evidence (detailed investigative reports, case histories, etc.) showing that a representative sample of such putative neurotics are completely healthy that Szasz, perhaps understandably, fails to offer his readers. Persons in a so-called catatonic stupor who are apparently oblivious of the world around them; others who are convinced that they are being relentlessly persecuted by unidentified enemies out to poison or otherwise destroy them; still others who believe that they are God's emissaries or angels—or even God himself—and that, as such, they have the power to destroy the world; so-called depressives who may lacerate and maim themselves, and for whom suicide may seem to be the obvious "solution" to all their problems; patients who are actively hallucinating and who may be wildly manic and assaultive—it is detailed reports of interviews and examinations conducted with a representative cross section of these putative psychotics which reveal that —*mirabile dictu*—they are as mentally healthy as you or I, that Szasz fails to offer to his readers.

Instead of providing such evidence, Szasz relies upon arguments concerning the words "mental illness" to prove that there is no such thing as neurosis, psychosis, insanity, "madness," and so on. In brief, he contends that there cannot be an illness unless physical signs or symptoms of it exist. And since (in his view) there are no physical signs or symptoms of the so-called mental illnesses, it follows that neurosis, psychosis, insanity, "madness," and the like do not exist.

Unfortunately for Szasz's argument, physical signs or symptoms of mental illness frequently *do* exist. For example, electroencephalograms have shown that the brain wave patterns of many persons whom psychiatrists regard as seriously ill often are highly erratic and abnormal. Further, a whole range of physical signs or symptoms ranging from facial tics and allergic reactions to serious gastric and pulmonary disorders have been shown to reflect the presence of mental disorders. Indeed, the whole area of psychosomatic medicine is concerned with the very close relationship that has been shown to exist between neurosis and psychosis and physical and bodily disorders. In fact, it may be contended that the very strange behavior of many neurotics and psychotics is itself "physical" evidence of mental illness.

But even if all this were not so, Szasz's argument in effect *assumes*, rather than proves, that there is no such thing as mental illness. That is, he *assumes* that there cannot be an illness unless physical signs or symptoms of it exist and having also made the assumption discussed above that there are no signs or symptoms of mental illness, he concludes that neurosis, psychosis, insanity, "madness," and the like, do not exist. As a logician might put it, Szasz's argument "begs the question."

Admittedly—as Szasz emphasizes when he discusses the word "illness"— when there is a physical illness, physical signs or symptoms of it usually appear. But it hardly follows that, as Szasz assumes, physical signs or symptoms are needed to prove the existence of *mental* illness. Indeed, an analysis of the definitions of the word "illness" offered in the unabridged edition of the Merriam Webster and other leading dictionaries soon reveals that Szasz's belief that physical signs or symptoms constitute a defining characteristic of the term is clearly idiosyncratic and amounts to an attempt to create a private definition of it.

But even if Szasz's definition of the word "illness" were shared by today's lexicographers, Szasz's *argument would still be unsound, since it attempts to do what is philosophically and epistemologically impossible; to define something out of existence.* As philosophers and logicians have pointed out to generations of students: "When you have stated the defining characteristics of X, you have proved nothing one way or the other about whether X exists. . . . When you are able to define a word in terms of characteristics A, B, and C, you have still not shown that there *exists* anything in the universe that has characteristis A, B, and C. You cannot legislate centaurs into existence by defining a word, any more than you can legislate black swans out of existence by redefining the word 'swan.' From defining X, you can draw no conclusions whatever about whether there are any X's in the world; that is not a matter for definition but for scientific investigation." In short, to determine whether or not mental illness (or anything else) exists, empirical evidence is needed. Szasz's attempt to define mental illness in terms of physical signs or symptoms—coupled with his assumption that there are no such signs or symptoms and that therefore there is no such thing as mental illness is an outrageously highhanded attempt to do what is philosophically and epistemologically impossible; to define mental illness out of existence.

To try to determine at this point why as well-educated and philosophically sophisticated a person as Szasz would attempt to define mental illness out of existence would be to delay unduly consideration of the second element of Szasz's basic thesis detailed at the beginning of this paper. Still it ought to be noted that by seeking to define mental illness out of existence, Szasz may be revealing the presence and influence of a belief that words can actually create or destroy—a possibility that finds considerable support in numerous statements by Szasz overestimating greatly the power of words, such as: "In ordinary life, the struggle is not for guns but for words: whoever first defines the situation is the victor; his adversary, the victim."; "In the animal kingdom, the rule is, eat or be eaten; in the human kingdom, define or be defined." In any event, to believe that words can be used to create or destroy is to believe in *word magic*: something which, as psychoanalysts have learned, is typical at the age of two or so, but which becomes increasingly unsual thereafter.

To the extent that conditions now labeled mental illness may actually exist, they are really "problems in living" (ethical, social, legal, political, and other problems).

Aware, perhaps, that the conditions psychiatrists label mental illness may reveal that "something" is amiss, Szasz asserts that insofar as these conditions actually exist (a matter upon which he is vague and equivocal at times), they are really "problems in living."

Unfortunately, the phrase "problems in living" is so very vague and general that it can be used to describe practically every problem a person may have. One man may have contracted a disease, another may be unable to meet his financial obligations, a third may be in the midst of getting a divorce, a fourth may find it impossible to pass the courses he is taking at school, a fifth may have been arrested for murder, rape or whatever – all of them may be said to have "problems in living." Yet it is *also* true – and far more meaningful and helpful – to say that the first man has a health problem, the second an economic problem, the third a marital problem, the fourth a learning problem, and the fifth a legal problem. Not only does the phrase "problems in living" fail to prove helpful when someone attempts to understand or resolve the problems so described, but its very vagueness and generality – its essential meaninglessness – imposes its own confusion.

Possibly in an attempt to help to overcome this objection, Szasz sometimes tries to be more specific concerning the meaning of "problems in living" by stating that what he is really talking about are ethical, social, legal, political, and other problems. Unfortunately, however, Szasz *assumes* – rather than proves – that what psychiatrists now term mental illness may be some other problem. One looks in vain for evidence (detailed investigative reports, case histories, and the like) demonstrating that a representative sample of the persons whom psychiatrists now regard as neurotic or psychotic are really suffering from the effects of ethical, social, legal, political, and other problems. Moreover, Szasz seems unable to accept the possibility that the conditions psychiatrists label neuroses or psychoses may reflect not only ethical, social, legal, political, or other "problems in living," *but mental illness as well.* As David P. Ausubel has put it: "There is no valid reason why a particular symptom cannot both reflect a problem in living *and* constitute a manifestation of disease." Or as another analyst of Szasz's writings has noted, there seems to be a strange quirk in Szasz's reasoning which repeatedly leads him to the conclusion that 'phenomenon A belongs either to class (category) X or to class (category) Y, but never to both."

What may be the most telling objection to Szasz's assertion that the conditions psychiatrists label neuroses and psychoses are not mental illnesses, but are instead "problems in living," is that this assertion fails to take into account the huge amount of evidence that has accumulated (particularly during the past hundred years or so) which certainly seems to reveal that these conditions are indeed mental illnesses. For example, there is a veritable mountain of evidence—including what are literally tens of thousands of highly detailed clinical reports, case histories, and the like—which clearly appear to demonstrate that *neuroses and psychoses frequently emerge as a result of the developmental difficulties occurring in infancy and childhood when the problems that arise can hardly be described as ethical, social, legal, or political.*

Psychiatrists who diagnose and treat what they regard as mental illnesses are really persecutors, oppressors, and torturers, who sometimes even create the conditions they are supposed to cure.

Szasz's charge that psychiatrists who diagnose and treat what they regard as mental illnesses are really persecutors, oppressors, and torturers, who sometimes even create the conditions they are supposed to cure, is so dramatic, idiosyncratic, and extreme, that one would suppose that Szasz would be prepared to back it up with a plethora of irrefutable evidence. Unfortunately, however, one finds that he makes little or no effort to meet this burden of proof. For example, he offers little or no evidence that psychiatrists have either exacerbated or created mental illnesses. And, by the same token, he avoids dealing with the huge amount of evidence that psychiatrists have helped to ameliorate and cure mental illnesses.

Had Szasz been able to adduce convincing evidence that neuroses and psychoses are non-existent, he would have been better able to justify his failure to prove that psychiatrists are persecutors, oppressors, and torturers. After all, if neuroses and psychoses do not exist, it·may well be justifiable to suggest that psychiatrists who attempt to treat these conditions are, in actuality, persecutors, oppressors, and torturers. As has been seen, however, Szasz's "word magic" cannot begin to be considered an adequate substitute for the clinical evidence needed to support the contention that there is no such thing as mental illness.

It should be noted here that when Szasz discusses psychiatry and psychiatrists, he sometimes distinguishes between what he terms private or voluntary psychiatry (psychiatric services that a person voluntarily secures for himself) and involuntary or "institutional" psychiatry (psychiatric services that are imposed upon a person alleged to be emotionally ill, most usually in a state mental institution). Szasz utterly condemns institutional psychiatry, often in such statements as: "There are and can be, no abuses *of* institutional psychiatry, because institutional psychiatry *is,* itself, an abuse, just as there were, and could be, no abuses *of* the Inquisition, because the Inquisition *was,* itself, an abuse. Indeed, just because the Inquisition was the characteristic and perhaps inevitable abuse of Christianity, so institutional psychiatry is the characteristic and perhaps inevitable abuse of medicine." Szasz is more equivocal concerning voluntary psychiatry, sometimes lumping it together with institutional psychiatry, but sometimes admitting that it may have limited value as a form of "applied secular ethics."

When discussing both voluntary and involuntary psychiatry, however, Szasz—characteristically—fails to offer what one would suppose to be the "best evidence" of his charges. That is, he fails to interview or to examine a representative cross section of the persons whom private—and especially institutional—psychiatrists have treated, and to show that a large percentage of these patients have been persecuted, oppressed, and tortured. Instead—and, once again, characteristically—he relies on the *repetition of dramatic but unsupported charges* of persecution, oppression, and torture by psychiatrists to "prove" his point.

Examples of this technique of *alleging rather than proving* abound in Szasz's book *The Manufacture of Madness,* in which he presents what he conceives of as "historical evidence" to justify his charge that psychiatrists are persecutors, oppressors, and torturers. For instance, he declares that today's so-called mental patients are the equivalent of or analogous to yesterday's witches and heretics, and that today's psychiatrists are the equivalent of or analogous to yesterday's Inquisitors who persecuted, oppressed, and tortured witches and heretics. Now, it is undoubtedly true that *some* persons alleged in the past to be witches and heretics were persecuted, oppressed, and tortured by *some* religious leaders; and it may even be true that *some* of these alleged witches and heretics were persons whom *some* psychiatrists today would be likely to regard as mentally ill. By no means does it follow, however—as Szasz certainly implies—that *most or all* persons alleged in the past to be witches and heretics would be considered mentally ill by *most or all* of today's psychiatrists. And, in addition, it certainly does not follow; indeed, there is not a scintilla of evidence to show that, as Szasz asserts, today's psychiatrists are the equivalent of yesterday's Inquisitors.

●   ●   ●

Persons now labeled mentally ill should not be sent involuntarily to so-called mental institutions; if they commit crimes, they should be prosecuted and punished like everyone else.

As has been seen, Szasz's thesis that there is no such thing as mental illness is, to say the least, dubious. Nevertheless, because the non-existence of mental illness is the premise upon which Szasz bases his conclusion that persons now labeled mentally ill should not be sent involuntarily to so-called mental institutions—as well as his further conclusion that if such persons commit crimes, they should be prosecuted and punished like everyone else— it is perhaps understandable that Szasz offers comparatively little data to support these conclusions. After all, if mental illness is simply a "myth" (a term Szasz stresses in his seminal work *The Myth of Mental Illness*), it is hard to imagine an acceptable reason for labeling people mentally ill, sending them against their wishes to mental institutions, and freeing them from the restraints and penalties normally imposed by the law. Indeed, on this basis it may even be possible to defend Szasz's failure to confront what is surely a veritable mountain of evidence—psychoanalytic and historical particularly—which casts the most serious doubts upon his view that the involuntary commitment of the "insane" to mental institutions ought to be abolished; and that instead, these unfortunates ought to be subjected to the processes and penalties of the criminal law. Also, in line with the foregoing, there is no consideration by Szasz that prison might be just one of those institutions where these various abuses, oppressions, persecutions, and tortures that he seeks to avoid actually take place, and in fact probably to a far greater degree toward disturbed people than is the case in mental institutions. . . .

To turn now . . . to a discussion of the merits of his views that persons now labeled mentally ill should not be sent involuntarily to so-called mental institutions—and that if they commit crimes, they should be prosecuted and punished like everyone else—would be to extend this paper far beyond its intended limits. After all, these are matters which hundreds—if not thousands of books and articles touch upon. Nevertheless, a few brief comments concerning Szasz's views seem required here.

To begin with, "all societies we know of have classified some of their members into categories analogous to our term 'mentally ill.'" And, indisputably, the so-called mentally ill present extremely troublesome social problems that "will not vanish by sleight of hand or pen."

Szasz states repeatedly that he wants to shield persons who are labeled mentally ill from discrimination and oppression by society. Yet he seems unaware that subjecting these persons to prosecution and punishment under the criminal law, especially if they are unable to control the urges that beset them, or lack the mental clarity or capacity needed to aid their counsel in preparing an adequate defense, may itself be a form of discrimination and oppression. Szasz's stated desire to protect persons accused of being mentally ill also presumably finds reflection in his demand that their involuntary commitment to mental institutions be prohibited. Yet Szasz seems to fail to realize that commitment to a mental institution may offer desperately needed help and protection to persons who are so disorganized and bewildered that they cannot take care of themselves.

In addition, Szasz seems to be unaware that, historically, his "solution" to the problems posed by the presence in society of persons considered to be mentally ill—insisting upon their "freedom" to sleep in doorways and to wander in confusion and bewilderment through the streets, and his demanding that they be prosecuted and punished for the crimes they commit — was tried for centuries and found wanting. Szasz somehow seems to forget that the crimes which he himself alleges the mentally ill were once accused of, such as heresy and witchcraft, were once punished in such horrible ways as stoning to death and burning at the stake. And as the investigations of Dorothea Dix reveal, the "freedom" enjoyed by the mentally ill before the creation of the modern mental institution was the "freedom" to be locked away in an attic, cellar, or outhouse, and the "freedom" to wander lost and neglected through the countryside, without family, friends, sustenance, or hope.

The point is that, as Norman Dain has stressed, "eliminating involuntary commitment will not eliminate the social problems created, especially in a mass society, by the existence of people who cannot function at a certain level or in certain socially prescribed ways." Or as Robert Scharf has so movingly put it: "A person who is in danger because of a lack of insight into his own mental illness is a special case before society and the law. It is unbrotherly and unloving to think that his safety and treatment are less important than his personal freedom, when his ability to choose is hobbled or absent. Only an ideological zealot can contend that a person's life is worth the philosophical purity of having every individual, whatever his state of mind, entirely determine his own fate."

●   ●   ●

In Response to the Critics

Lee S. Weinberg and Richard E. Vatz

The Mental Illness Dispute:
the Critical Faith Assumptions

The writings of Thomas Szasz over the past twenty years comprise over a score of books and hundreds of articles and reviews. Although the upshot of Dr. Szasz's writings is most often represented as simply the belief that mental illness is a myth, the broad array of historical, philosophical, medical, and legal issues involved does not lend itself to easy distillation. Consequently, much of the debate over the issues that Szasz has raised over the years seems to focus in piecemeal fashion on limited and perhaps arbitrarily chosen components of Szasz's arguments. Two articles published in the *Archives* in recent years by Michael S. Moore and Ronald Pies are exceptions to this trend; they offer penetrating and extensive criticism of what the authors regard as the philosophical underpinnings of Szasz's criticisms of traditional views of mental illness and psychiatry.

Analysis of assumptions which underlie Szasz and his critics' positions reveals that the arguments regarding the ontological status of mental illness are based on faith assumptions which do not lend themselves to confirmation or disconfirmation, but whose resolutions will have major consequences for psychiatry. Thus, the permanent impasse in the issues does not negate the fact that certain points of view in the competition will win out and have crucial and far-reaching impacts. In this article we will demonstrate the basic incompatible starting points or assumptions which characterize the points at issue in debates on mental illness and examine the consequences of the adoptions of these different perspectives. In doing so, we will also indicate

From *Journal of Psychiatry and Law* 9 (Fall, 1981): 305–311.

some of the interesting but basically parenthetical issues which have cluttered consideration of the seminal questions. What follows are analyses of two such questions—ontological and epistemological respectively—which represent the *sine qua non* of the disputes over the status of mental illness and its determination.

What are the necessary and sufficient conditions warranting the conclusion that a person is sick?

Assumptions about the nature of illness itself are at the core of the debate over mental illness. Efforts to define the necessary and sufficient conditions for the ascription of illness have generally emphasized either the presence of demonstrable lesions, on the one hand, or complaints of suffering on the other. As Pies correctly points out, there has always been a tension between these opposing views, Virchow representing the former to a large degree, and Hippocrates the latter. More recently, John Coulehan has identified these competing models of illness as the Western Biomedical Model and the Holistic Systems Model.

As with many critics, Pies includes in his discussion of this issue his interpretation of the historical development of the concept of illness which is different from Szasz's, but the issue of historical accuracy or lineage is not a critical one in the debate. What is critical is the question of what conditions will be taken as necessary and sufficient for the conclusion that illness is present.

Szasz's claim that mental illness is a myth, a metaphor mistakenly taken literally, seems to assume that a measurable lesion *is* a necessary and sufficient condition for the presence of illness. Indeed, his point that cadavers retain the evidence that real disease was present in the living person seems to reflect this assumption. Pies suggests that·Szasz makes what philosophers call a category error, by believing that cadavers can be sick; in doing so, Pies somewhat distorts Szasz's point, which pertains to the question of evidence of manifestations of illness, rather than the issue of whether or not illness survives the patient in some philosophical sense. Nonetheless, Szasz is in the camp of those insisting that an illness requires some pathoanatomic deviation. Pies speculates that such a view might lead Szasz to conclude that obesity is a mythical illness as well; in fact Szasz *has* expressly taken this position.

Pies and others, on the other hand, claim that the necessary conditions for illness are few and nebulous, and the sufficient conditions may include the patient's simply reporting himself to be suffering. He does not address the issue of whether, in the absence of *both* lesions and complaints, a person may be sick, *e.g.,* the case in which someone *other* than the sick person identifies the person as suffering, and the person disagrees. This is a critical question because this type of identification is employed frequently by mental health professionals in diagnosing cases of mental illness.

The foregoing disputes on definitions of illness rely on faith assumptions which are arbitrary and incompatible, but the implications of the definitional biases in current practice are, of course, quite significant. Let us now identify the major extant approaches and their implications.

The following are the major criteria approaches for defining or diagnosing illness:

1. Measurable lesion and complaint of suffering are necessary and sufficient conditions.
2. Measurable lesion is necessary and sufficient condition.
3. Complaint of suffering is sufficient condition.
4. Physician diagnosis of suffering is sufficient condition.

The above four possibilities show the major definitional approaches to illness in generally descending order of restrictiveness. Looking at a case, for example, of myocardial infarction, one would consider it a disease by all of the above, unless the infarct were without complaint of pain. In that case, it would not be an illness by the most restrictive standard (and standards may shift for different diseases by different physicians or even by the same physician for different diseases or for different patients for the same disease). In the case of cardiac neurosis with no measurable lesions, the patient would have an illness only according to definition 3 and 4. All disputes on the proper definition of illness thus reflect disagreements over which criterion or criteria to apply, leaving only the problem of expertise in lesion detection a separate concern. For consideration of functional mental illness in which no one claims detection of histopathologic or pathophysiologic change, we have, if not what Pies criticizes Szasz for calling a "uniquely mythological" *term*, a unique *definition* operating. This is the first unique aspect of what we call *mental* illness. For there are no other illnesses in which the fourth set of necessary and sufficient conditions, *i.e.,* absence of both lesions and complaints, is taken as constituting illness, in many instances when only the *physician's* claim of discovery of patient suffering is indicated.

As the restrictiveness of the definition decreases, the power of the physician to define illness by his judgment alone increases. The implication of this increased power points to the second unique component of the alleged illness we call "mental illness." It is also the only illness in which we often may not allow the patient to refuse treatment, since the determination of rationality of the patient is part or all of the final diagnosis of illness. This leads us to our second seminal question, a two-part question:

What is rationality, and can purpose be inferred from claims?

The heart of Moore's analysis of Szasz revolves around this second question to which an answer must be assumed and whose implications must be recognized before taking sides in the debate. For Moore, irrationality ". . . means an incapacity to act so as to further intelligible desires in the light of rational beliefs." His description of the ways in which the actions of people reflect irrationality rests entirely on judgments made about ". . . the agent's conscious beliefs." Thus, "conscious beliefs" becomes the cornerstone on which his case must rest. But this, in turn, requires an assumption that we can correctly infer one's beliefs from one's actions, and/or that one's claims about one's beliefs are to be taken as an accurate portrayal of one's beliefs. If Moore does not make one or both of these assumptions, it is not possible for him to ever have access to a person's beliefs or, therefore, to a person's purpose in acting in a particular manner. This distinction between claims and beliefs must be glossed over by Moore if his conception of rationality is to be valid.

The implication of these assumptions, therefore, must be that Moore accepts that a person's claims *do* reflect his beliefs, that these beliefs reflect his purpose for acting as he has, and that this purpose can be subjected to certain criteria for an assessment of its rationality on objective bases.

On the contrary, Szasz assumes that claims may or may not reflect beliefs and that, as a result, we may not have access to the beliefs which we must have in order to know patients' purposes and make a decision on the question of their rationality. This view also implies that illness cannot be inferred from only a claim of suffering since we cannot infer suffering from that claim. Moreover, Szasz argues that objective standards of rationality do not exist regardless.

These questions of the ability to infer people's cognitions from their claims and/or behavior and the ability to assess the rationality of those cognitions according to objective standards or rationality are unanswerable, but they pose issues whose resolutions have tremendously important consequences. If we cannot infer beliefs from claims, then the less restrictive definitions of illness become moot, and a patient should always be free to refuse treatment. If we *can* infer beliefs from claims *and* if we can also assess rationality by physician assessment or otherwise, then one can well justify involuntary treatment. But, finally, even if we can infer beliefs from claims, if we cannot assess rationality, then the right to refuse medical treatment for *any* illness, including alleged "mental illness" (by whatever definition), is a question of political freedom.

As we have shown, the seminal points at issue or questions in the debates over the ontological status of mental illness and the epistemological status of its determination are essentially based on different approaches to definitions of illness and rationality and are based on faith assumptions that do not lend themselves to objective resolution any more than the definitions of "meaningful life" do in debates on abortion. Still, the answers we choose will have inestimable consequences for matters of medicine, morals, law, and individual freedom.

Lee S. Weinberg and Richard E. Vatz

Szasz and the Law: An Alternative View

In the Summer 1976 issue of *The Journal of Psychiatry and Law,* Mr. C. G. Schoenfeld offers "An Analysis of the Views of Thomas Szasz." In his article, Mr. Schoenfeld attempts to disprove Dr. Szasz's theses regarding the existence of "mental illness" and to dispute the accuracy of Szasz's description of the attitudes and actions of those who serve institutional psychiatry. In this answer to Mr. Schoenfeld, we will argue that he fails in the former because he simply does not understand Szasz's argument and is only partially successful in the latter which, in any event, is less crucial to an understanding of Szasz's theory. . . .

The major problem in Schoenfeld and in many other critiques of Szasz is a failure to perceive the rich theoretical perspective being offered. Szasz intertwines traditional theories of psychiatry and forensic psychiatry with theories of semiotic behavior. The problem in Schoenfeld's critique, however, can be seen in his reliance on dictionary definitions of "illness," an approach which ignores all anthropological, rhetorical, and meta-linguistic analyses of the way in which language functions to create the reality which we "see." His derisive reference to "word magic" further reveals his inability to grasp Szasz's rhetorical perspective. In asserting that Szasz attempts to achieve the ". . . philosophically and epistemologically impossible . . . [feat of defining] something out of existence," Schoenfeld has overlooked, for example, the action of the American Psychiatric Association in defining the "disease" of homosexuality out of existence.

From *Journal of Psychiatry and Law* 4 (1977): 551–558.

...In asking for "clinical evidence [of] ... persons whom psychiatrists usually judge to be neurotic or psychotic, but whom he [Szasz] has interviewed or examined as a psychiatrist, and whom he has demonstrated to be completely normal," Schoenfeld again misses the entire point of the argument. Szasz does not maintain that such people are "normal"; indeed, he would find the question meaningless and irrelevant. The central point that Szasz makes is simply that such people and their behavior cannot be understood by use of a medical framework or medical language. That is, the medicalization of language is a pretense by which psychiatrists claim they understand behavior but which, in fact, only serves to accredit or discredit it. If a man machine-gunned infants in a maternity ward, Szasz would surely not say that it is "normal." He would say, however, that you will not shed light on this behavior by discussing it in medical terminology. Szasz would never argue that "they are as healthy as you or I," a point which Schoenfeld believes must be made to sustain Szasz's position. Again, Schoenfeld misunderstands. Szasz rejects the term "mental health" as well as "mental illness" since he rejects medical metaphors for understanding behavior.

Had Schoenfeld understood the foregoing, he would not have asked for "evidence" that mental illness does not exist. You cannot prove the nonexistence of anything, and in particular, you cannot, of course, prove the nonexistence of a metaphor. This confusion in Schoenfeld accounts for his analogizing Szasz's contention that mental illness is a myth to legislating "black swans out of existence by redefining the word 'swan.'" Szasz says that mental illness (unlike swan) is a metaphor. What sorts of evidence does one proffer to disprove a metaphor? Usually, one does not need any evidence at all since most metaphors are recognized as such. If we say that someone who is ugly is a "dog" we would not call a kennel since we realize that "dog" here is a metaphor. With mental illness, however, Szasz contends that we mistake the metaphor for reality and thereby enfranchise the medical field to deal with aberrant behavior. In essence, Szasz doesn't think that killers are "normal"; he simply doesn't think their problem is medical. You don't prove the inappropriateness of a medical metaphor for understanding unusual behavior by disputing that the behavior is unusual or abnormal. You show it by fully accounting for the behavior in nonmedical ways.

The "... developmental difficulties occurring in infancy and childhood" which Schoenfeld outlines are precisely what Szasz would agree are often involved. What are these problems if they are not "problems in living"? Schoenfeld attacks the "vagueness and generality" of Szasz's notion of "problems in living." However, the term accurately reflects Szasz's position; namely, that such problems are diffuse and general and only appear to be specific and discrete as a consequence of the psychiatric categories used to describe them. Once more, Schoenfeld's criticism stems from a misreading of the Szasz's position.

In sum, it is simply not Szasz's position at all that Schoenfeld's list of strange and/or dangerous people are "as mentally healthy as you or I." The whole point is that they are communicating in unconventional idiom or acting in a manner understandable, perhaps, only to them. When Schoenfeld describes "exhibitionists who cannot resist exposing their genitals in public" or others "who are compelled . . . to perform bizarre rituals" he begs the question of the person's alleged lack of control of his own behavior. More significant, however, he misses Szasz's point which is not that such people are normal, but that their behavior cannot be made understandable by reference to a medical model. Szasz prefers the model of game playing. . . . As to the rituals, they may be seen as "bizarre" or "uplifting" depending upon who has the power to define what symbolic behavior is legitimate. It is this very point which Schoenfeld mistakenly interprets when he says that Szasz implies ". . . that most or all persons alleged in the past to be witches and heretics would be considered mentally ill by most or all of today's psychiatrists." In fact, Szasz is merely making the argument that behavior perceived to be strange by those in power at any particular point in history will be discredited by whatever discrediting mechanism is operative at the time.

To prove the existence of mental illness, Schoenfeld uses the same illogic that he attributes to Szasz; in fact, he uses the exact such logical fallacies. He accuses Szasz of begging the question, that is, proving a conclusion by assuming it in the premise. He says Szasz attempts to ". . . define something out of existence." This assumes that "mental illness" *does* exist, which is precisely the point in question. This elementary logical error is ubiquitous in Schoenfeld's article, and again results from his lack of understanding of Szasz. Another logical error is Schoenfeld's argument that those labelled neurotic or psychotic are mentally ill in view of physical signs which are present:

> Unfortunately for Szasz's argument, physical signs or symptoms of mental illness frequently *do* exist. For example, electroencephalograms have shown that the brain wave patterns of many persons whom psychiatrists regard as seriously mentally ill are often highly erratic and abnormal. Further, a whole range of physical signs or symptoms ranging from facial tics and allergic reactions to serious gastric and pulmonary disorders have been shown to reflect the presence of mental disorders.

This is to argue *a posteriori*. We rarely look for such disturbances in what we consider normal behavior. In addition, if we found such physical evidence in a person whose behavior was conventional, we would not call it mental illness. Furthermore, when a person is "stricken" with mental illness and we discover certain EEG patterns, we rarely have prior EEG information on that individual. Quite possibly, he had the same EEG patterns when he was considered "mentally healthy." Szasz argues that the unconventional behavior itself is not a sign or symptom of illness, but rather necessary and often sufficient evidence of "mental illness." Certainly, unusual behavior can be seen as "physical evidence" of mental illness only through the use of Schoenfeld's own peculiar type of "word magic." For Szasz, then, the fact that the symptoms of mental illness *are* the disease shows the falsity of the medical model. Moreover, even in cases of brain disease such as brain tumors or Huntington's chorea, the metaphor of mental illness is totally misleading. As Szasz maintains throughout *The Myth of Mental Illness,* even in the small percentage of those people who demonstrate organic brain disease, their *behaviors* cannot be understood through chemical-neurological terms.

[It is true that many psychiatrists counter that over the past 10 years or so, schizophrenia has been correlated with a number of physiological and bio-chemical abnormalities. Various studies of dopamine and serotonin imbalances in the brains of schizophrenics as well as endorphin (brain opiates) deficiencies and excesses have led to claims of new proof of the disease and possible cures of the disease of schizophrenia.

All of such efforts leave Dr. Szasz unimpressed regarding mental illness, if not brain disease, for a number of reasons. First, he argues, such findings occur in only a small number of those labeled "mentally ill" and even those cases often do not tell us about whether chemical-neurological changes are causes or effects of the admittedly unusual behavior of "schizophrenics." As one Johns Hopkins psychiatrist notes, "No one knows the answer to that."

Moreover, studies are often inconclusive, contradictory, or problematic. For example, a Hopkins neurobiologist, Dr. Solomon Snyder, writes that studies on increases in dopamine receptors of schizophrenics must be interpreted with caution, as so many complex systems are interacting, such as the effects of neuroleptic drugs taken by the patients. Moreover, regarding studies on endorphins, *Science* magazine concluded recently that "the most certain thing that can now be said of the relationship between brain opiates and mental illness is that nothing is settled."

Second, Dr. Szasz states, if certain behaviors are found to be caused by actual brain diseases, such diseases and behaviors will no longer be considered mental illnesses. In this regard, Dr. Paul Lemkau, professor emeritus of mental hygiene at Hopkins and not a supporter of Dr. Szasz, ruefully acknowledges that when chemical-neurological disorders have been discovered as the reason for behaviors considered to be symptoms of mental illnesses, as was true in the cases of epilepsy or central nervous system syphilis, these disorders have been removed from the purview of psychiatry and no longer considered "mental illnesses."

Last, Dr. Szasz notes, if mental illness were ever defined on physiological or biochemical bases alone, a lot of people who behave "normally" would be diagnosed as mentally ill, including many psychiatrists, and an extraordinary number of people now defined as "mentally ill" would have to receive a clean bill of health. (*The Baltimore Sun* (August 22, 1982): K2)]

•   •   •

Schoenfeld's suggestion that Szasz is unaware that ". . . prison might be just one of those institutions where these various abuses, oppressions, persecutions and tortures that he seeks to avoid actually take place . . ." is both inaccurate and irrelevant. Szasz not only agrees with that but has often argued the need for major change in the prison system himself. However, the inadequacy of the prison system has absolutely nothing to do with the validity or invalidity of Szasz's contention concerning mental illness. It only means that society probably will continue to ignore the inhumane treatment of those in prison just as it ignores what occurs in mental institutions. Szasz's question concerns the notion of medical persons dealing with nonmedical problems and justifying it through the clever, if unconscious, use of language; he is not attempting to prove that prisons are more humane than mental institutions.

In an effort to dispute Szasz's argument that many administrators are servants of the state, not the "patients," Schoenfeld raises the well-established fact that clientele groups have frequently captured the agencies which supposedly regulate them in the public interest. However, the analogy is a poor one. Quite unlike the groups Schoenfeld sees as being able to influence the administrative agencies which regulate them, mental patients do not have their people sitting as administrative judges, administrators, and staff researchers.

Unfortunately, Mr. Schoenfeld, who is a competent scholar with a solid background in problems of law and psychoanalysis, fails to come to grips with the nature of the Szaszian position he seeks to destroy. . . . Again, we find Schoenfeld remiss in his comprehension of Szasz's concepts. . . . It certainly comes as no surprise to us that psychiatrists, and especially institutional psychiatrists, those most threatened by the implications of Szasz's theory, would vociferously denounce him and defend their continued ability to practice a lucrative, high status trade. Nor does it surprise us that many lawyers who criticize Szasz find it difficult to deal with his broad perspective. We feel that if more people actually understood what Dr. Szasz has said, they would be better equipped to handle his arguments; they are simply too important to be dealt with inaccurately or illogically.

Richard E. Vatz, Jonas Rappeport, and Lee S. Weinberg

Comment and Controversy

VATZ: Our topic for tonight deals with the theories of psychiatrist, Dr. Thomas Szasz, professor of psychiatry at the State University of New York in Syracuse, New York. We shall be discussing his views on mental illness as well as other topics. Dr. Szasz's prolific writings are considered by many psychiatrists to be radical and irresponsible, but by many social observers to be both penetrating and enlightening. With me tonight are Professors Jonas Rappeport and Lee S. Weinberg. Dr. Rappeport is the chief medical officer of the Supreme Bench of Baltimore, as well as clinical associate professor of law at the University of Maryland School of Law and assistant professor of psychiatry at the Johns Hopkins University. Professor Weinberg, a colleague and friend of mine, is associate professor of administration of justice and associate director of legal studies at the University of Pittsburgh, and a member of the Pennsylvania bar.

   Gentlemen, Dr. Thomas Szasz has written extensively on psychiatry and mental illness as well as many related areas. His basic premise, I suspect, may be somewhat shocking to our audience. He argues, simply enough, that there is no such thing as mental illness; it is a myth. In our discussion we shall hope to cover at least three questions and their implications regarding this position. First, what if anything is mental illness? Second, what is the proper rule of mental illness in our society; and third, what is the proper role of psychiatry in the courtroom? I should like to begin our discussion by asking Dr. Weinberg to explain

Transcript of a radio program on WBAL, Baltimore, Maryland, February, 1979.

to us what Dr. Szasz means by stating that "mental illness is a myth."
Then I should like to hear Dr. Rappeport's reaction.

WEINBERG: Thank you. I will be representing the views of Dr. Szasz on the
program and trying to explain them in a way that people can understand. I will try to indicate why Dr. Szasz believes institutional
psychiatry to be unethical, immoral, and illegal. His basic position can
be summed up in the claim that mental illness is a myth. For Szasz,
behaviors that are peculiar, difficult to understand, threatening, or
even dangerous, cannot be understood by reference to medical terminology or medical diagnoses; that is, physicians have no particular
expertise which might permit them (any better than anyone else) to deal
with problems of behavior. Dr. Szasz argues that the medicalization of
language is the mechanism by which physicians attempt to regulate
behavior—to deal with what are, in fact, political and social issues.
Basically, I think that the consequences of this are: 1) that there is an
appearance created that the behaviors are being explained; 2) that doctors are enfranchised to take away people's liberties under the guise of
medical treatments; and 3) that there is a belief that because people
behave in "sick" ways we have a duty to do something about it, just as
there is a general belief that we ought to do something about physical
illness when it occurs.

The difference, Dr. Szasz would argue, is that illnesses of the body
reflect a general consensus on the definition of health. However, the
behavior which people come to criticize and view as mental illness is
simply a disagreement on whether or not such behavior should be
permitted.

VATZ: Dr. Rappeport, may we have your comment?

RAPPEPORT: I think that Dr. Thomas Szasz has made some very excellent
contributions towards our taking a new look at institutionalized
psychiatry. On the other hand, I feel that he has used a bunch of fancy
rhetoric and illogical attempts at logical arguments; that is, he has confused the issue and distorted it. There are a tremendous number of
severe errors of fact in the information that he furnishes and, furthermore, he does not furnish us with any acceptable model as a replace-
ment for the one which is generally in use today. There is no question
or doubt about the fact that much of the behavior of the mentally ill is
definitely sickness and may, in fact, in the near future be clearly explained on an organic as well as psychosocial basis. I have no argument
with Szasz saying that some of our conditions in hospitals are horrible;
I have no argument with him saying that on rare occasions psychiatry
has been abused. But he is writing as an adversary, not as a scientist,

and he is just dishonest; he says mental illness is a myth and I say Thomas Szasz's medical honesty is a myth.

VATZ: Let me ask you about one thing that you said which I found to be particularly interesting. You have said that even in a situation within which we cannot discern a medical illness or a physiological imbalance accompanying strange behavior, this does not mean that we will not eventually find such a condition to account for this behavior. Do I understand that to be one of the points which you are making?

RAPPEPORT: That is exactly correct.

VATZ: Dr. Weinberg, would you respond to this?

WEINBERG: First, the notion that behavior is caused by chemical imbalances or neurological conditions is one that Dr. Szasz would find highly questionable, as do I. When we begin to hypothesize that there is a particular chemical or neurological condition which causes a person to act in a particular way, we run into a number of serious logical and methodological problems. For one, we only look for these chemical or neurological conditions in persons whose behavior we find unacceptable for one reason or another. We do not go out and look for these conditions in so-called "normal" people. Also, even if we could show that there was a chemical imbalance associated with a specific behavior, it is likely that other people have the same chemical imbalance, but do not exhibit the strange behavior and, conversely, many other people exhibiting the exact same strange behavior do not share the chemical imbalance. Dr. Szasz would not, I am sure, maintain that behavior occurs in a chemical vaccum. Rather, he would say that there is no way in which a one-to-one correspondence has ever been or could ever be established between chemical-neurological facts and behavior.

VATZ: So Szasz's point is that even if we had full knowledge of an individual's chemical-neurological status, we would still be unable to predict specific behaviors or beliefs from that.

RAPPEPORT: Yes, but the very same thing applies to all medical situations. We don't go around taking blood sugars and blood pressures of people unless they have a complaint. We don't run laboratory tests unless there is some indication of a problem. We're certainly not going to examine the chemistries of people unless they show the symptoms of illness. The symptoms may clearly be in terms of behavior, however. This is the simplistic part of Dr. Szasz's argument that behavior differs from, for example, bleeding or headache. He implies that behavior is not an expression of many other complex mechanisms.

VATZ: In other words, behavior is a symptom, in your view, just like headache is a symptom? And there is no reason, you would argue, Dr. Rappeport, that behavior cannot be a symptom? Is that correct?

RAPPEPORT: Behavior *may* or *may not* be a symptom and I think that Szasz makes a significant contribution when he says to his psychiatric colleagues, "be careful" about explaining student radicalism in the sixties, for instance, in psychiatric terms.

VATZ: That would be an example, then, where you would agree with Dr. Szasz that political analysis is disguised as medical analysis?

RAPPEPORT: Right. If you start putting technical labels on political behavior and explaining it other than in the broadest psycho-social terms, then I think that you are engaging in a very questionable activity. On the other hand, there are certainly behaviors that are unarguably sick.

WEINBERG: I think that Dr. Szasz, however, is not simply saying that the problem with the psychiatric or medical model is that it is abused. He goes beyond that to argue that it is inappropriate because behavior cannot constitute a disease. He points out that in true physiological diseases a person feels pain, for example, which is symptomatic of a medical condition; for instance, a narrowing of the aorta results in chest pain. But behavior, by contrast, is purposive, not symptomatic, although we may not understand these purposes. His point is that this inability to understand motives is the very reason that the behavior is labelled "sick."

VATZ: Well, Dr. Weinberg, isn't it true, as Dr. Rappeport says, that we can view behavior as a symptom of a *mental* illness. What is objectionable or inaccurate about that position?

WEINBERG: First of all, Dr. Szasz would say that so-called mental illness is the only "illness" in which the behavior is the symptom and the symptom is, itself, the disease. The "symptom" does not point to any underlying pathology.

VATZ: In other words, his view would be that mental illness is the only illness in which the appearance of the symptom is sufficient for an inference that a disease is present; in other disease situations one would have to further inquire and collect further evidence of the presence of disease. Symptoms alone would not permit the conclusion that disease was present.

WEINBERG: That is an accurate statement of Dr. Szasz's view.

VATZ: Let me go over one other point that Dr. Rappeport was making. You suggest that Dr. Szasz is overzealous in implying that there are constant political motives in psychiatric diagnosis. You feel he is simply incorrect in this assessment of psychiatrists and that he totally misperceives the situation?

RAPPEPORT: I think that when certain social issues have come up that psychiatrists have been asked to give opinions and that they have been too free in giving them. They may have used certain kinds of professional jargon in these opinions, but I don't believe that they were really saying, "hey, that's a severe illness." Granted, when one does look at behavior and especially deviant behavior you open a large area when you start ascribing labels. You can label all sorts of behavior.

VATZ: So one point I infer from your comments is that Szasz is so general and vague in his conceptions of categories of behavior that he really doesn't leave us with much meaning to understand behavior at all, much less to abandon a medical model.

RAPPEPORT: Szasz favors the same thing that R. D. Laing does and the same thing that certain youth movements do: let it all hang loose; anybody can do whatever they want to do at any time under any circumstances so long as it does not impinge on anyone else.

WEINBERG: I think that is a misreading of both Szasz and Laing. It is a misreading of Szasz in the sense that Szasz would not argue that one should do anything he or she pleases or that there are no consequences. He would argue the opposite, in a sense—namely, that people must recognize that their actions do have consequences and that they must be held responsible for these consequences. The problem with the psychiatric model is that it disguises these matters as medical, when they should be seen as moral and political. Szasz is critical of Laing for his denial that there is such a thing as schizophrenia and then going ahead to treat it nonetheless! Of course, this terminology itself would pose a problem for Szasz in that you cannot treat someone who does not have a disease. Whereas Szasz places the responsibility for human behavior on those who "behave," Laing blames society for the behavior of some schizophrenics who have been victimized by society. Laing, of course, leans to the left of the political spectrum, while Szasz leans to the right.

VATZ: So Szasz would argue, as opposed to Laing, that there is no reason to presume the righteousness of the patient anymore than there is reason to presume the righteousness of the doctor. Let me ask you something, Dr. Weinberg. Dr. Rappeport says that Szasz rails against the medical model and yet does not provide any particular suggestions to replace it. He simply says that people have "problems in living." That seems vague to me too. If everything is a problem in living, then you may as well put everything under that umbrella and you'll have no critical apparatus with which to deal with any types of behavior. How do you, Dr. Weinberg, reconcile your support of Dr. Szasz with Dr. Rappeport's criticism in this area?

WEINBERG: It seems to me that you are asking for new categories and new models to replace the old ones when Dr. Szasz's point is not that we need new categories and new models but *no* categories and *no* models. Or, to put it slightly differently, it seems to me that it is kind of like asking the Nazi death camp operators, "Can you think of a new and better way to solve the Jewish problem?" That question just cannot be answered if you do not believe that there is a problem. And I think that is analogous to what Dr. Szasz is saying.

RAPPEPORT: You are saying that there are human problems, but you also said that Dr. Szasz's suggestion for dealing with them is on an ethical, moral, or social basis. But I feel that he ducks the issue and fails to give us any guidance on *how* to handle these problems in living. As far as I know, he doesn't make any attempt to categorize or organize, but just makes these sort of global suggestions that, well, somehow we will deal with these problems. But, how will we do this? Szasz has said that we should recognize the right of the suicidal individual to take his own life. We should not call this person's severe depression a disease; we should treat this person's decision to kill himself as a competent and rational decision just like the decisions that we and other normal people make every day.

WEINBERG: I think that the suicide issue is one of the more difficult that Szasz has to deal with. I agree with you that it is very difficult to maintain that people have the right to destroy themselves for any reason that they feel warrants such drastic action. I think that if a person came to Dr. Szasz's office, however, and threatened suicide, Dr. Szasz might try to persuade the person not to commit suicide and to work with him to solve his problems in living.

VATZ: Why, if he says that suicide is an inherent right of the individual, would he try to persuade the person not to commit suicide?

WEINBERG: I am just speculating, but I imagine that Dr. Szasz might tell this person, "You obviously have not come here simply to notify me that you are about to commit suicide, because if you want to commit suicide you can do this without me. The fact that you are here suggests that you wish to talk with me about this problem which I will be happy to do."

RAPPEPORT: Now wait a minute. This is merely an assumption you are making. What about the patient who is dropped off at the psychiatrist's office by his spouse or someone else?

WEINBERG: Dr. Szasz would find that objectionable in that the patient has not presented himself for help.

RAPPEPORT: What of the person who is going to commit suicide who says, "I don't want anybody to stop me; I don't want Dr. Szasz; I don't want anybody to interfere."

WEINBERG: I assume Dr. Szasz would respect this person's wishes. But the suicide question presents the most difficult and emotional of Dr. Szasz's ideas.

VATZ: Let me interrupt for just a second. Just to restate, you are saying specifically that Dr. Szasz does not oppose a freely chosen suicide on the grounds that to oppose such an act compromises an individual's autonomy. An individual, in his view, has a singular human right to terminate his own life. Consequently, when convicted murderer Gary Gilmore said that he wished to be executed in accordance with the sentence imposed on him by the judge, and when the American Civil Liberties Union filed a suit to try to stop the execution without Gilmore's compliance, Szasz would say, "Look, just let him alone. If he wishes to commit suicide, let him do it." Is that a correct statement of Dr. Szasz's view?

WEINBERG: That is a correct restatement of this particular point of view, I believe. I think that many, and I would hope the majority, of American psychiatrists would say that in a case such as Gilmore, this is, indeed, his own choice and is similar to the rational decision to commit suicide by a person suffering tremendous pain as a result of terminal cancer. This is a rational choice and should be respected. One of the problems, Dr. Szasz says, is that he does not believe that a psychiatrist can determine on a valid and reliable basis where the line is between a rational and an irrational decision to commit suicide, or anything else for that matter.

VATZ: What do you think about that, Dr. Rappeport?

RAPPEPORT: My contention is that within certain limits one can make a reliable decision as to where the line should be drawn. The lack of perfect knowledge in this situation is not much different from most other decision-making situations which we face individually and collectively as a nation.

WEINBERG: I think that this brings us to the very heart of Dr. Szasz's position. It may or may not be possible to argue that it is rational for a particular person to elect to commit suicide. But what Dr. Szasz would argue to the death (if you will excuse the term in this context) is that whether or not it is a rational decision is not a matter of medicine. That is the crucial idea. It is a matter of religion, ethics, philosophy, morality, or law, but not medicine. The psychiatrist has no better insight as to where to draw the line between rational and irrational choices than does the family, the judge, the neighbor, or the individual himself.

RAPPEPORT: I would strongly disagree. I think at the very least the psychiatrist has the knowledge and understanding or the ability to attain the knowledge of what is going on in the patient sufficiently to inform others if they are empowered to make such decisions.

VATZ: Dr. Rappeport, let me ask you a question on that particular point. Dr. Weinberg has argued, along with Dr. Szasz, that determinations of rationality, whatever else they are, are not medical questions. I don't believe that that is a particular area of dispute between you.

WEINBERG: Excuse me, but I think that it is.

VATZ: Oh, in other words, Dr. Rappeport, you would argue that the determination of rationality, then, *does* have much to do with medicine and medical expertise?

RAPPEPORT: Dr. Weinberg is saying that medical people have nothing to contribute. He is saying that he does not think that the mental health professionals have any particular knowledge that will help in evaluating rationality.

VATZ: Well, then let me ask you this. Let us take an example of a suicidal individual who is brought to a psychiatrist by some friend or relative. Is it your belief that the psychiatrist is uniquely able to evaluate the rationality of that decision to commit suicide? Is there some reason to believe that a psychiatrist has that ability or has it above others in society?

RAPPEPORT: In general terms, yes. There are clearly situations in which many other people would be capable of judging rationality. But I think that there are also particular situations where clinical judgment is necessary. I am not saying that non-psychiatrists cannot develop that clinical judgment when they have been exposed to the clinical experience under the guidance of a trained psychiatrist.

WEINBERG: It seems to me that to the extent that a psychiatrist is better equipped than the cab driver who drove the suicidal individual to the hospital, it may well be a function of his having seen distraught people bent on self-destruction many times before. It is not, therefore, a function of medical school courses or an understanding of which portion of the brain is related to memory, speech, or motor development. It is merely because they have done this over and over again. So, in a sense, I suppose I am agreeing with you, but for a different reason.

RAPPEPORT: I am going to disagree and fall back on something that I don't think you or Dr. Szasz or anyone else can refute, but I can't prove. And that is that I believe there is a certain quality to the experience of medical education that separates those who have it from those who have not been exposed to that experience.

VATZ: With respect to rationality?

RAPPEPORT: With respect to all of the decisions that a physician is expected to make; with respect to a certain understanding of the qualitative dimensions of human suffering that affect various appraisals of human behavior. Now whether some of this can be achieved by others with sufficient experience I am not certain. But I do believe that in appraising the quality of depression in a patient, the medical knowledge of a psychiatrist is of value. We have had pretty good proof of this from the commitments that have been done now by judges and hearing officers, and there is some evidence that once they are educated by experience, and I do not mean merely the experience of seeing it over and over again, but rather hearing the patients and being told what it means, following it up and getting follow-up information and so on, that under those circumstances they attain the ability to make good decisions. Now you are correct; they did not have to go to medical school to do that in a very limited area. They also have been educated by the patients and the psychiatrists.

VATZ: There are many who claim that Szasz escapes through his generalities. They say, "Look, this discussion is academically invigorating, but it is perfectly irrelevant in a practical sense. We have people who are clearly dangerous, whose behavior is extremely peculiar and incomprehensible. What difference does it make what you call them—whether you call them mentally ill or whether you call them unhappy. The fact is that they have to be dealt with by society regardless of what we call them."

WEINBERG: Dr. Szasz believes that there are serious consequences flowing from the labels which we attach to people and their behavior. For instance, when Sarah Jane Moore attempted to assassinate former President Gerald Ford, she was taken to a psychiatrist immediately following her arrest. When a man drove his car through the White House gates, he was sent to a psychiatrist. Why? I think the answer lies in the label attached to their behaviors. Because we call these people "sick" as opposed to political radicals or political dissidents, we believe they should be "examined" by psychiatrists.

RAPPEPORT: Now wait a minute. Don't pull a Szaszian mistake like that. What about individuals who are not politically motivated at all and give the sickest of sick reasons, such as that voices told them to deliver the Koran and the New Testament and the Old Testament. . . .

VATZ: Let me just make sure that I understand exactly the opposing points here. Your argument, Dr. Rappeport, as I understand it, is that the examples of Dr. Weinberg may be fairly discernible in terms of motivation. In fact, however, there are some actions that are committed for no discernible motivation whatsoever. They are simply sick—people acting in a way that is totally incomprehensible. Now surely we are talking here about people whose behavior is sick. Dr. Weinberg, what is your reaction to that?

WEINBERG: That begs the entire question because the issue is, can behavior in any way be interpreted as a matter of illness or disease, or is the use of the term "illness" here really a metaphoric one. It seems to me that the behaviors which are the most outrageous and infuriating are the very ones most likely to be called sick. So, therefore, I disagree that a psychiatrist, having talked with a person such as we are discussing here, and probably not at great length at that, can determine the motives for his acts. The person claims to have heard voices. We know that we have not heard these voices, that the psychiatrist has not heard these voices; all we know and all the psychiatrist can know is that the person says he has heard voices. But, why do we believe this?

VATZ: But aren't there people who act incomprehensibly and without any reasonable motivation, such as "Son of Sam"?

WEINBERG: Well, they act incomprehensibly to most observers, yes. But the fact that it is totally incomprehensible does not prove that it is not reasonable to the person himself or that it is related to any illness. All it means is that we are not able to understand or to condone the behavior.

RAPPEPORT: But psychiatry does just that. We say and attempt to understand just what and why the patient's behavior is what it is. The difference may be that we give it a label and in framing it we then state that their sickness is unrealistic behavior. In every paranoid delusional system, you know, there is a bit of reality. There is always a core of reality. Those people who can read schizophrenia well enough can read and give meaning to the oddest, most bizarre expressions of the schizophrenic patient.

VATZ: Dr. Rappeport, let me interject a few questions here if I may. One of the implications I infer from Dr. Weinberg's comments is that the fact that an act appears to be singularly incomprehensible does not mean that there *is* no meaning. It simply means that the observers are not competent to impose the correct meaning. In other words, Son of Sam, to use perhaps an unfortunate and overused example, may have been motivated by matters that may not have motivated you, me, Dr. Weinberg, or Dr. Szasz. We cannot infer, however, that there was no motivation; all we can say is that we do not see how he could have done what he did.

WEINBERG: He may have wanted a tremendous amount of attention; he may have wanted to commit suicide, but preferred that the state execute him; there may have been a great number of reasons. But, and this is the point, they were not medical and it is not a physician's job to assess the rationality of those reasons.

RAPPEPORT: Why not?

WEINBERG: Because, as Dr. Szasz argues, medical training is not based on ethics, morality, and politics. It is based on physiology, biology, and chemistry.

RAPPEPORT: Why must all human behavior be based on ethics, morality, and politics?

WEINBERG: Because that, in Szasz's view, is the very nature of "humanness." To be autonomous, to make decisions, is what life is all about and why it is so difficult to deal with problems in living.

VATZ: Well, then, what really are the consequences of looking at behavior as medical? Doesn't Szasz argue that unrequested medical intrusions are criminal?

WEINBERG: I think Dr. Szasz's position is that this may well be criminal in cases where people are drugged, imprisoned, or otherwise "treated" against their will. But I don't think he is really advocating going around and arresting psychiatrists right off the bat.

RAPPEPORT: That's reassuring.

WEINBERG: I think that what he might want to do is to make known to people that this type of thing is going on—that liberties are being infringed in the name of medicine. And he believes that once they are recognized as a facade—a disguised form of oppression—they will be rejected by patients and society.

VATZ: Do you agree, Dr. Rappeport?

RAPPEPORT: Do I agree that the patients will be less willing to accept it?

WEINBERG: The people you call patients.

VATZ: Why do you say the people that you call "patients"?

WEINBERG: Because to call someone a patient, first of all, suggests that he has some sort of disease or illness.

RAPPEPORT: Well, I don't think the patients will have any trouble being called patients. I have observed too much horrible human suffering in people, some of whom say, "No, I don't want help, I don't want medicine," and then they stand there with their arm extended and say "give me a shot."

VATZ: Dr. Rappeport's point is important. Let us say that a person gives an initial indication of lack of desire to have a drug and yet, after you inject him with the drug, you can get a person who is very depressed to feel better and thank you profusely.

WEINBERG: In the first place, Dr. Szasz would agree that the drug might make this person feel better. Drugs do affect mood and behavior. What he would say is that the question is not whether the drug will work, the question is whether the person was willing to ingest it.

RAPPEPORT: Tom Szasz argues from a rigid philosophical position and I think that the "thank you theory" is based on the practical fact that people who are hurting badly may be so confused that they refuse what will eventually help them and for which they will say thank you. It is like what children sometimes do to their parents when they grow up; they sometimes say thank you, even though they may have cussed at them quite a bit while they were growing up.

WEINBERG: In your discussion of the "thank you theory" you analogized people with problems in living to children and I think that Dr. Szasz and John Stuart Mill and others would agree that children are not always the best judge of what is in their own interests. But I think that they would also maintain that adults are the best judges of what is in their interest. Further, I don't think that Szasz would disagree that people do, sometimes, say thank you for medication they have been forced to take. But there is a great danger in allowing the "thank you theory" into our lives; namely, that we then allow government or psychiatry or a combination of the two to justify all sorts of policies on the basis that we will later say thank you! That kind of paternalistic thinking scares me.

VATZ: Let me bring up a point that Szasz makes which is critical. He has often objected to involuntary incarceration in mental hospitals. Does Dr. Szasz believe that there are no circumstances under which we should allow a person to be involuntarily committed to a mental hospital? Do you agree, Dr. Weinberg?

WEINBERG: Dr. Szasz is opposed to involuntary civil commitment in all cases. Most states now use some type of system of predicted dangerousness as a basis for commitment and psychiatrists play the key role in this prediction. Szasz would rather deal with dangerousness along the same lines as we deal with the crime of attempt. Until someone actually does something dangerous to others, he should not be deprived of his liberty. And if he only does something dangerous to himself he should not be deprived of his liberty either.

RAPPEPORT: Szasz wouldn't put them in a hospital anyhow. Szasz would put them in jail!

WEINBERG: And I agree with him on that point.

VATZ: One of the interesting things that may strike our listeners is the implication that Dr. Szasz sides with political conservatives on the issue of punishment. Those who believe we have too many lenient judges may find a great deal of camaraderie with Thomas Szasz. We are arguing that our penal system should be much more rigorous, much harder on criminal offenders and this is, I take it, what Dr. Szasz is advocating Dr. Rappeport, let me throw you the question I asked Dr. Weinberg.

Under what conditions would you say that a person should be involuntarily committed to a mental hospital?

RAPPEPORT: I can make a very general statement on that issue. That is, I think in our society someone has to be in the position of making the decision to commit a person where the person is unable to adequately care for himself and to look out for his own health and safety, and possibly the safety of others. This decision-making needs to be done by someone before he does something which places him in the criminal justice system. At what level the decision is made, when the decision is made, and who makes the decision must, of course, all be determined by law and within the constitutional order. Now the pendulum in the history of our society has swung back and forth between a very liberal theory of giving this responsibility to medical people, to a very rigid demand that the criminal justice system handle these issues. At the moment, we have swung pretty much to the judicial determination of these issues.

VATZ: Let me ask you this question, Dr. Rappeport. I do not recall the particulars of the matter, but during the past year, Maryland released a mental patient who had committed a violent act against a child. There were cries from the public and in the newspapers that the procedures for releasing such people are too lax. Now, I am wondering if psychiatrists are charged with the responsibility for predicting future dangerousness, is there not a substantial risk that they may become rather conservative; that to err on the side of keeping people from their freedom may be to their ultimate advantage? As long as a person is not released early, the psychiatrist cannot be held responsible.

RAPPEPORT: No. I can state that psychiatrists cannot predict long-term future behavior better than anyone else. Short-term behavior, yes—days, weeks, a couple of months, absolutely. But long-term behavior I do not feel can be predicted by anyone, and, therefore, I think that it has been made very clear that whoever is the decision maker—whether it is the parole board, the psychiatrist, the judge, anyone—is going to err on the side of caution.

WEINBERG: Dr. Vatz, I just have one comment. Dr. Rappeport indicates his own skepticism of the abilities of psychiatrists to predict long-term behavior patterns. Recently, attorney Melvin Belli stated that he thinks much more of your abilities than you apparently do. He says that psychiatry and psychology have progressed far enough that we are now able to tell those who should never be let out. He goes further to say that we might even be able to do this before they run afoul of the law.

So there are many people, I believe, who have a great deal more faith in the expert predictions of psychiatrists than you do.

RAPPEPORT: Well, having Melvin Belli, bless his heart, have more faith in us is not, I suspect, necessarily useful.

VATZ: I think this leads us into a critical aspect of psychiatry that Szasz is quite concerned with in his work: the role of the psychiatrist in the courtroom with respect to the insanity plea. I think that the public, somewhat incorrectly, perceives the insanity plea as a method through which dangerous criminal defendants are freed.

WEINBERG: In fact, often the defendant acquitted by reason of insanity is subject to a commitment process which keeps him incarcerated for long periods of time, even life.

RAPPEPORT: The use of the insanity defense is exceedingly rare. In Baltimore, we have something in the area of 4000 criminal trials per year and I think between 2 and 5 people were found not guilty by reason of insanity. There are cases, of course, where a person found not guilty by reason of insanity will spend more time in hospitals than he would have had he been found guilty and sentenced under the criminal law. I can't say that this will never happen again, although most state laws have altered this situation in recent years.

VATZ: One of the beauties of Thomas Szasz's views is that he is so unambiguous in many of his claims including his view that the insanity defense should be abolished. What do you both think of that suggestion?

RAPPEPORT: My reaction to Szasz's idea that people should be held responsible regardless of whether or not they are horribly mentally deficient? I totally disagree. I think that the insanity plea supports many of society's purposes. It is a socio-legal decision whether or not a person is responsible and I think that professional psychiatrists can assist. I give opinions: I do not make decisions in these areas. By the way, note that Szasz is willing to make exceptions to this rigid responsibility model for the young, growing mind, but not for the sick mind. This is where I challenge his purpose and his logic, for if we recognize the one (as we do and should) why not recognize the other?

●   ●   ●

VATZ: O.K., I would like to get to one final point which is important in the legal aspect of psychiatry. One of the aspects about which the public is not substantially informed is the declaration of a defendant as competent or incompetent to stand trial in the first place. I would like to know what Dr. Szasz feels about this procedure?

WEINBERG: Dr. Szasz would probably argue that whether or not a person is competent to stand trial due to his mental state is not a medical matter. People are assumed to be competent. The question, of course, is really whether or not the client understands the charges against him and can assist his attorney in the preparation of his legal defense. And whether or not one can play the role of client and defendant adequately is not a matter of medicine.

RAPPEPORT: But does Szasz even accept this as an issue? Doesn't he say we should never allow a finding of incompetence? Isn't he really saying that if you are charged with a crime you should stand trial. If you can't assist your lawyer and do not understand what is going on, that is tough luck? That seems to be what he is saying.

WEINBERG: His central point is that this is not medical. I am not sure if he would agree with your characterization of his position on this one, i.e., that there are literally no circumstances in which a trial should be delayed because the defendant cannot meaningfully participate.

RAPPEPORT: I agree. The final decision is not medical. This is a legal and social question to be determined by legislatures, judges, and lawyers. I do feel, however, that the psychiatrist has a great deal to contribute to that decision by examining and explaining facts to the court.

VATZ: Let me summarize the two positions here. As I understand Dr. Weinberg's point, there may be questions of competency, but the psychiatrist's expertise is irrelevant to such a determination; and I understand Dr. Rappeport's position to be that psychiatrists do have substantial expertise in this area and should be allowed to testify in court on this issue.

Our time is up. I want to thank both of you for this enlightening and lively discussion of the views of Thomas Szasz. Good night.

References to Works by Thomas S. Szasz

Chapter 1

Autonomy

1. *The Second Sin* (Garden City, New York: Doubleday Anchor, 1973), p. 38.
2. Ibid., p. 39.
3. *The Theology of Medicine: The Political-Philosophical Foundations of Medical Ethics* (New York: Harper Colophon, 1977), pp. xiii–xv.
4. Ibid., pp. xvi–xix.
5. Ibid., pp. xix–xxii.
6. Ibid., pp. 68–75.
7. Ibid., pp. 81–85.
8. *Law, Liberty, and Psychiatry: An Inquiry into the Special Uses of Mental Health Practices* (New York: Macmillan, 1963), pp. 5–6.
9. *The Ethics of Psychoanalysis: The Theory and Method of Autonomous Psychotherapy* (New York: Basic Books, 1965), pp. 22–25.

Chapter 2

Authenticity and Humanism

1. *The Second Sin*, p. 70.
2. Ibid., p. 88.

3. *Heresies* (Garden City, New York: Doubleday Anchor, 1976), p. 127.
4. *The Theology of Medicine*, pp. 76–78.
5. *Law, Liberty, and Psychiatry*, pp. 14–15.
6. Ibid., pp. 54–56.
7. *The Theology of Medicine*, pp. 86–88.
8. Ibid., pp. 89–95.
9. Ibid., pp. 95–96.
10. Ibid., pp. 96–99.
11. *The Ethics of Psychoanalysis*, pp. 13–18.

Chapter 3

Mental Illness Is a Myth

1. *The Second Sin*, p. 87.
2. Ibid., p. 88.
3. *The Myth of Mental Illness: Foundations of a Theory of Personal Conduct* (New York: Harper and Row, 1974), pp. 1–2.
4. Ibid., pp. 11–13.
5. Ibid., pp. x–xii.
6. *Ideology and Insanity: Essays on the Psychiatric Dehumanization of Man* (Garden City, New York: Doubleday Anchor, 1970), pp. 21–24.
7. *The Myth of Mental Illness*, pp. 101–102.
8. Ibid., pp. 222–230.
9. Ibid., pp. 125–140.
10. Ibid., pp. 141–147.
11. *Schizophrenia: The Sacred Symbol of Psychiatry* (New York: Basic Books, 1976), pp. xii–xiv.
12. Ibid., pp. 9–17.
13. "Schizophrenia: A Category Error," *Trends in NeuroSciences* 1 (July, 1978): 26–28.

Chapter 4

Mental Therapy Is a Myth

1. *Heresies*, p. 167.
2. *The Myth of Psychotherapy: Mental Healing as Religion, Rhetoric, and Repression* (Garden City, New York: Doubleday Anchor, 1978), pp. xvii–xxiii.
3. Ibid., pp. 3–10.

4. Ibid., pp. 11–16.

Chapter 5

Deviant Behavior Is Freedom of Choice

1. *The Second Sin*, p. 71.
2. *Ceremonial Chemistry: The Ritual Persecution of Drugs, Addicts, and Pushers* (Garden City, New York: Doubleday, 1974), pp. 164–170.
3. Ibid., pp. 50–51.
4. "The Ethics of Addiction," *Harper's* (April, 1972): 74–79.
5. *Ceremonial Chemistry*, pp. 53–54.
6. "Bad Habits Are Not Diseases: A Refutation of the Claim that Alcoholism Is a Disease," *The Lancet* [London] 2 (July 8, 1972): 83–84.
7. *Sex By Prescription* (Garden City, New York: Doubleday, 1980), pp. xi–xvi.
8. Ibid., pp. 4–9.
9. "Some Call It Brainwashing," *The New Republic* (March 6, 1976): 10–12.

Chapter 6

Forensic Psychiatry Is Fraudulent

1. *Heresies*, p. 53.
2. "Psychiatric Diversion in the Criminal Justice System: A Critique," in Randy Barnett and John Hagel III, (eds.) *Assessing the Criminal: Restitution, Retribution, and the Legal Process* (Cambridge, Massachusetts: Ballinger, 1977), pp. 110–120.
3. *Law, Liberty, and Psychiatry*, pp. 228–230.
4. "Reagan Should Let the Jurors Judge Hinckley," *The Washington Post* (May 6, 1981): A-19.
5. *Law, Liberty, and Psychiatry*, pp. 45–48.
6. Ibid., pp. 226–228.
7. Ibid., pp. 230–236.

Chapter 7

Three Questions and Answers on Contentions

1. *The Ethics of Psychoanalysis*, pp. 130–136.

2. *Sex By Prescription,* pp. 9-10.
3. *Schizophrenia,* pp. 98-102.
4. Ibid., pp. 125-127.
5. Ibid., pp. 48-53.
6. Ibid., pp. 212-214.

The Complete List of the Works of Thomas S. Szasz

1. "The 'Schemm Regime' in the Treatment of Extreme Congestive Heart Failure: A Case Report." *Ohio State Medical Journal* 43 (September, 1947): 926–928. [with S. Elgart]
2. "The Role of Hostility in the Pathogenesis of Peptic Ulcer: Theoretical Considerations with the Report of a Case." *Psychosomatic Medicine* 9 (September–October, 1947): 331–336. [with E. Levin, J. B. Kirsner, and W. L. Palmer]
3. Psychiatric Aspects of Vagotomy: A Preliminary Report." *Annals of Internal Medicine* 28 (February, 1948): 279–288.
4. "Psychiatric Aspects of Vagotomy: II. A Psychiatric Study of Vagotomized Ulcer Patients with Comments on Prognosis." *Psychosomatic Medicine* 11 (July–August, 1948): 187–199.
5. "Psychiatric Aspects of Vagotomy: IV. Phantom Ulcer Pain." *Archives of Neurology and Psychiatry* 62 (December, 1949): 728–733.
6. "Factors in the Pathogenesis of Peptic Ulcers." *Psychosomatic Medicine* 11 (September–October, 1949): 300–304.
7. "Psychosomatic Aspects of Salivary Activity: I. Hypersalivation in Patients with Peptic Ulcer." In *Life Stress and Bodily Disease: Proceedings of the Association for Research in Nervous and Mental Disease* 29 (1950): 647–655.
8. "Psychosomatic Aspects of Salivary Activity: II. Psychoanalytic Observations Concerning Hypersalivation." *Psychosomatic Medicine* 12 (September–October, 1950): 320–331.
9. "A Theory of the Pathogenesis of Ordinary Human Baldness." *Archives of Dermatology and Syphilis* 61 (January, 1950): 34–48. [with A. Robertson]
10. "Physiologic and Psychodynamic Mechanisms in Constipation and Diarrhea." *Psychosomatic Medicine* 13 March–April, 1951): 112–116.
11. "Oral Mechanisms in Constipation and Diarrhea." *International Journal of Psycho-Analysis* 32 (1951): 196–203.

237

12. "On the Psychoanalytic Theory of Instincts." *Psychoanalytic Quarterly* 21 (January, 1952): 25–48.
13. "Psychoanalysis and the Autonomic Nervous System." *Psychoanalytic Review* 39 (April, 1952): 115–151.
14. Psychiatric Aspects of Vagotomy: III. The Problem of Diarrhea After Vagotomy." *Journal of Nervous and Mental Disease* 115 (May, 1952): 394–405.
15. "The Psychosomatic Approach in Medicine." In *Dynamic Psychiatry,* edited by Franz Alexander and Helen Ross. Chicago: The University of Chicago Press, 1952. Chapter 12, pp. 369–400.
16. "Psychosomatic Research." In *Twenty Years of Psychoanalysis,* edited by Franz Alexander and Helen Ross. New York: W. W. Norton & Co., 1953, pp. 248–280.
17. "Entropy, Organization, and the Problem of the Economy of Human Relationships." *International Journal of Psycho-Analysis* 36 (1955): 287–297.
18. "The Nature of Pain." *American Medical Association Archives of Neurology and Psychiatry* 73 (August, 1955): 174–181.
19. "The Ego, the Body, and Pain." *Journal of the American Psychoanalytic Association* 3 (1955): 177–200.
20. "On the Experiences of the Analyst in the Psychoanalytic Situation: A Contribution to the Theory of Psychoanalytic Treatment." *Journal of the American Psychoanalytic Association* 4 (1956): 197–223.
21. "Is the Concept of Entropy Relevant to Psychology and Psychiatry?" *Psychiatry* 19 (May, 1956): 199–202.
22. "Some Observations on the Relationship Between Psychiatry and the Law." *American Medical Association Archives of Neurology and Psychiatry* 75 (March, 1956): 297–315.
23. "A Contribution to the Philosophy of Medicine: The Basic Models of the Doctor-Patient Relationship." *American Medical Association Archives of Internal Medicine* 97 (May, 1956): 585–592. [with M. H. Hollender]
24. "Malingering: 'Diagnosis' or Social Condemnation? Analysis of the Meaning of 'Diagnosis' in the Light of Some Interrelations of Social Structure, Value Judgment, and the Physician's Role." *American Medical Association Archives of Neurology and Psychiatry* 76 (October, 1956): 432–433.
25. "Comments on 'The Definition of Psychosomatic Disorder.'" *British Journal of the Philosophy of Science* 7 (1956): 231–234.
26. "Some Observations on the Use of Tranquilizing Drugs." *American Medical Association Archives of Neurology and Psychiatry* 77 (January, 1957): 86–92.
27. "The Psychology of Bodily Feelings in Schizophrenia." *Psychosomatic Medicine* 19 (1956): 11–16.
28. "A Contribution to the Psychology of Bodily Feelings." *Psychoanalytic Quarterly* 26 (1957): 25–49.
29. "A Critical Analysis of the Fundamental Concepts of Psychical Research." *Psychiatric Quarterly* 31 (1957): 96–108.
30. Review of *The Criminal, the Judge, and the Public* by Franz Alexander and Hugo Staub (revised edition). Chicago: The Free Press, 1956. *American Medical Association Archives of Neurology and Psychiatry* 78 (July, 1957): 109–111.
31. "On the Theory of Psycho-analytic Treatment." *International Journal of Psycho-Analysis* 38 (1957): 166–182.

32. "A Contribution to the Psychology of Schizophrenia." *American Medical Association Archives of Neurology and Psychiatry* 77 (April, 1957): 420–436.
33. *Pain and Pleasure: A Study of Bodily Feelings.* New York: Basic Books, Inc., 1957; London: Tavistock Publications, 1957.
34. "Commitment of the Mentally Ill: 'Treatment' or Social Restraint?" *Journal of Nervous and Mental Disease* 125 (April–June, 1957): 293–307.
35. "The Concept of Testamentary Capacity: Further Observations on the Role of Psychiatric Concepts in Legal Situations." *Journal of Nervous and Mental Disease* 125 (July–September, 1957): 474–477.
36. "Psychiatric Expert Testimony: Its Covert Meaning and Social Function." *Psychiatry* 20 (August, 1957): 313–316.
37. Review of *Psychiatric Research Reports* Nos. 2, 4, and 6. Washington, D.C.: The American Psychiatric Association (1955–1956). *Mental Hygiene* 41 (October, 1957): 583–584.
38. "Normality, Neurosis, and Psychosis: Some Observations on the Concepts of Mental Health and Mental Illness." *Journal of Nervous and Mental Disease* 125 (October–December, 1957): 599–607. [with M. H. Hollender]
39. "The Problem of Psychiatric Nosology: A Contribution to a Situational Analysis of Psychiatric Operations." *American Journal of Psychiatry* 114 (November, 1957): 405–413.
40. Review of *Psychical Research* by R. C. Johnson. New York: Philosophical Library, Inc., 1956. *American Journal of Psychiatry* 114 (November, 1957): 475–476.
41. "Psychiatry, Ethics, and the Criminal Law." *Columbia Law Review* 58 (February, 1958): 183–198.
42. "Scientific Method and Social Role in Medicine and Psychiatry." *American Medical Association Archives of Internal Medicine* 101 (February, 1958): 228–238.
43. "Men and Medicine." *British Journal of the Philosophy of Science* 8 (February, 1958): 310–317.
44. "Psychoanalysis as Method and as Theory." *Psychoanalytic Quarterly* 27 (1958): 89–97.
45. "The Role of the Counterphobic Mechanism in Addiction." *Journal of the American Psychoanalytic Association* 6 (1958): 309–325.
46. Reply to Ian Stevenson, M.D. [correspondence] *American Journal of Psychiatry* 114 (March, 1958): 847–848.
47. "Recent Books on the Relation of Psychiatry to Criminology. *Psychiatry* 21 (August, 1958): 307–319. [a review article]
48. "Psycho-analytic Training: A Socio-psychological Analysis of Its History and Present Status." *International Journal of Psycho-Analysis* 39 (1958): 598–613.
49. "The Doctor-Patient Relationship and Its Historical Context." *American Journal of Psychiatry* 115 (December, 1958): 522–528. [with W. F. Knoff and M. H. Hollender]
50. Review of *Studies in Hysteria* by Joseph Breuer and Sigmund Freud. New York: Basic Books, Inc., 1957. *American Journal of Psychiatry* 115 (December, 1958): 568–569.
51. "Politics and Health: Some Remarks Apropos of the Case of Mr. Ezra Pound." *American Journal of Psychiatry* 115 (December, 1958): 508–511.

52. "A Critical Analysis of Some Aspects of the Libido Theory: The Concepts of Libidinal Zones, Aims, and Modes of Gratification." In *Conceptual and Methodological Problems in Psychoanalysis*. L. Bellak, Cons. Editor. *Annals of the New York Academy of Science* 76 (January 23, 1959): 975-990. [Discussion, pp. 990-1009]
53. "The Classification of 'Mental Illness': A Situational Analysis of Psychiatric Operations." *Psychiatric Quarterly* 33 (January, 1959): 77-101.
54. "Law for the Mentally Ill." [Letter to the Editor] *The New York Times* (Friday, February 20, 1959): 24 [with R. Seidenberg]
55. "Psychoanalysis and Medicine." In *Readings in Psychoanalytic Psychology*, edited by Morton Levitt. New York: Appleton-Century-Crofts, Inc., 1959. Chapter 24, pp. 355-374.
56. "Pound, Politics, and Mental Health." [correspondence] *American Journal of Psychiatry* 115 (May, 1959): 1040-1041.
57. Review of *Economics of Mental Illness* by Rashi Fein. New York: Basic Books, Inc., 1958. *American Medical Association Archives of General Psychiatry* 1 (July, 1959): 116-118.
58. "Language and Pain." In *American Handbook of Psychiatry*, edited by S. Arieti. New York: Basic Books, Inc., 1959. Vol. I. Chapter 49, pp. 982-999.
59. "Introduction." In *The Analysis of Sensations, and the Relation of the Physical to the Psychical* by E. Mach. (Translated from the First German Edition by C. M. Williams; revised and supplemented from the Fifth German Edition by S. Waterlow; with a New Introduction by T. S. Szasz.) New York: Dover Publications, Inc., 1959, pp. v-xxxi.
60. "Recollections of a Psychoanalytic Psychotherapy: The Case of 'Prisoner K.'" In *Case Studies in Counseling and Psychotherapy*, edited by A. Burton. Englewood Cliffs, New Jersey: Prentice-Hall, Inc., 1959. Chapter 4, pp. 75-100.
61. "What Is Malingering?" *Medical Trial Technique Quarterly* 6 (September, 1959): 29-40.
62. "Psychiatry, Psychotherapy, and Psychology." *American Medical Association Archives of General Psychiatry* 1 (November, 1959): 455-463.
63. "The Communication of Distress Between Child and Parent." *British Journal of Medical Psychology* 32 (1959): 161-170.
64. "Mach and Psychoanalysis." *Journal of Nervous and Mental Disease* 130 (January, 1960): 6-15.
65. "Psychiatry Shouldn't Interfere with the Law." [Letter to the Editor] *The New York Herald Tribune* (Friday, February 5, 1960): 10.
66. "Calls Recent Request 'Abuse of Psychiatrist.'" [Reader's Forum] Reprinted from *The New York Herald Tribune* (Friday, February 5, 1960): 10. *The Tablet* (Saturday, February 13, 1960): 6.
67. "The Myth of Mental Illness." *American Psychologist* 15 (February, 1960): 113-118.
68. "Freedom and the Physician's Role." [correspondence] *Journal of the American Medical Association* 173 (May 7, 1960): 84-85.
69. "Hospital Refusal to Release Mental Patient." *Cleveland-Marshall Law Review* 9 (May, 1960): 220-226.
70. "Moral Conflict and Psychiatry." *Yale Review* 49 (June, 1960): 555-566.

71. "Three Problems in Contemporary Psychoanalytic Training." *American Medical Association Archives of General Psychiatry* 3 (July, 1960): 82-94.
72. "Civil Liberties and Mental Illness: Some Observations on the Case of Miss Edith L. Hough." *Journal of Nervous and Mental Disease* 131 (July, 1960): 58-63.
73. "Civil Liberties and the Mentally Ill." *Cleveland-Marshall Law Review* 9 (September, 1960): 399-416.
74. "The Right to Commit a Crime." [Reprint-condensation of "Moral Conflict and Psychiatry." *Yale Review* (Summer, 1960)]. *Current* (September, 1960): 53-54.
75. "The Ethics of Birth Control. Or: Who Owns Your Body?" *The Humanist* 20 (November-December, 1960): 332-336.
76. "The Uses of Naming and the Origin of the Myth of Mental Illness." *American Psychologist* 16 (February, 1961): 59-65.
77. "Hospital-Patient Relationships in Medicine and Psychiatry." *Mental Hygiene* 45 (April, 1961): 171-179.
78. "Psychoanalysis — Modified, Purified, and Basic." [Reviews of *Psychoanalysis and the Family Neurosis* by Martin Grotjahn, New York: W. W. Norton, 1960; *The Structure of Psychoanalytic Therapy: A Systematizing Attempt* by David Rapaport, New York: International Universities Press, 1960; and *Basic Theory of Psychoanalysis* by Robert Waelder, New York: International Universities, Press, 1960.] *Contemporary Psychology* 6 (April, 1961): 118-121.
79. "And One For All." [Review of *The Couch and the Circle* by Hyman Spotnitz, New York: A. A. Knopf, 1961.] *New York Times Book Review* (May 14, 1961): 7.
80. "The Meaning of Suffering in Therapy: A Round Table Discussion." *American Journal of Psychoanalysis* 21 (1961): 12-17.
81. *The Myth of Mental Illness: Foundations of a Theory of Personal Conduct.* New York: Hoeber-Harper, 1961.
82. "Two Types of Therapy." [Reply to Letters to the Editor] *New York Times Book Review* (June 11, 1961): 28-30.
83. "Criminal Responsibility and Psychiatry." In *Legal and Criminal Psychology,* edited by H. Toch. New York: Holt, Rinehart and Winston, Inc., 1961. Chapter 7, pp. 146-148.
84. "The Problem of Privacy in Training Analysis: Selections from a Questionnaire Study of Psychoanalytic Practices and Opinions." *Psychiatry* 25 (August, 1962): 195-207.
85. "Psychiatry as a Social Institution." In *Psychiatry and Responsibility,* edited by H. Schoeck and J. W. Wiggins. Princeton, New Jersey: D. Van Nostrand Co., 1962. Chapter 1, pp. 1-18.
86. Review of *Pain: Its Modes and Functions* by F. J. J. Buytendijk. Chicago: University of Chicago Press, 1962. *American Medical Association Archives of General Psychiatry* 7 (September, 1962): 220.
87. "Bootlegging Humanistic Values Through Psychiatry." *Antioch Review* 22 (Fall, 1962): 341-349.
88. "Mind Trapping: Psychiatric Subversion of Constitutional Rights." *American Journal of Psychiatry* 119 (October, 1962): 323-327.
89. "Human Nature and Psychotherapy: A Further Contribution to the Theory of

Autonomous Psychotherapy." *Comprehensive Psychiatry* 3 (October, 1962): 283.

90. "Open Doors or Civil Rights for Mental Patients?" *Journal of Individual Psychology* 18 (November, 1962): 168-171.

91. "Psychiatry's Threat to Civil Liberties." *National Review* 14 (March 12, 1963): 191-192.

92. "Mind Trapping." [correspondence] *American Journal of Psychiatry* 119 (March, 1963): 900.

93. "Psychiatry in Public Schools." *The Humanist* 23 (May-June, 1963): 89-93.

94. "Freud as a Leader." *Antioch Review* 23 (Summer, 1963): 113-144.

95. "Psychoanalytic Treatment as Education." *American Medical Association Archives of General Psychiatry* 9 (July, 1963): 46-52.

96. "Foreword." In *A Textbook of Abnormal Psychology* by N. H. Pronko. Baltimore: Williams & Wilkins Co., 1963, pp. vii-viii.

97. "Psychoanalysis and Suggestion: An Historical and Logical Analysis." *Comprehensive Psychiatry* 4 (August, 1963): 271-280.

98. "A Questionnaire Study of Psychoanalytic Practices and Opinions." *Journal of Nervous and Mental Disease* 137 (September, 1963): 209-221. [with R. A. Nemiroff]

99. *Law, Liberty, and Psychiatry: An Inquiry into the Social Uses of Mental Health Practices.* New York: Macmillan Co., 1963.

100. "The Concept of Transference." *International Journal of Psycho-Analysis* 44 (1963): 432-443.

101. "Discussion of Papers on Schizophrenia by Drs. Arieti, Azima, Bychowski, and Mme. Sechehaye." *Psychiatric Research Report* 17 (November, 1963): 57-60.

102. "Should 'Insanity' Be an Excuse for Crime?" *North American Newspaper Alliance* (December 28, 1963).

103. "What Psychiatry Can and Cannot Do." *Harper's Magazine* 228 (February, 1964): 50-53.

104. "What Psychiatry Can Do." *Harper's Magazine* 228 (April, 1964): 100. [a reply]

105 "A Question of Identity." *New York Times Book Review* (April 5, 1964): 14, 16.

106. Review of *The Birth and Death of Meaning* by Ernest Becker. New York: The Free Press, 1962; and *The Revolution in Psychiatry.* New York: The Free Press, 1964. *The Behavioral Sciences Book Service* (October, 1964).

107. "Psychoanalysis and Taxation: A Contribution to the Rhetoric of the Disease Concept in Psychiatry." *American Journal of Psychotherapy* 18 (October, 1964): 635-643.

108. "Criminal Insanity: Fact or Strategy?" *The New Republic* (November 21, 1964): 19-22.

109. "The Moral Dilemma of Psychiatry: Autonomy or Heteronomy?" *American Journal of Psychiatry* 121 (December, 1964): 521-528.

110. "Psychiatry as Ideology." In *The Rationalist Annual, For the Year 1965,* edited by H. Hawton. London: Pemberton Publishing Co., Ltd., 1965, pp. 43-52.

111. "Legal and Moral Aspects of Homosexuality." In *Sexual Inversion: The Multiple Roots of Homosexuality,* edited by J. Marmor. New York: Basic Books, Inc., 1965. Chapter 7, pp. 124-139.

112. "A Strategy of Freedom: The Moral Dimension of Freudian Therapy." *Transaction* 2 (May-June, 1965): 14-19.
113. *The Ethics of Psychoanalysis: The Theory and Method of Autonomous Psychotherapy.* New York: Basic Books, Inc., 1965.
114. "A Note on Psychiatric Rhetoric." *American Journal of Psychiatry* 121 (June, 1965): 1192-1193.
115. *Psychiatric Justice.* New York: Macmillan Co., 1965.
116. "Portrait of a Secular Moralist." *The New Republic* (November 27, 1965): 32-33.
117. "Toward the Therapeutic State." *The New Republic* (December 11, 1965): 26-29.
118. Review of *The Addict and the Law* by Alfred R. Lindesmith. Bloomington, Indiana: Indiana University Press, 1965. *American University Law Review* 15 (December, 1965): 163-168; Reprinted in *International Journal of Addictions* 1 (January, 1966): 150-155.
119. "Equation of Opposites." *The New York Times Book Review* (February 6, 1966): 6.
120. "Discussion of 'The New Technology and Our Ageless Unconscious.'" *Psychoanalytic Forum* 1 (1966): 15-16.
121. "Unending Challenge." *The New York Times Book Review* (April 17, 1966): 18, 20, 22.
122. "The Mental Health Ethic." In *Ethics and Society: Original Essays on Contemporary Moral Problems,* edited by R. T. DeGeorge. Garden City, New York: Doubleday-Anchor, 1966, pp. 85-110; reprinted in part in *The National Review* (June 14, 1966): 570-572.
123. "Mental Illness Is a Myth." *The New York Times Magazine* (June 12, 1966): 30, 90-92; reprinted in *Popular Psychology* 1 (May, 1967): 22, 25, 57-58.
124. "Is Mental Illness a Myth?" [Replies to Letters to the Editor] *The New York Times Magazine* (July 3, 1966): 4, 33; (July 10, 1966): 2.
125. "Psychotherapy: A Sociocultural Perspective." *Comprehensive Psychiatry* 7 (August, 1966): 217-223.
126. Review of *Medical Orthodoxy and the Future of Psychoanalysis* by K. R. Eissler. New York: International University Press, 1965. *The Village Voice* (September 1, 1966): 5, 10-11.
127. "The Ethics of Abortion." *The Humanist* 26 (September-October, 1966): 147-148.
128. "The Social Situation of the Hospitalized Mental Patient." *Journal of American Association of University Women* 60 (October, 1966): 31-32.
129. "Whither Psychiatry?" *Social Research* 33 (Autumn, 1966): 439-462.
130. "There Was No Defense." *The New York Times Book Review* (November 13, 1966): 4, 34; reprinted in *Psychiatry and Social Science Review* 1 (January, 1967): 21-24.
131. "Ezra Pound." [Reply to Letters to the Editor] *The New York Times Book Review* (December 11, 1966): 65.
132. Review of *The Trial of Ezra Pound* by Julien Cornell. New York: The John Day Company, 1966. *Rutgers Law Review* 21 (Winter, 1967): 367-374.
133. "Alcoholism: A Socio-ethical Perspective." *Western Medicine* 7 (December, 1966): 15-21; reprinted in *Washburn Law Journal* 6 (1967): 255-268.

134. Discussion of "A Historical Review of Classification of Behavior and One Current Perspective," by Lewis L. Robbins. In *The Classification of Behavior Disorders,* edited by L. D. Eron. Chicago: Aldine Publishing Company, 1966, pp. 38–41.
135. "The Psychiatric Classification of Behavior: A Strategy of Personal Constraint." In *The Classification of Behavior Disorders,* edited by L. D. Eron. Chicago: Aldine Publishing Company, 1966, pp. 123–170.
136. "Woodrow Wilson: A Study by Freud." *The Boston Sunday Herald* (February 5, 1967): 17.
137. "The Hazards of Zeal." *The National Review* (March 21, 1967): 307–310; reprinted in *Psychiatry and Social Science Review* 1 (February, 1967): 5, 10–12.
138. "Murder and Violence in the Affluent Society." *The Boston Sunday Herald* (April 30, 1967): 18.
139. "How Sick Is Sick?" *The New Republic* (May 6, 1967): 21–23.
140. "The Doctor in the Case." *The New York Times Book Review* (May 28, 1967): 8.
141. "The Destruction of Differences." *The New Republic* (June 10, 1967): 21–23.
142. "Behavior Therapy and Psychoanalysis." *Medical Opinion and Review* 3 (June, 1967): 24–29.
143. "Mental Illness." [Letter to the Editor] *The Economist* [London] (June 17, 1967): 1192.
144. "The Insanity Plea and the Insanity Verdict." *Temple Law Quarterly* 40 (Spring-Summer, 1967): 271–282.
145. "Moral Man: A Model of Man for Humanistic Psychology." In *Challenges of Humanistic Psychology,* edited by James F. T. Bugental. New York: McGraw-Hill Book Co., 1967. Chapter 5, pp. 45–51.
146. Reply to Dr. Vladimir G. Eliasberg. [Letters to the Editor] *American Journal of Psychiatry* 124 (September, 1967): 163.
147. "Freedom and Goals." [Reply to the Letter to the Editor] *Medical Opinion and Review* 3 (September, 1967): 119–123.
148. "Mental Illness as an Excuse for Civil Wrongs." *Notre Dame Lawyer* 43 (October, 1967): 24–38. [with George J. Alexander]
149. "The Psychiatrist as Double Agent." *Transaction* 4 (October, 1967): 16–24.
150. "The Psychiatrist: A Policeman in the Schools." *This Magazine Is About Schools* (October, 1967): 114–134.
151. "Psychoanalysis and the Rule of Law." *Washburn Law Journal* 7 (Fall, 1967): 25–34.
152. "The College Psychiatrists." [Reply to Letters to the Editor] *Transaction* 5 (December, 1967): 4.
153. "Involuntary Mental Hospitalization: A Crime Against Humanity." *The Exchange* (December, 1967): 1–4.
154. "The Painful Person." *The Journal Lancet* 88 (January, 1968): 18–22.
155. "Some Remarks on Autonomous Psychotherapy." *Psychiatric Opinion* 5 (January, 1968): 4, 6–8.
156. "College Psychiatry: A Critique." *Comprehensive Psychiatry* 9 (January, 1968): 81–85.
157. "Medical Ethics: A Historical Perspective." *Medical Opinion and Review* 4 (February, 1968): 115–121.

158. "Subversion of the Rule of Law." *National Review* (March 12, 1968): 247-248.
159. "Science and Public Policy: The Crime of Involuntary Mental Hospitalization." *Medical Opinion and Review* 4 (May, 1968): 24-35.
160. "Mental Illness as an Excuse for Civil Wrongs." *Journal of Nervous and Mental Disease* 147 (August, 1968): 113-123. [with George J. Alexander]
161. "Justice and Psychiatry." *The Atlantic* (October, 1968): 127-132.
162. Review of *The Insanity Defense* by Abraham S. Goldstein. New Haven: Yale University Press, 1967; and *Criminal Justice* by Abraham S. Blumberg. Chicago: Quadrangle Books, 1967. *Boston University Law Review* 48 (Winter, 1968): 151-155.
163. "Problems Facing Psychiatry: The Psychiatrist as Party to Conflict." In *Ethical Issues in Medicine: The Role of the Physician in Today's Society*, E. Fuller Torrey, editor. Boston: Little, Brown and Company, 1968. Chapter 13, pp. 265-284.
164. "The Psychology of Persistent Pain: A Portrait of L'Homme Douloureux." In *Pain*, edited by A. Soulairac, J. Cahn, and J. Charpentier. (Proceedings of the International Symposium on Pain, organized by the Laboratory of Psychophysiology, Faculty of Sciences, Paris, April 11-13, 1967). London: Academic Press, 1968, pp. 93-113.
165. "Hysteria." In *International Encyclopedia of the Social Sciences, Vol. 7*, edited by David L. Sills. New York: Macmillan & Free Press, 1968, pp. 47-52.
166. "The Crime of Commitment." *Psychology Today* 2 (March, 1969): 55-57.
167. "The Right to Health." *Georgetown Law Journal* 57 (March, 1969): 734-751.
168. "An 'Unscrewtape' Letter: A Reply to Fred Sander." *American Journal of Psychiatry* 125 (April, 1969): 1432-1435.
169. "The Right to Health." *The Freeman* 19 (June, 1969): 352-362.
170. "Psychiatry, the Law, and Social Control." *University Review* 2 (Summer, 1969): 8-11.
171. "Interview: Thomas S. Szasz, M.D." *The New Physician* 18 (June, 1969): 453-461, 476.
172. "Enigmas of Violence." [Letter to the Editor] *Science* 164 (June 27, 1969): 1465.
173. "Social Control and Legal Psychiatry." *The Journal of the Albert Einstein Medical Center* 17 (Summer, 1969): 52-59.
174. "Abortion Law Reform." [Letter to the Editor] *The Humanist* 29 (September-October, 1969): 34.
175. "Justice in the Therapeutic State." *Indiana Legal Forum* 3 (Fall, 1969): 14-34.
176. "Mental Illness Is Not a Disease." *Science Digest* 66 (December, 1969): 7-14.
177. "The Mad Scene: Who Is Dangerous to Whom?" *Medical Opinion and Review* 6 (February, 1970): 111.
178. "A Psychiatrist Views Mental Health Legislation." *Wabash Law Journal* 9 (Winter, 1970): 224-243.
179. "Blackness and Madness." *Yale Review* 59 (Spring, 1970): 333-341.
180. *Ideology and Insanity: Essays on the Psychiatric Dehumanization of Man.* Garden City, New York: Doubleday Anchor, 1970.
181. *The Manufacture of Madness: A Comparative Study of the Inquisition and the Mental Health Movement.* New York: Harper and Row, 1970.
182. "The Mad Scene: Diagnosis—Black or White? *Medical Opinion and Review* 6 (March, 1970): 46-47.

183. "The Mad Scene: Brothers' Keepers." *Medical Opinion and Review* 6 (April, 1970): 52–53.
184. "Introduction." In *The Ordeal of Stephen Dennison* by Lucy Freeman and Lisa Hoffman. Englewood Cliffs, New Jersey: Prentice-Hall, 1970, pp. ix–xii.
185. "Blackness and Madness: Images of Evil and Tactics of Exclusion. In *Black America,* edited by John F. Szwed. New York: Basic Books, 1970, pp. 67–77.
186. "Justice in the Therapeutic State." In *The Administration of Justice in America.* The 1968–1969 E. Paul du Pont Lectures on Crime, Delinquency, and Corrections, pp. 75–92, Copyright 1970 by the University of Delaware.
187. "Psychiatry as Tactic." [Letter to the Editor] *The New York Times* (July 25, 1970): 22.
188. "The Right to Drugs: A Matter of Freedom?" *Newsday* (October 21, 1970): 3B.
189. "R. F. K. Must Die!" *The New York Times Book Review* (November 15, 1970): 8, 74.
190. "'Mental Illness' Myth Cruel Fraud." *Twin Circle* (March 14, 1971): 15.
191. "Fairness and Folly." *Medical Opinion and Review* 7 (April, 1971): 65.
192. "From the Slaughterhouse to the Madhouse." *Psychotherapy* 8 (Spring, 1971): 64–67.
193. "The Sane Slave." *American Journal of Psychotherapy* 25 (April, 1971): 228.
194. "The Ethics of Suicide." *The Antioch Review* 31 (Spring, 1971): 7–17.
195. "The Negro in Psychiatry: An Historical Note on Psychiatric Rhetoric." *American Journal of Psychotherapy* 25 (July, 1971): 469–471.
196. "The American Association for the Abolition of Involuntary Mental Hospitalization." *The Abolitionist* 1 (Summer, 1971): 1–2. [with George J. Alexander]
197. "Involuntary Commitment: A Form of Slavery." *The Humanist* 31 (July–August, 1971): 11–14.
198. "Psychiatric Torts." In *American Trial Lawyers Association, 1970, Freeport and Miami Beach.* Cincinnati, Ohio: W. H. Anderson Co., 1971.
199. "In the Church of America, Psychiatrists Are Priests." *Hospital Physician* (October, 1971): 44–46.
200. "The Ethics of Addiction." *The American Journal of Psychiatry* 128 (November, 1971): 541–546.
201. "Under Mind." [Review of *A Question of Madness* by Zhores A. Medvedev and Roy A. Medvedev. London: Macmillan, 1971.] *New Society* (December 16, 1971): 1213–1215.
202. "Scapegoating 'Military Addicts': The Helping Hand Strikes Again." *Transaction* 9 (January, 1972): 4–6.
203. "Drugs, Doctors, and Deceit." [Letter to the Editor] *New England Journal of Medicine* 286 (January 13, 1972): 111.
204. "The Ethics of Addiction." *Harper's Magazine* 244 (April, 1972): 74–79.
205. "Psychosis, Psychiatry, and Homicide." [Letter to the Editor] *Journal of the American Medical Association* 220 (May 8, 1972): 864–865.
206. "Tragic Failures." [Review of *In a Darkness* by James A. Wechsler, with Nancy F. Wechsler and Holly W. Karpf. New York: W. W. Norton, 1972.] *National Review* (May 26, 1972): 591, 593.
207. "Reply to J. W. Goppelt." [Letters to the Editor] *American Journal of Psychiatry* 128 June, 1972): 1588.

208. "Reply to R. D. Blair." [Letters to the Editor] *American Journal of Psychiatry* 128 (June, 1972): 1589.
209. "A Dissent." [Letter to the Editor] *National Catholic Reporter* (May 12, 1972): 10.
210. Remarks, in Symposium on the Aging Poor (Current Comment) *Syracuse Law Review* 23 (1972): 78-82, 84-85.
211. "Law, Property, and Psychiatry." *American Journal of Orthopsychiatry* 42 (July, 1972): 610-626.
212. "Bad Habits Are Not Diseases: A Refutation of the Claim that Alcoholism Is a Disease." *The Lancet* (London) 2 (July 8, 1972): 83-84.
213. "Voluntary Mental Hospitalization: An Unacknowledged Practice of Medical Fraud." *New England Journal of Medicine* 287 (August 10, 1972): 277-278.
214. "Introduction." In *Prisoners of Psychiatry: Mental Patients, Psychiatrists, and the Law* by Bruce Ennis. New York: Harcourt, Brace, Jovanovich, 1972, pp. xi-xix.
215. "Psychiatric Stigmatization." [Letter to the Editor] *The New York Times* (December 26, 1972): 32.
216. "Fanaticism." [Letter to the Editor] *The Times Literary Supplement* [London] (February 3, 1973): 124.
217. "Medicine and the State: The First Amendment Violated. An Interview with Thomas Szasz." *The Humanist* 33 (March-April, 1973): 4-9.
218. "The Physician as a Spy." [Letter to the Editor] *The New York Times* (March 24, 1973): 32.
219. "Mental Illness as a Metaphor." *Nature* 242 (March 30, 1973): 305-307.
220. "La Liberta del Malato Mentale." *Enciclopedia della Scienze e della Tecnica Mondadori* (Milano; Mondadori, 1973): 368-369.
221. "From Contract to Status Via Psychiatry." *Santa Clara Lawyer* (Spring, 1973): 537-559. [with George J. Alexander]
222. *The Second Sin.* Garden City, New York: Doubleday, 1973.
223. *The Age of Madness: The History of Involuntary Mental Hospitalization Presented in Selected Texts.* Garden City, New York: Doubleday Anchor, 1973.
224. "Panel Discussion: Do Solutions to Drug Problems Threaten Our Civil Liberties?" *Villanova Law Review* 18 (May, 1973): 875-895.
225. "Drugs and Freedom." (Transcript of the "Firing Line" program taped at WKPC in Louisville, Kentucky, on May 16, 1973, and originally telecast on PBS on July 15, 1973. Host: William F. Buckley, Jr., Guest: Dr. Thomas S. Szasz.) Columbia, South Carolina: Southern Educational Communications Association, 1973.
226. "The Dominion of Psychiatry." *The New York Times* (August 5, 1973): E-15.
227. Interview. *Penthouse* (October, 1973): 68-74.
228. "The A.C.L.U.'s 'Mental Illness' Cop-Out." *Reason* 5 (January, 1974): 4-9.
229. "Freedom for Patients: A Dialogue." *The Bulletin of the New York State District Branches of the American Psychiatric Association* 16 (January, 1974): 1, 9.
230. "Language and Humanism." *The Humanist* 34 (January-February, 1974): 25-30.
231. "Illness and Indignity." *Journal of the American Medical Association* 227 (February, 1974): 543-545.

232. "When History Comes Home to Roost." *The New York Times* (March 6, 1974): 33.
233. "The A.C.L.U. and Involuntary Commitment: A Reply." *Reason* 5 (April, 1974): 29.
234. "Crime, Punishment, and Psychiatry." In *Current Perspectives on Criminal Behavior, Original Essays on Criminology,* edited by Abraham S. Blumberg. New York: Alfred A. Knopf, 1974, pp. 262-285.
235. "Medicine and Madness." (Special report) In *The Encyclopedia Brittanica Yearbook, 1974.* Chicago: The Encyclopedia Brittanica, 1974, pp. 454-455.
236. "Objectionable Psychologizing. [Letter to the Editor] *The New York Times Magazine* (April 21, 1974): 8.
237. "The Psychiatric Perspective on Pain and Its Control." In *The Treatment of Chronic Pain,* edited by F. Dudley Hart. London: Medical and Technical Publishing Co., Ltd., 1974, pp. 39-61.
238. *The Myth of Mental Illness: Foundations of a Theory of Personal Conduct.* (revised edition) New York: Harper & Row, 1974.
239. "Psychiatry: A Clear and Present Danger." *Mental Hygiene* 58 (Spring, 1974): 17-20.
240. *Ceremonial Chemistry: The Ritual Persecution of Drugs, Addicts, and Pushers.* Garden City, New York: Doubleday, 1974.
241. "The Myth of Mental Illness: Three Addenda." *Journal of Humanistic Psychology* 14 (Summer, 1974), no. 3.
242. ECT [Letter to the Editor] *The Listener* (July 25, 1974).
243. "Introduction." *The Stoned Age: A History of Drugs in America* by John Rublowsky. New York: G. P. Putnam's Sons, 1974, pp. 9-11.
244. "Might Makes the Metaphor." *Journal of the American Medical Association* 229 (September 2, 1974): 1326.
245. "Straight Talk from Thomas Szasz." An interview in *Reason* 6 (October, 1974): 4-13.
246. "The Myth of Psychotherapy." *American Journal of Psychotherapy* 28 (October, 1974): 517-526.
247. "Your Last Will and Your Free Will." *The Alternative* 8 (November, 1974): 10-11.
248. "Our Despotic Laws Destroy the Right to Self-Control." *Psychology Today* 8 (December, 1974): 19-29, 127.
249. Review of *About Behavior* by B. F. Skinner. *Libertarian Review* 3 (December, 1974): 6-7.
250. "Sargant and Szasz." [Letter to the Editor] *The Spectator* (February 22, 1975): 197.
251. "The Moral Physician." *The Center Magazine* 8 (March-April, 1975): 2-9.
252. "Stop Poking Around in Your Patients' Lives!" [Interview] *Medical Economics* (June 9, 1975): 106-128.
253. "The Age of Madness." [Letter to the Editor] *Times Literary Supplement* (July 25, 1975): 841.
254. "On Involuntary Psychiatry." [Op-Ed] *The New York Times* (August 4, 1975): 19.
255. "Medical Metaphorology." *American Psychologist* 30 (August, 1975): 859-861.

256. "The Age of Madness." [Letters to the Editor] *The Times Literary Supplement* [London] (August 29, 1975): 971.
257. "To Review Stand on Drugs." [Letters to the Editor] *The New York Times* (August 31, 1975): 14-E.
258. "The Danger of Coercive Psychiatry." *American Bar Association Journal* 61 (October, 1975): 1246-1249.
259. "The Control of Conduct: Authority vs. Autonomy." *Criminal Law Bulletin* 11 (September–October, 1975): 617-622.
260. "Some Call It Brainwashing." *The New Republic* (March 6, 1976): 10-12.
261. "Mercenary Psychiatry." *The New Republic* (March 13, 1976): 10-12.
262. "APA and Zionism." [Letter to the Editor] *Psychiatry News* 11 (April 2, 1976): 2.
263. "Psychiatry in Courtrooms." [Letter to the Editor] *The New Republic* (May 8, 1976).
264. *Heresies.* Garden City, New York: Doubleday Anchor, 1976.
265. "Anti-psychiatry: The Paradigm of the Plundered Mind." *The New Review* [London] (1976): 3-14.
266. "Male Women, Female Men." *The New Republic* (October 9, 1976): 8-9.
267. "Ezra Pound." [Letter to the Editor] *Times Literary Supplement* [London] (1976): 1306.
268. "Abortion: Punish the Women?" [Guest comment] *Daily Orange* of Syracuse University (October 9, 1976): 6-8.
269. "Twice-Brainwashed." *The New Republic* (October 23, 1976): 6-8.
270. "Political Torture and Physicians." [Letter to the Editor] *The New England Journal of Medicine* 295 (October 28, 1976): 1018.
271. "Schizophrenia: The Sacred Symbol of Psychiatry." *British Journal of Psychiatry* 129 (October, 1976): 308-316.
272. *Schizophrenia: The Sacred Symbol of Psychiatry.* New York: Basic Books, 1976.
273. "Patriotic Poisoners." *The Humanist* 36 (November–December, 1976): 5-7.
274. "Anti-psychiatry." [Letter to the Editor] *The New Review* (November, 1976): 71.
275. *Paresis and Plunder: The Models of Madness in Psychiatry and Anti-Psychiatry.* (The Noel Buxton Lecture, 1975) Colchester: The University of Essex, 1976.
276. *Karl Kraus and the Soul-Doctors: A Pioneer Critic and His Criticism of Psychiatry and Psychoanalysis.* Baton Rouge, Louisiana: Louisiana State University Press, 1976.
277. "Involuntary Psychiatry." *University of Cincinnati Law Review* 45 (1976): 347-365.
278. "The Right to Die." *The New Republic* (December 11, 1976): 8-9.
279. "The Theology of Therapy: The Breach of the First Amendment Through the Medicalization of Morals." In *American Law: The Third Century,* edited by Bernard Schwartz. Hackensack, New Jersey: Fred B. Rothman & Co., 1976, pp. 365-376.
280. "A Different Dose for Different Folks: We Should Treat Drug Taking in the Same Way We Treat Speech and Religion, as a Fundamental Right." *Skeptic* (January–February, 1976): 47-49, 63-70.
281. *Psychiatric Slavery: When Confinement and Coercion Masquerade as Cure.* New York: The Free Press, 1977.

282. *The Theology of Medicine: The Political-Philosophical Foundations of Medical Ethics.* Baton Rouge: Louisiana: Louisiana State University Press, 1977; New York: Harper Colophon, 1977.
283. "A Dialogue on Drugs." *Psychiatric Opinion* 14 (March-April, 1977): 10-12, 44-47.
284. "Szasz on Schizophrenia." [Letter to the Editor] *British Journal of Psychiatry* 130 (May, 1977): 520-524.
285. "Donaldson." [Letter to the Editor] *Psychiatric News* 12 (May 2, 1977): 2.
286. "What Do Psychiatrists Know About Terrorism?" [Letter to the Editor] *The New York Times* (June 19, 1977): 16-E.
287. "Aborting Unwanted Behavior: The Controversy on Psychosurgery." *The Humanist* 37 (July-August, 1977): 7, 10-11.
288. "The Child as Involuntary Mental Patient: The Threat of Child Therapy to the Child's Dignity, Privacy, and Self-Esteem." *San Diego Law Review* 14 (1977): 1005-1027.
289. "On the 'Incarceration' of Martha Mitchell." [Letter to the Editor] *The New York Times* (September 25, 1977): 14-E.
290. "Christmas Book Recommendations." *The American Spectator* 11 (December, 1977): 29.
291. "Models of Madness." *The Listener* [London] (December 1, 1977): 721-723.
292. "Soviet Psychiatry: The Historical Background." *Inquiry* (December 5, 1977): 6-7.
293. "Foreword." In *Therapeutic Partnership: Ethical Concerns in Psychotherapy* by Carl Goldberg. New York: Springer Publishing Company, 1977, pp. vii-viii.
294. "Psychiatric Diversion in the Criminal Justice System: A Critique." In *Assessing the Criminal: Restitution, Retribution, and the Legal Process,* edited by Randy E. Barnett and John Hagel, III. Cambridge, Massachusetts: Ballinger Publishing Co., 1977, pp. 99-120.
295. "The Concept of Mental Illness: Explanation or Justification?" In *Mental Health: Philosophical Perspectives,* edited by H. T. Engelhardt, Jr. and S. F. Spicker. Dordrecht-Holland: D. Reidel Publishing Co., 1977, pp. 235-250.
296. "Healing Words for Political Madness: A Conversation with Dr. Thomas Szasz." *The Advocate* (December 28, 1977): 37-40.
297. "Soviet Psychiatry: Its Supporters in the West." *Inquiry* (January 2, 1978): 4-5.
298. "Drug Prohibition." *Reason* 9 (January, 1978): 14-18.
299. "The Soviets Are Worse." [Letter to the Editor] *Inquiry* (February 20, 1978): 32.
300. "State Mental Hospitals: Orphanages for Adults." *Pacific News Service Syndicate* (February 23, 1978).
301. *The Myth of Psychotherapy: Mental Healing as Religion, Rhetoric, and Repression.* Garden City, New York: Doubleday Anchor, 1978.
302. "Condoning Psychiatric Slavery." *Inquiry* (March 6, 1978): 3-4.
303. "Why Do We Fear the Retarded?" *Newsday* (March 16, 1978): 93.
304. "The Psychiatrist as Accomplice." *Inquiry* (April 3, 1978): 4-5.
305. "Prescription for Control." *Inquiry* (May 1, 1978): 4-5.
306. "The Case Against Compulsory Psychiatric Interventions." *The Lancet* [London] (May 13, 1978): 1035-1036.

307. "New Addictions for Old." *Inquiry* (May 29, 1978): 4–5.
308. "The Rapist as Patient." *Inquiry* (June, 1978): 3–4.
309. "Criminal Intent." [Letter to the Editor] *Inquiry* (June 26, 1978): 32.
310. "The Ethics of Therapy." *National Forum* 58 (Spring, 1978): 25–29.
311. "Schizophrenia—A Category Error." *Trends in NeuroSciences* 1 (July, 1978): 26–28.
312. "Nobody Should Decide Who Goes to the Mental Hospital: Dr. Thomas Szasz Talking with Governor Jerry Brown and Dr. Lou Simpson." *The Co-Evolution Quarterly* (Summer, 1978): 56–69.
313. "Should Psychiatric Patients Ever Be Hospitalized Involuntarily—Undei Any Circumstances—No." In *Controversy in Psychiatry,* edited by J. P. Brady and H. K. H. Brodie. Philadelphia: W. B. Saunders, 1978, pp. 965–977.
314. "The Abortionist as Fall Guy." *Inquiry* (July 24, 1978): 4–5.
315. "The Psychiatric Presidency." *Inquiry* (September 18, 1978): 4–6.
316. "Pilgrim's Regress." *The Spectator* (September 23, 1978): 72–73.
317. "Psychiatry: The New Religion." [Interview with Professor Thomas Szasz] *Cosmos* [Australia] 6 (October, 1978): 6–7.
318. "Peter Bourne's Quaalude Caper." *Inquiry* (October 30, 1978): 4–7.
319. "A Dialogue About Drug Education." *Psychiatric Opinion* 15 (October, 1978): 10–14.
320. "The Concept of Schizophrenia." [Commentary] *Trends in NeuroSciences* 1 (November, 1978): 129.
321. "Bourne's Quaalude Caper." *Inquiry* (November 27, 1978): 4–6.
322. "Gifts That Could Change the World." *Newsday* (December 24, 1978): 8.
323. "The Devil's Fool." *Inquiry* (December 25, 1978): 4–5.
324. "Behavior Therapy: A Critical Review of the Moral Dimensions of Behavior Modification." *Journal of Behavior Therapy and Psychiatry* 9 (1978): 199–203.
325. "Insanity and Responsibility: Psychiatric Diversion in the Criminal Justice System." In *Psychology of Crime and Criminal Justice,* edited by Hans Toch. New York: Holt, Rinehart and Winston, 1979, pp. 133–134.
326. "Jones as Jesus." *The Libertarian Review* (January, 1979), pp. 34–35.
327. "The Freedom Abusers." *Inquiry* (February 5, 1979): 4–6.
328. "What Is Most Humane Commitment to the Mentally Ill?" [Letter to the Editor] *The Milwaukee Journal* (February 8, 1979): 8.
329. "Torsney and Our 'Psychiatric Executioners.'" [Letter to the Editor] *The New York Times* (February 24, 1979): 20.
330. "Should the FDA Ban H₂O?" *Inquiry* (April 2, 1979): 5–6.
331. "'Mental Illness' and Police Brutality." *The Libertarian Review* (April, 1979): 32–33.
332. "Male and Female Created He Them." *The New York Times Book Review* (June 10, 1979): 11, 39.
333. "Psychiatric Diversion in the Criminal Justice System." In *Mentally Ill Offenders and the Criminal Justice System,* edited by Nancy J. Beran and Beverly G. Toomey. New York: Praeger Publishers, 1979, pp. 54–73.
334. "Power and Psychiatry." In *Power: Its Nature, Its Use, and Its Limits,* edited by Donald W. Harward. Cambridge, Massachusetts: Schenkman Publishing Co., 1979, pp. 153–158.
335. "Dreyfus Redux, in Reverse." *The New York Times* (August 4, 1979): 19.

336. "J'Accuse: How Dan White Got Away with Murder, and How American Psychiatry Helped Him Do It." *Inquiry* (August 6 & 20, 1979): 17-21.
337. "A.A.A.I.M.H. – R. I. P." *The Abolitionist* 9 (September, 1979): 1, 4.
338. "Critical Reflections on Child Psychiatry." *Children and Youth Services Review* 1 (1979): 7-29.
339. "The Lying Truths of Psychiatry." In *Lying Truths: A Critical Scrutiny of Current Beliefs and Conventions,* edited by R. Duncan and M. Weston-Smith. London: Pergamon Press, 1979, pp. 121-122.
340. "The Lying Truths of Psychiatry." *The Journal of Libertarian Studies* 3 (Summer, 1979): 121-139.
341. "Psychodrama in the White House." *The Libertarian Review* (December, 1979): 24-31.
342. "Ein kritischer Blick auf die Psychiatrie." *Neue Zürcher Zeitung* 18 (February, 1980): 17-18.
343. "Therapeutic Tyranny." *Omni* (March, 1980): 43.
344. "Our Fear and Trembling Through the Ages." *Saturday Review* (March 15, 1980): 39-40.
345. "Would You Give Tranquillizers to King Lear?" [Interview] *New Zealand Listener* (April 19, 1980): 38-39.
346. "'Back Wards to Back Streets.'" *TV Guide* (May 17-23, 1980): 32-36.
347. "Das Recht des Menschen auf sein Heroin." *Penthouse* [Germany] (June, 1980): 52-53.
348. "Voyeurism as Science." *Inquiry* (June 9 & 23, 1980): 15-16.
349. "Diagnostician or Accuser?" *The Spectator* (September 13, 1980): 15-16.
350. *Sex By Prescription.* Garden City, New York: Doubleday, 1980.
351. "Schlechte Gewohnheiten sind keine Krankheiten." [Letter to the Editor] *Penthouse* [Germany] (October, 1980): 82.
352. "The A.C.L.U. vs. Walter Polovchak." *Inquiry* (October 27, 1980): 6-8.
353. "A Critical Look at Psychiatry." *News from Gracie Square Hospital* 11 (December, 1980): 1, 4.
354. "The Case Against Sex Education." *Penthouse* (January, 1981): 124-125.
355 "Tea and Sympathy on the Way to Mecca." *Free Inquiry* 1 (Spring, 1981): 16-17.
356. "A Talk with Thomas Szasz, by Lawrence Mass, M.D." *Christopher Street* (March-April, 1981): 32-39.
357. "Criminals' 'Sickness in Our Minds.'" [Interview] *The Syracuse Post-Standard* (April 6, 1981): C-1.
358. "The Sadness of Sex." *Inquiry* (April 27, 1981): 22-24.
359. "Reagan Should Let the Jurors Judge Hinckley." *The Washington Post* (May 6, 1981): A-19.
360. "Power and Psychiatry." *Society* 18 (May-June, 1981): 16-18.
361. "The Protocols of the Learned Experts on Heroin." *The Libertarian Review* (July, 1981): 14-17.
362. "The Case of John Hinckley." *Spectator* [London] (July 11, 1981): 9-10.
363. "Mental Illness: A Myth?" In *The ABC of Psychology,* general editor L. Kristal. London: Michael Joseph, 1981, pp. 150-155.
364. "Szasz on the Dangerous Patient." [Discussion] *The American Journal of Forensic Psychiatry* 2 (1981-1982): 6-7, 17.

365. "Interview: Thomas Szasz." *High Times* (September, 1981): 32–38, 69–70.
366. "Le combat de Thomas Szasz contre les 'tortures psychiatriques.'" [Interview with Alexandre Szombati] *Le Monde Dimanche* (October 11, 1981): xii–xiii.
367. "Viewpoint: From Pathogenic to Therapeutic." *Sexual Medicine Today* (February 10, 1982): 33.
368. "The Lady in the Box." *The New York Times* (February 16, 1982): A-19.
369. "The War Against Drugs." *Journal of Drug Issues* 12 (Winter, 1982): 115–122.
370. "The Psychiatrist as Moral Agent." *Whittier Law Review* 4 (1982): 77–85.
371. "Purifying America." *Inquiry* (April 12, 1982): 26–30.
372. "Building the Therapeutic State." *Contemporary Psychology* 27 (April, 1982): 297.
373. "Writing People Off as Crazy." *The Washington Post* (April 16, 1982): A-29.
374. "Shooting the Shrink," *New Republic* (June 16, 1982): 11–15.
375. Interview. *The Review of the News* (July 14, 1982): 39–48.
376. "The Psychiatric Will: A New Mechanism for Protecting Persons Against 'Psychosis' and Psychiatry," *American Psychologist* 37 (July, 1982): 762–770.
377. "The Right to Refuse Treatment: A Critique." In *Who Decides: Conflicts of Rights in Health Care,* edited by Nora K. Bell. Clifton, New Jersey: Humana Press, 1982.
378. Foreword in *Psychiatry and Freedom* (special issue), guest editor Thomas S. Szasz. *Metamedicine* 3 (October, 1982): 313.
379. "On the Legitimacy of Psychiatric Power," *Metamedicine* 3 (October, 1982): 315–324.
380. "Speaking About Sex: Sexual Pathology and Sexual Therapy as Rhetoric," *Syracuse Scholar* 3 (Fall, 1982): 15–19.
381. "Tylenol Killer: Mad or Just Bad?" *Washington Post* (November 3, 1982): A23.
382. "Was Virginia Woolf Mad?" *Inquiry* (December, 1982): 44–45.
383. "Literature in Medicine," *Literature in Medicine* 1 (1982): 36–37.
384. "Lunatic Reform," *The Spectator* (December 4, 1982): 16.
385. *Essays in Mental Health Policy.* Buffalo, New York: Prometheus Books, 1983.